TROPICAL

AESTHETICS

OF

BLACK

MODERNISM

THE VISUAL ARTS OF AFRICA AND ITS DIASPORAS

A series edited by Kellie Jones and Steven Nelson

TROPICAL

✳

AESTHETICS

✳

OF

✳

BLACK

✳

MODERNISM

Samantha A. Noël

DUKE UNIVERSITY PRESS DURHAM AND LONDON 2021

Designed by Amy Ruth Buchanan
Typeset in Arno Pro and Trade Gothic by
Copperline Book Services

Library of Congress Cataloging-in-Publication Data
Names: Noël, Samantha A., [date] author.
Title: Tropical aesthetics of black modernism /
Samantha A. Noël.
Other titles: Visual arts of Africa and its diasporas. Description:
Durham : Duke University Press, 2021. | Series: The visual arts of
Africa and its diasporas |
Includes bibliographical references and index.
Identifiers: LCCN 2020031386 (print) |
LCCN 2020031387 (ebook) | ISBN 9781478010333 (hardcover) |
ISBN 9781478011408 (paperback) | ISBN 9781478012894 (ebook)
Subjects: LCSH: Art, Black—Caribbean Area—Themes, motives
—20th century. | African American artists—
20th century. | Art, Caribbean—Themes, motives. | Art, Caribbean
—20th century. | Tropics—In art.
Classification: LCC N6591 .N645 2021 (print) |
LCC N6591 (ebook) | DDC 704.03/960730904—dc23
LC record available at https://lccn.loc.gov/2020031386
LC ebook record available at https://lccn.loc.gov/2020031387

Cover art: Edouard Duval-Carrié, *After Heade—
Moonlit Landscap*e, 2013, detail. Mixed media on
aluminum, 96 × 144 in. Courtesy of the artist.

DUKE UNIVERSITY PRESS GRATEFULLY ACKNOWLEDGES
THE VICE PRESIDENT FOR RESEARCH AT WAYNE STATE
UNIVERSITY, DR. STEPHEN LANEIR; THE DEAN OF
THE COLLEGE OF FINE, PERFORMING, AND
COMMUNICATION ARTS AT WAYNE STATE UNIVERSITY,
DR. MATTHEW SEEGER; AND THE JAMES PEARSON DUFFY
DEPARTMENT OF ART AND ART HISTORY AT WAYNE STATE
UNIVERSITY, WHICH PROVIDED FUNDS TOWARD THE
PUBLICATION OF THIS BOOK.

For Peter and Roslyn Noël

CONTENTS

ILLUSTRATIONS

ACKNOWLEDGMENTS

I embarked on this project about eight years ago, but preparations for my career as a scholar and teacher started many years prior. I pursued my undergraduate education at Brooklyn College, City University of New York, and it will always be a part of my scholarly DNA. Professor William T. Williams's art classes propelled me to interrogate art philosophically and still influence me to this day. I took my very first art history course with Mona Hadler, who showed me a new way of viewing art. The Honors Academy is a breeding ground for academic excellence at Brooklyn College and I could never thank the following people enough for recognizing my potential and for encouraging me to take the road less traveled: Tucker Farley, Robert Scott, Roni Natov, Margarita Fernandes-Olmos, and Paul Montagna.

At Duke University, my adviser, Richard J. Powell, supported the unconventional and interdisciplinary nature of my work and never ceased in pushing me to think more creatively and critically. Kristine Stiles has been a dedicated mentor, and I will always be grateful for her commitment to my scholarly and personal development. Sheila Dillon encouraged me to think outside the box when writing about women and performance. Finally, Michaeline Crichlow not only was a compassionate mentor but also demonstrates how Caribbean scholars can contribute to the region even when not living there. I am grateful to two other individuals who aided me in formulating ideas for the early stages of my research. Deborah Thomas was selfless and dedicated in her efforts to help me create a compelling critical stance. I am also thankful for the invaluable conversations I had with the late, great Pat Bishop, an iconic artist, art historian, musical director, and, more important, a true national treasure of Trinidad and Tobago.

I am deeply appreciative of the institutional support I received from Wayne State University. I would like to thank the vice president for research, Stephen Laneir, and the dean of the College of Fine, Performing and Communication Arts, Matthew Seeger, for their assistance in this regard. I am also grateful for the support that the chair of the James Pearson Duffy Department of Art and Art History, Sheryl Oring, provided while preparing this book. I am fortunate to have the encouragement of great colleagues at Wayne State University who have championed the development of this book through its many stages: Dora Apel, Jeffery Abt, Judith Moldenhauer, Danielle Aubert, Siobhan Gregory, Brian Kritzman, Derek Coté, Adrian Hatfield, Evan Larson-Voltz, Jennifer Olmsted, Brian Madigan, Melba Boyd, and Simone Chess. I also owe a special thank you to Amy Hays and Ted Duenas, whose assistance has been unmatched.

The two years I spent at the University of Notre Dame thanks to the Moreau Postdoctoral Fellowship provided a means for me to grapple with ideas that set the foundation for this book. I am particularly thankful for the support, encouragement, and counsel of Julia Douthwaite during that period. I continued to develop these ideas while holding a visiting position in the art department at Davidson College, and my exchanges with C. Shaw Smith proved to be fruitful in unpacking many theoretical entanglements. My research strengthened with opportunities to present at symposia held at Davidson College, the University of Notre Dame, and Wayne State University. I am also indebted to the Dark Room forums and the Exposure Symposia founded and organized by Kimberly Juanita Brown, a fellow comrade in academia. My arguments in chapters 1 and 2 appeared in an earlier form in *Art Journal*. When I submitted the article to be considered for publication in this journal, I received a generous amount of constructive feedback from its former editor Rebecca Brown. Her careful reading of the text, along with those of the reviewers, was instrumental in my critical elucidating of crucial ideas for this book. Also, an earlier version of chapter 3 appeared in *Small Axe*.

This research project benefited immensely from numerous libraries and archives around the world. I am indebted to the staff members at the following institutions: Wayne State University Libraries; New York Public Libraries, Schomburg Center for Research in Black Culture; National Library of Trinidad and Tobago; National Archives of Trinidad and Tobago; Bibliothèque Nationale de France; SDO Wifredo Lam Archive in Paris, France; Stuart Hall Library, Institute of International Visual Arts in London, England; the British Library in London, England; the Special Collections and Archives at Franklin Library, Fisk University, Nashville; Wolfsonian Library and Museum, Florida International University; and the Davidson College Library.

It is every writer's dream to have a committed and compassionate editor. I am beyond thankful to Ken Wissoker for his enthusiasm for my book at its early stages and for his patience and support when I needed them most. I would also like to thank his editorial associate, Kate Herman, for her immeasurable efforts. I immensely valued the keen and meticulous responses of the reviewers. E. Patrick Johnson has been a long-standing locus of support and encouragement throughout my career, and I am grateful for the support of Eddie Chambers. I owe a special thank you to Tanya Shields, who offered unparalleled feedback on portions of this book.

Despite the fact that the majority of my friends are based throughout the United States, Europe, and the Caribbean, they are my community without whom I am unable to thrive. I met Uraline Septembre and Martina Scimeca in college and graduate school, respectively, and I am grateful for the ways in which my friendships with them has helped sustain me. Chera Reid and I met during a college summer program many moons ago, but my years in Detroit would have been burdensome without her unwavering and loyal friendship. Another friend, Valerie Mercer, has been a warm and supportive presence as a fellow black art historian here in Detroit. I am also thankful for my high school friends Candace Jarrette and Chantelle Cobham, with whom I am always connected and who are always sources of encouragement. Although we lived only five minutes apart in Trinidad, Marissa Archibald and I did not meet and become friends until we were pursuing our tertiary education in North Carolina. Another Trini, Ria-Ann Borel, has been a loyal friend for decades, and we are always able to reconnect during our travels or virtually despite living on different continents. I met Simone Walker my first year in this country and she continues to be my close friend and confidante.

Finally, and certainly not least, I would not have made it this far were it not for my family. My great uncle Ashton Charles, who passed on only months before the publication of this book, had always been a pillar of love and support throughout the years. Words cannot express how thankful I am for the undying love and support of my mother, Roslyn Noël. Thank you for always being there no matter the issue or time of day. To my brother, Peter Noël II, your boundless dedication to your music has always inspired me. Thanks for your words of encouragement. Daddy, although you have passed on, your presence in my life is always felt.

A photograph by Carl Van Vechten, the famed Harlem Renaissance photographer, features an arresting portrait of acclaimed Trinidadian dancer and choreographer Beryl McBurnie (figure I.1). Wearing a black long-sleeved sweater, a gold choker, and a multicolored beaded necklace, McBurnie is positioned in three-quarter view facing to her right, while her head is tilted in the opposite direction. Her hair is elaborately coiffed and accented with a colorful band. Her training as a dancer is reflected in her pose, which seems to echo a choreographed stance and conveys her natural penchant for corporeal expression. This color Kodachrome of McBurnie is one of more than one thousand portraits from "Living Portraits: Carl Van Vechten's Color Photographs of African Americans, 1939–1964."[1] Although not African American, her inclusion in the collection is indicative of her prominent position in the New York art and cultural scene, and of the diasporic reaches of the Harlem-based cultural movement. In 1941, the year Van Vechten took this photograph, McBurnie headed to New York to continue her studies in dance. She eventually gained significant acclaim for her creative talents, being hailed as one of the first female calypso singers in the United States, using the sobriquet La Belle Rosette. McBurnie is also considered a major influence in the evolution of American modern dance.[2]

While we can sense McBurnie's affinity to transcultural malleability as a modern colonial subject from Trinidad, visual cues like the straw hat and colorful necklace seem to also convey her as embodying a prescribed tropical persona. The inclusion of the straw hat, for example, as a prop was most likely due to Van Vechten's curious approach to the rendering of many of his sitters. Yet when La Belle Rosette performed at the Museum of Modern Art and other venues, McBurnie may have represented the tropical, exotic, and primitive other. During the early years of the calypso craze in America, Black calypso entertainers from the Caribbean

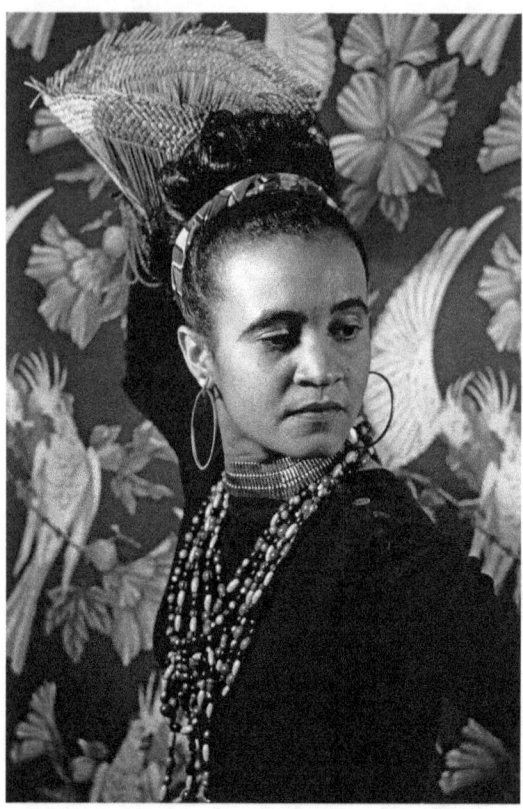

I.1 Carl Van Vechten, *La Belle Rosette*, 1941. © Van Vechten
Trust. Carl Van Vechten Papers Relating to African
American Arts and Letters, James Weldon Johnson
Memorial Collection in the Yale Collection of American
Literature, Beinecke Rare Book and Manuscript Library,
Yale University, New Haven, CT.

were expected to embody an exoticized Black other that made them distinct from their American counterparts yet akin to the servitude typical in
Caribbean tourist destinations.[3] However, in Van Vechten's photograph,
McBurnie seems to be circumscribed within a primitive-versus-modern
dialectic. Defying categorization and geographic specificity, McBurnie
exemplifies a cosmopolitan, Pan-African sensibility that was quite prevalent in the first half of the twentieth century. McBurnie's portrait evinces
the overwhelming presence of visual references and various accoutre-
ments in the arts and popular culture of the early twentieth century that
can be attributed to the tropics. This tropicalia was also visible or sug-

gested in literature, theater productions, and film, and they all inferred the non-West, nontemperate regions of the world. In a number of ways, McBurnie's presentation in the photograph embodies the creative manifestations of Black modernism of this era, given how it conveys the ways in which tropicality functioned as a key unifying element among peoples of the Black Atlantic. She exemplifies the unique yet complex relationship that Black people have with the terrain they inhabit.

At the same time, the tropicality-oriented exoticism that McBurnie embodies in the photograph and would have embodied in her calypso performances can to a certain extent signify what Martinican writer René Ménil referred to as colonial exoticism. This is a type of exoticism in which "Caribbean people have an exotic vision of themselves and offer up an exotic expression of themselves," a condition that for Ménil stems from the colonial situation.[4] Ménil declared that the essential characteristics of a person's existence in a colonial society are separation from oneself as well as an exile and even an alienation from oneself that ultimately suppresses its particular national soul and is eventually replaced by the "soul-of-the-mainland-other."[5] Although McBurnie's comportment is one of a woman who is self-aware and possesses a sense of purpose, given the immense accomplishments she would achieve in years to come, the straw hat she holds behind her head along with the beaded necklace are markers of an imposed representation of Caribbeanness that was prevalent in the early to mid-twentieth century. While there was a concerted effort in the Caribbean region to define the parameters of a cultural nationalism that countered the imposed exoticism of the West, of which McBurnie was certainly a part, what often emerged was a "form of an anti-exoticism that unfortunately is itself situated in exoticism."[6] This tendency of anti-exoticized exoticization that rendered Caribbean people picturesque also included the overall practice of exoticizing any art conveying the tropical landscape, so much so that one develops an exotic vision of one's own environment.

This could often lead to a kind of trivialization of oneself and one's natural surroundings. Ménil astutely expressed the importance of an individual existing in her own terrain as a profound and rich subject. Such an endeavor has tended to be challenging for people of African descent, particularly in the Americas, given the legacy of slavery and colonialism. These two institutions had an immense effect on Black people of the Western Hemisphere and ultimately affected their relationship to nature. Compounding this predicament is the troubling characterization of African people's affinity to nature as being vile, backward, and therefore inferior to what transpires in Europe. Yet efforts to challenge this delineation of Black people's connectivity to nature by means of a counternarrative emerged in the writings of Martinican Suzanne Césaire that were concurrent to McBurnie's New York years. As I examine in chapter 2, Césaire's concept of the "plant-man" venerates a way of living that is nature-centered as well as a source of empowerment and self-awareness.[7]

This book aims to make sense of these overlooked cultural phenomena and conundrums. In particular, it seeks to illuminate the imaginative ways in which Black visual artists and performers of the Caribbean and the United States sought to create art that was representative of their respective milieus in the early twentieth century. *Tropical Aesthetics of Black Modernism* offers a thorough investigation of how Caribbean and American artists of the early twentieth century responded to the colonial and hegemonic regimes through visual and performative tropicalist representation. It privileges the land and how a sense of place is critical in the identity formation of early twentieth-century artists as well as their creative processes. While this book offers ideas about Black modernism that are new to the discipline of art history in particular, it is important to acknowledge its address to studies of Black modernity more broadly.[8]

By proposing an alternative understanding of the tropics, this book shows how Aaron Douglas, Wifredo Lam, Josephine Baker, Maya Angelou, and some masqueraders and designers of Trinidad Carnival effectively contributed to the development of Black modernity and even Black sonic modernity. My theoretical intervention demonstrates how tropicality calls for a new understanding of the African diasporic experience, a unifying element connecting the Black Atlantic that is not generic but creates a linkage between this enclave and the land of origin—Africa. This notion of tropicality thus disrupts the construction of Africa as the antithesis of Europe and the embodiment of the past and renders the Pan-African world as a purposeful interlocutor of modern life.

In his formative work *The Other America*, literary scholar J. Michael Dash grapples with the reductive conceptualization of the New World within the realm of the natural. For him, the conventional idea that Europe is the domain of culture will always be a crucial aspect of the exotic discourse imposed on any attempt to engender a counterdiscourse situating the New World and more specifically the Caribbean in terms of culture. More importantly, "since the realm of nature within which the New World is inscribed is itself the product of representation ... the natural will become a significant and problematic terrain within which a counterdiscursive practice will be situated."⁹ *Tropical Aesthetics of Black Modernism* recognizes this conundrum and examines these challenges, given the disposition from which tropical and subtropical terrains and the Black bodies that occupy them have been perceived and represented by European interlopers over time. Despite the predicament that works of art and literature have consistently represented these regions in a singular manner, this book aims to show how Black Atlantic visual artists and performers of the early twentieth century unabashedly set about not only redefining themselves but also recontexualizing the portrayals of equatorial territories with which they are often associated.

This book grapples with the ways in which visual tropes of tropicality complicated the conveyance of modernity for Black people in different locations throughout the Black Atlantic. For this reason, the crucial artworks of the Caribbean modern art movement and of the Harlem Renaissance ought not be viewed as being particular to their geopolitical parameters but as part of a larger African diasporic mission. As Brent Hayes Edwards reminds us, the Pan-Africanist movement that emerged in the advent of the twentieth century was both political and cultural in its efforts to fully galvanize the people of African descent around the world.¹⁰ Pan-Africanism is also viewed as being at the forefront of the global movement against imperialism. Furthermore, Black radicals connected the struggles of Black people in the West to those in Africa.¹¹ Given this reality, I contend that this discourse of internationalism also existed in the realm of visual art. This book therefore examines the creative manifestations of Black modernism in the early twentieth century and explicates how tropicality functioned as a key unifying element in African diasporic art. By examining the works of Wifredo Lam, Aaron Douglas, Maya Angelou, and Josephine Baker as well as the costumed bands prevalent in Trinidad Carnival, I explicate how their representations of tropical and subtropical landscapes are reflective of the unique yet complex relationship that Black people of these respective regions have with the terrain they inhabit—land on which many of their enslaved ancestors labored.

Despite this traumatic legacy, these works nonetheless show how this land is revered by its inhabitants, who recognize it for its beauty, with the intention not to transform it but to accept it. This ideological heeding of nature should be viewed as an alternative modernity that counters the idea of transforming "undeveloped" nature for the sake of capitalist expansion.¹² In so doing, there is a particular political enterprise at stake, one that dissociates the land with the history of slavery and thereby reclaims it. Artists such as Wifredo Lam and Josephine Baker are thus highlighting the internationalist ethos of Pan-Africanism through their visual and performed explorations of landscapes—terrains that are mostly tropical—and are therefore geopolitically uniting areas such as the southern United States and the Caribbean. Ultimately, this book seeks to illuminate the desire for early twentieth-century Black Atlantic peoples to engender a sense of belonging to the citizenry and a particular kind of claim to the land that they inhabit, which speaks to a desire for home.

TROPICALIZING THE LANDSCAPE

Historically, the relationship between Europe and the non-West has always been characterized by discourses of imperialism and colonialism. The power dynamic thus established the West as the dominant and superior power that stood in opposition to the non-West as the inferior other. Much scholarship has examined the political, cultural, and historical paradigms of this relationship and how it has shaped the ways in which non-Europeans are viewed.[13] However, the physical environments where these people resided possessed just as much significance in the way non-Western people and their cultures have been represented. The Europeans considered these landscapes to be quite alien and a major contributing factor to the supposed degeneracy and savagery of these alien peoples.[14] This kind of geographical discourse undoubtedly justified the view that it was the Western world's utmost responsibility to bring these terrains and the people who occupied them into assiduous subordination.

It is for this reason that the Caribbean and the southern region of the North American continent have been designated as part of the tropics. The tropics are located in the middle latitudes of Earth between the Tropics of Cancer and Capricorn and also go beyond these latitudes to include proximate areas that experience tropical and subtropical conditions. The tropics can thus be interpreted as a Western way of stating difference and unfamiliarity in cultural forms and environment, cultures and landscapes that are distinctly alien from the normality of the northern temperate zone. This is implied in the use of the word *tropic* in the name of the latitudinal lines differentiating the tropical and temperate zones of the world; the word is an institutionalized term that has become part of the English language. Still, tropicality is a form of othering that encapsulates "an ambivalent body of ideas, representations, and experiences," all of which exist

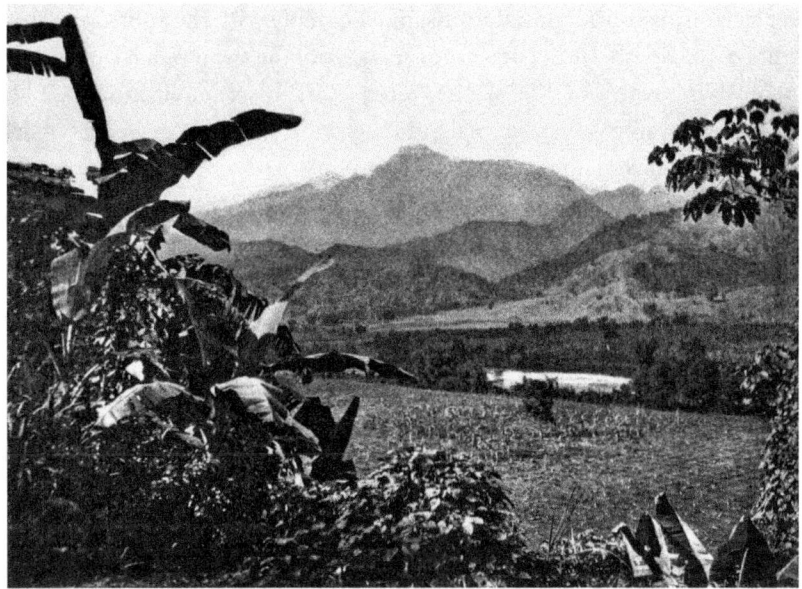

I.2 *Golden Vale*, ca. 1913. From *Jamaica: British West Indies* (Boston: United Fruit Company, 1913).

in mental juxtaposition to something else; or, simply stated, tropicality is a social construction rather than a material reality.[15]

Since the fifteenth century, Europeans viewed these zones as tropical Edens characterized by an exotic otherness, since for them the tropical world invoked images of the Garden of Eden and reflected an abundance of nature (figure I.2). Visitors to places like the Caribbean and South Asia were so amazed by the bountiful vegetation and the diversity of tropical birds and animals, so much so that equatorial regions constituted the antithesis of the bleak existence of the humanized environment in the temperate regions of the world. Their perception of non-Western peoples who lived in harmony with their environment contrasted the destruction of the environment by European intervention, and an abundance seemed to contrast a Europe that was scarcely free of famine and plague. However, by the eighteenth century, an association between tropical climate and disease was established since the term *tropical* now connoted negativity and darkness.[16] A similar perception emerged in the United States, where the semitropical environments of the rural South were characterized by swamps, jungles, and marshes. The nationalist romanticism once reserved for terrains of the North slowly attenuated and was eventually replaced by escapist connotations, most notably with the subtropical locales of the South. In fact, it was the imagery of the swamp that captivated people's interest, and it was interpreted as an elusive environment. The American swamp was the domain of sin, death, decay, the locale for witchcraft as well as ferocious creatures.[17]

It is clear that what was perceived as tropical was rooted in the mind's eye. The German traveler and naturalist Alexander von Humboldt was more influential than any other figure in Europe in his invention of the notions of the tropics both "as a field of scientific enquiry and an aesthetic domain."[18] From 1799 to 1804, Humboldt embarked on an extensive scientific exploration of the New World. Eventually, he published thirty volumes on these findings in 1827, and he lectured widely throughout Europe.[19] His writings reflect the awe of his experience of the tropics, which he saw as being full of "organic richness" and "abundant fertility." Humboldt firmly declared that the tropics epitomized the wonders of nature: "Nowhere does she more deeply impress us with a sense of her greatness, nowhere does she speak to us more forcibly."[20] In fact, he was far more inspired by the landscape than the inhabitants while traveling throughout the Americas in the late eighteenth century.[21]

While tropicalia was an imposing spectacle for people like Humboldt, it proved to be an adverse environment for others. Noted figures such as Walter Raleigh grew weary of the dangers of thunder and lightning, earthquakes, diseases, and the many beasts that roam the forests. Indeed, disease became a defining characteristic of the tropics in the minds of Europeans, since many worried that the heat and humidity would likely produce gruesome miasmas that could have devastating effects on the European body. It was also believed that the tropical climate elicited physical laxity and relaxed one's moral fiber.[22] In one account of the Jamaican landscape, Raleigh's disposition is heightened by fear and apprehension due to a supposed parasitic plant that is represented as an all-encompassing means of death and likened to a voracious animal.[23] And, as with the jungles of the tropical world, many believed in the morbid implications from what lurked beneath the swamp's waters of the southern United States. William Wirt experienced Virginia's and North Carolina's Great Dismal Swamp as "an immense morass" that "had become the secure retreat of ten thousand beasts of prey."[24] Such disparaging imagery conjured from these interpretations of the southern United States and the Caribbean speak to the extent to which tropical regions were constructed from a psychological urge on the part of these writers who greatly influenced visual artists to create psychological landscape paintings. Since writers, explorers, and scientists began to view various natural elements as no longer utopic but more unnerving, these terrains soon encouraged efforts to look inward and explore oneself beyond the province of social conventions.[25]

Given the visual and experiential mode in which the tropics have been interpreted by the West historically, I am interested in the sensory and intellectual reaches of viewing the tropics as "a realm of aesthetic experience."[26] It is clear that from very early on, visitors to tropical regions were fully engaged with the imagistic features of the equatorial landscape. However, when artists and writers who ventured to tropical zones represented these terrains, their perceptions of the physical arrangements were compounded by projections of values and ideals as well as certain fears and prejudices.[27] Historian Nancy Leys Stepan reminds us that the word *landscape* refers to "a manner of perceiving space in terms of a scene situated at a distance from the observer [that] is rooted . . . in a Western way of organizing the visual field" and that the "designation of a site as one of 'nature' often results in our ignoring the social matrices that frame or produce it . . . or the realities and textures of human activities necessary to make it work as a site of nature."[28] Undeniably, this is what artists who aspired to render their visual perception of the tropics sought to accomplish. Frederic E. Church, a prominent nineteenth-century American landscape painter associated with the Hudson River School, was among the first group of artists who traveled to South America and the Caribbean to explore the aesthetic possibilities of tropical terrains, paying particular attention to mountain scenery. The writings of Humboldt proved to be a significant impetus for this sojourn, especially the scientist's challenge that artists "should be enabled far in the interior of continents, in humid mountain valleys of the tropical world, to seize . . . on the true image of the varied forms of nature."[29] Humboldt's writings celebrated the link between physical life on Earth and the character of its inhabitants, and Americans would have taken those ideas to heart during the age of Manifest Destiny.[30]

Over the course of several months, Church traversed tropical territories creating works such as *The Heart of the Andes* (1857), *The Veil of St. Thomas, Jamaica* (1867), *and Morning in the Tropics* (1876). Church's compositions featured grandiose panoramas of tropical scenery, painted with microscopic detail and a level of accuracy that reflected the prevailing geological theory of the time. A key philosophical notion among the Hudson River School was a privileging of nature that many believed to be synonymous with God. This kind of Christianized naturalism transcended theological parameters that separated God and nature, thereby replacing the Bible with nature.[31] Constructing a landscape composition was thus a moral endeavor, and tropical landscapes were often composed of dark and shadowy regions of jungle in the lower portions that gave way to sun-drenched and sublime heights of the mountain ranges and sky. Church, however, was far too enthusiastic about the visual appeal of tropical vege-tation to convey the supposed macabre elements of the jungle.[32] Also, for late nineteenth-century American landscape painters and photographers alike, a key aspect of creating these compositions was offering viewers the "best general view" that quantifies the natural formations of the terrain, thereby asserting a European American value system that stipulated that certain features exemplified what were perceived as the unique qualities of the environment.[33] These paintings that showcased the panoramic vistas of tropical foliage and seascapes therefore shaped the signification of this type of imagery for years to come.

Eventually, idealized perceptions of the tropics influenced how natural landscapes in tropical parts of the world were reconstituted to meet these expectations. In *An Eye for the Tropics*, art historian Krista Thompson de-fines such constructions of "place-images" as they pertain to the Anglo-phone Caribbean as tropicalization. The term refers to "the complex visual systems through which the islands were imaged for tourist consumption and the social and political implications of these representations on actual physical space on the islands and their inhabitants."[34] Hoteliers, colonial administrators, and local white mercantile elites physically transformed or tropicalized many aspects of the islands so that they mimicked picturesque, photographic representations created by British, American, and local pho-tographers that became symbolic of specific islands. These picturesque im-ages rendered the terrain as rural, exotic, primitive, and unmodern.[35]

This preoccupation with tropicalia continued well into the twentieth century. Artists such as Henri Rousseau of France created lush jungle scenes full of exotic vegetation and wild animals on canvases. Rousseau's *The Dream* (1907) was not painted in the tropics but was inspired by the Jardin des Plantes in Paris, from where he was able to envisage a tropi-cal vision that was experiential at its core.[36] Many artists of the Art Deco style also incorporated tropical elements into their work. This iconic style found in the design and architecture of the 1920s and 1930s was created out of concern that the new century should produce an appropriate style. Much inspiration for Art Deco came from the imagery of empire present in the picture palaces and amusements halls of late Victorian Britain, for example, as well as ancient Egyptian and Native American imagery.[37]

The bas-relief created for the Musée des Colonies, which was the only permanent edifice built for the 1931 Colonial Exposition in Paris, epitomizes such imagery of colonial empire that was prevalent in early twentieth-century Europe. Alfred Janniot's bas-reliefs featured colonial subjects of Africa and Asia immersed in agricultural and artisan work, laboring to exploit the colony's natural bounty for the good of the metropole.[38] Indeed, these European artists aestheticized the Western construct of the tropics as a means to visually convey an "experience" of being in an exotic location, which was characterized by colonial conquest and capitalist exploitation. And these sites located in the non-West epitomize, according to cultural theorist Édouard Glissant, "antispace" that is limited in scope yet "diverse enough to multiply it into infinity. It is . . . like an anthology of landscapes."[39] Like the conflation of African and Asian rain forests in Janniot's bas-reliefs, visual renderings of tropicality were universalizing, with each tropical image rendered indistinguishable.[40] Furthermore, exoticism became the discursive means through which Europe could decipher the strange terrains and cultures it colonized.[41] And the exotic otherness of the colonies also provided avant-garde artists and writers a chance to embody that romanticist primitivism they believed the inhabitants possessed.

ON BLACK MODERNISM

Nonetheless, how are we to interpret the conveyance of tropicality by members of a racial group often associated with tropical terrains? In what ways can one identify and grapple with the aesthetic register of tropicality, and, more important, what can this tell us about the Black Atlantic experience in the first half of the twentieth century, which was unmistakably modern yet not always perceived in this way? Although the artistic and cultural forms of Africa and its diaspora contributed significantly to the development of modernism, they were seldom seen as having a fundamental role in the shaping of modernism.[42] Studies of modernism often omit the Harlem Renaissance or negritude, for example, thereby never considering the circulation of artists and ideas across regions, continents, and racial and cultural lines.[43]

Modernism is often described as the rebellious artistic and literary movements of the late nineteenth- and early twentieth-century Europeans and European Americans, whose sense of dissatisfaction with industrialization was reflected in the breakdown of the representational in art and literature. Nonetheless, modernism is concomitant with the sociological processes referred to as modernity, which is defined as social forces such as industrialization, urbanization, commodification, and technological innovations that reflect the rise of the machine age in Western Europe and America. Yet when histories of colonial conquest, the annihilation of indigenous populations, and the enslavement of African peoples are considered in the historical mapping of modernity, as literary scholar Simon Gikandi attests, Eurocentric narratives of modernity are postulated as that which happens to rather than that which is effected by non-European peoples.[44]

Undoubtedly, artists of the African diaspora were united in their steadfastness to visualize the complications of Black modernism and in so doing contributed to an existing global modern art movement. In the Caribbean, the desire for evidence of Black indigeneity that fueled cultural nationalist and anticolonialist movements went hand in hand with substantiating claims that the respective islands of the Anglophone Caribbean, for example, could be self-governed modern nation-states. Soon the iconography that was instituted in artworks became emblematic of Caribbeanness as well as a particular modern Caribbean aesthetic. Similarly, the development of an aesthetic that reflected the ethos of African American identity was key to the ideological framework of the New Negro movement. Alain Locke, the leading figure of the movement, expertly recognized a new self-awareness among Black Americans that was akin to modernity in the early decades of the twentieth century.[45] Yet artists and performers were able to go beyond these nationalist preoccupations and offer through their work a visual rendering of a unified African diasporic experience.

A number of scholars have pushed for a more pluralistic approach to the canonical framing of modernism through their articulations of African diasporic modernisms, and these often call for a privileging of the social, political, and economic underpinnings of cultural production. Art historian Richard J. Powell identifies Black modernism as the conveyance of modernity filtered through the colored lens and focus of a subjective, African American urban perspective, which would often incorporate cubist and expressionist forms in addition to an African American–derived "blues aesthetic" into scenographies.[46] Literary scholar Houston A. Baker Jr. recognizes the rise of Booker T. Washington as a national leader as the dawn of African American modernism.[47] Caribbean modernism, according to J. Michael Dash, begins with the 1804 Haitian Revolution, since this is the first time Caribbean thought challenged the "reductive mystification of colonialism."[48] And modern art in the Caribbean, as art historian Veerle Poupeye attests, also features representations that are particular to the development of cultural nationalism in already independent countries such as Haiti and Cuba, as well as the conveyance of the desire for independence from still-colonized entities such as Martinique and Barbados.[49]

But these competing modernisms are nationalist and regionalist in their concerns. Rather than reprise the marginalizing tactics of the Eurocentric model, Glissant calls for alternative modernisms to be more collective and not singular in their rethinking of these narratives. And he encourages these constructions to embrace the complications that already exist: "They must include all at once struggle, aggressiveness, belonging, lucidity, distrust of self, absolute love, contours of the landscape, emptiness of the cities, victories, and confrontations. That is what I call our irruption into modernity."[50] This line of inquiry speaks to the importance of recognizing a diversity of experiences in modernism but in particular the diverse experiences of Black modernism. As Glissant further elucidates, the human spirit yearns for a cross-cultural relationship without universalist transcendence, and diversity requires the presence of peoples with the intention of creating a new relationship.[51] In this vein, art historian Kobena Mercer characterizes modernism as global or cosmopolitan, given the interactive relationships that have always been present between the Western center and societies hitherto placed on the periphery.[52] Given these realities, art historian Lowery Stokes Sims argues that, for Black artists, "modernism affirmed the notion that a modern individual could be an agent of change or transformation. Whereas for white artists modernism was reflected in the breakdown of the representational and the familiar in literature and art, for Black artists that rupture represented a potential revolution in self-definition and self-image as they assumed the role of proactive rather than reactive agents in contemporary society."[53]

Sims's bold assertion intimates the potentiality and promise of identity formation and self-making that the creative community throughout the Black Atlantic recognized in modernism. Apart from revealing the manifold experiences of Black Atlantic peoples of the early twentieth century that Glissant and Mercer explicate, the visual art and performances examined in this book offer transformative meditations of the terrains on which Black people occupied and, in so doing, conceive a new understanding of "home" that went in tandem with the new ways in which Black people perceived themselves.

TROPICAL AESTHETICS

The tropics along with the values the term connoted in the West were always considered to be antithetical to the European models of civilization, industrialization, and progress.[54] At the same time, because of efforts by avant-garde artists to challenge the art establishment's parameters of what constitutes art, tropical flora and other natural motifs became integral in the development of modern art and design movements such as Arts and Crafts, Art Deco, Art Nouveau, and Jugendstil (German version of Art Nouveau). From the late nineteenth century, the use of tropical plants to accent the interior design of one's living quarters was a key indicator of one's socioeconomic status.[55]

Undeniably, the artists and performers I discuss in this book created artistic evocations of tropicality that were in dialogue with parallel explorations of the intersection of tropicality and the Black experience of the early twentieth century in literature and theater. A fecundity of tropicality was present in novels such as *Cane* by Jean Toomer, *Porgy* by DuBose Heyward, *Tropic Death* by Guyanese-born Eric Walrond, and *Banana Bottom* by Jamaican-born Claude McKay. However, much of these meditations echoed predominant conceptions of the tropical landscape in the Western imaginary. Other early twentieth-century artists of the Black Atlantic have incorporated tropical aesthetics to expound their own experiences of Black modernism. American Doris Ulmann's photography conveyed how a southern Black subjectivity hinged with a southern landscape encapsulated what Powell calls "a modern 'ancestorism.'"[56] This emphasis of the cultural bond these subjects have with their ancestors is evident in photographs such as *Nun with Girl, New Orleans*; there is an undeniable recognition of the common Black folk and their cultural importance. While Ulmann's imagery captured early twentieth-century African Americans who retained their cultural heritage, it also celebrated the quiet tenacity of a people who persevered through great political, social, and economic transformations. Alternatively, African American Richmond Barthé's sculptural representations of African-descended peoples were largely informed by reductive perceptions of Africa and other tropical locations as exotic yet fearsome.[57]

Jamaican sculptor Edna Manley created arresting carvings that celebrated the Black working class. During the impassioned 1930s that were characterized by the West Indian labor movement during which working-class men and women protested relentlessly for better working conditions and fair wages in the workplace, Manley's sculptures such as *Negro Aroused* echoed the sentiments of the anticolonialist movement and a modernity that was quintessentially Caribbean.[58] Known mostly for paintings he created during his stay in Haiti, African American artist William Edouard Scott also created American landscape paintings that feature the subtropical terrains of South Carolina and West Virginia with introspective portrayals of its Black inhabitants.[59] The striking compositions of Haitian artist Hector Hyppolite present imagery associated with the Vodun religion, of which he was a devout practitioner. Using bright colors and visionary scenes, Hyppolite's art is an example of cultural nationalism, the movement that saw the cultural contribution of the Black masses as indigenous to the region and intrinsic in modern Caribbean art.[60] The manifestation of tropicalia in the African American imaginary of this era emerged in theater productions such as *Voodoo Macbeth* (1936) and *Haiti* (1938). Josephine Baker's performances at Les Folies Bergère and Théâtre des Champs-Élysées featured primitivist embodiments of blackness that incited in her Parisian audience a reductive reading of the "other." These provocative performances, often staged in a tropical setting, were largely characterized by a history of European colonial conquest. Yet they reflected Baker's ability to transform herself and exert a level of self-agency as a modern Black woman.[61]

The works created by these artists are clearly interconnected and reveal evident exchanges that would have occurred across space and medium. This dialogic interplay between literature, theater, blues, and even calypso was crucial to the evolution of creative movements such as Black modernism in the early twentieth century. Furthermore, the intersectionalities of these various disciplines of the arts confirm the benefits to be gained by art history once other artistic constituents are seen as integral to its evolution. This book thus aspires to broaden the epistemological reaches of the discipline of art history by acknowledging the interdisciplinarity inherent in the study of creative production of any kind.

Apart from challenging the parameters of art-making, Black Atlantic artists such as Wifredo Lam and Maya Angelou defied early twentieth-century conventional understandings of tropicalia by re-presenting tropical terrains in art and performance in new and radical ways. They employed what I call "tropical aesthetics" in an effort to enact the *naming of place*. Women's studies scholar Katherine McKittrick asserts that such naming, "regardless of expressive method and technique . . . is also a process of self-assertion and humanization."[62] The tropical aesthetics that these artists and performers use function in this vein, proving to be an aesthetic that makes possible a "sayability" of geography that enables agency; there is no aspiration for "material ownership and Black repossession but rather . . . a grammar of liberation."[63] Tropical aesthetics thus allowed these artists to visually articulate a different way of knowing and imagining the world.[64] Since geography in a material and discursive sense is never fully secure, given that three-dimensional space is socially produced, the idea that belonging to a place could lead to a sociospatial liberation is seldom realized for many Black people.[65]

Due to these limitations, tropical aesthetics allows for a critical imaging and reclaiming of space, and through art one can reify social geographies through the manifestation of what McKittrick calls alternative geographic formulations. Indeed, as the artists and performers explored in this book have proven, art can bring into fruition a different sense of place. This was certainly needed in the United States during the dreaded Jim Crow era that Black Americans endured in the South.[66] The Great Migration ultimately proved to be a feasible means of defying the limitations that African Americans experienced of being reduced to an ungeographic existence. Their traversing across the American continent from the south to the north was a means of attaining sociospatial liberation. For Caribbean peoples, migrating from rural to urban centers within respective islands or to other islands in the archipelago as well as to the neighboring continents of North and Central America were all endured to escape poverty, servitude, and the institutionalized oppression that colonization mandated in order to achieve the same sociospatial liberation.[67] At the quotidian level, these Black Atlantic peoples created alternative geographic formulations in order to have a sense of place, a rootedness they desired in order to attain some semblance of sovereignty. Although their new environments may not have resembled what they were accustomed to, they could still envisage the possibility of agency and realize the promise of freedom in their natural surroundings. These notions are fully present in the works of Wifredo Lam, Aaron Douglas, Maya Angelou, Josephine Baker, and early twentieth-century Trinidad Carnival through the employment of tropical aesthetics.

The surrealist notion of the *marvelous real* is a crucial means through which tropical aesthetics can be galvanized. Cuban critic and novelist Alejo Carpentier asserted that the marvelous "arises from an unexpected alteration of reality (the miracle), from a privileged revelation of reality . . . an amplification of the scale and categories of reality, perceived with particular intensity by virtue of an exaltation of the spirit that leads it to a kind of extreme state."[68] René Ménil considered how one's relationship with the terrain can be recuperated through this notion. For him, the land of the marvelous is a stunning revenge against a disheartened life, since everything becomes possible in this existence. One can overcome spatial boundaries and therefore cross infinite distances, and one can also transgress temporal limitations, since, in the event of an inadvertent death, one can "be reborn into a more beautiful life."[69] Ménil believed that dreams ensure the advent of the marvelous and this imagined marvelous actualizes in time and space through the human body.[70] This empowering discursive trajectory is in tandem with the spirit of self-definition and transformation Black people believed modernism symbolized for them at the dawn of the twentieth century.

It can be argued that artists and performers I explore were looking to tropicality as a foundation for an aesthetic register through which they could visually grapple with the Black Atlantic experience. Despite the pejoration with which Black people, along with their histories and cultural practices, were viewed, tropical aesthetics offers an emboldened means to project affirmative identity politics for a people so often linked to equatorial regions of the world that were also disparaged. And the marvelous real would have certainly aided in fashioning the desired affinity Black people sought to have with the various spaces they inhabited in the early twentieth century. At times, Black people in the United States may have enacted the marvelous real to render temperate terrains of the northern metropoles subtropical, such as the landscapes of the rural South. And, like their American counterparts, Black people in the Caribbean could subvert their dehumanizing predicaments by crossing into the threshold of the marvelous to transform their experiences and emerge reborn.

On a more fundamental level, tropical aesthetics can be a strategic method used to disrupt the touristic gaze through which the Caribbean archipelago, for example, is viewed, given its potential for inducing agency and imagining new possibilities for one's natural surroundings. By eradicating reductive visual representations of Black Atlantic peoples and the land they inhabit, tropical aesthetics brings about a reclamation humanity and dignity. Tropical aesthetics can also aid in the reimagining of the land-scapes Black people live on with Black folk in mind, and, via the marvelous real, it can actualize the connectedness these landscapes have with other lands that members of the Black Atlantic occupy. In the realm of perfor-mance, tropical aesthetics stimulated an imperative in Black performers of the modern era who transformed their predicament not only through self-reinvention but also through reorienting their relationship with the physical world. Their bodily movements were means through which they created new ways of thinking about themselves as communities in their home countries or even in locations abroad.[71] These performances thus elicited a sense of symbolic belonging to Pan-Africa, since the countries in which they lived did not fully accept them as part of the citizenry or the nation-state. Indeed, many artists, intellectuals, and activists of this his-torical moment have articulated how restricting the classifications of na-tionality and ethnic affiliation were to their ambitious pursuits. Tropical aesthetics can certainly aid in understanding how various social and po-litical movements sought to mobilize people of the Black Atlantic during the early twentieth century, thereby allowing artists to experience a mar-velous liberation.[72]

✳

Through the examination of a phenomenon that has gone more or less unnoticed, *Tropical Aesthetics of Black Modernism* makes a substantial contribution to our understanding of Black people's relationship with their environment during the age of modernism and how this in turn con-tributed to their self-definition in the early twentieth century. This book strives to consider how early twentieth-century Black Atlantic visual art-ists, performers, and masqueraders were expressing the desire for a sense of belonging to the tropicalist terrains by redefining and thus claiming it through visual representation, embodied performances, or even simply by masquerading on the terrain.

Chapter 1 examines the work of artist Aaron Douglas. A number of Douglas's earlier works from the 1920s to the 1940s prioritized represen-tations of urbanity in an effort to emphasize African Americans' partic-ipation in American modernist enterprise. In this chapter, I argue that the compositions in which the natural landscapes predominate should be viewed not as a visual rebuttal of modernism but as a Black modern-ist re-presentation that envisages tropicalia as monumental and integral to early twentieth-century Black self-definition. One can certainly associate Douglas's tropical landscapes of the southern United States and of the Caribbean as evocations of the tropical regions of sub-Saharan Africa. For him, Africa was the common thread that connected Black people of all nationalities. And his tropical scenery served as an intermediary that geologically linked the southern United States and the Caribbean to the continent. I also explore artworks that reflect what I view as Douglas's aspiration to convey a people who desire an alternative to the capitalist order of the land, an alternative modernity that is not monopolizing but is egalitarian. Through the use of a tropical aesthetic, I demonstrate how Douglas's art makes visible and quite perceptible the complicated relationship that members of the Black Atlantic have with their environment, one that can be empowering despite history and integral to their self-definition.

A crucial aspect of blacks attaining self-definition in the early twentieth century was the belief in the possibility of Black political autonomy. Aspirations of Black sovereignty are certainly present in the works of Wifredo Lam, who created art upon his return to Cuba in the 1940s that reflected a desire to reclaim the landscape for the sake of gaining political autonomy, particularly for the Black masses. Building on the idea of the monumentality of the tropical terrain, chapter 2 investigates the ways the artist reinvented the Cuban landscape, particularly given how his compositions rendered a new kind of modernity that privileges nature and man's relationship with it. Given Lam's preoccupation with the land of Cuba and with Black Cuban culture, the chapter illuminates Lam's effort to insightfully represent the environment with a sense of rootedness, a sense of place for Black Cubans, many of whom were diminished by poverty and exploitation. The art he created is imbued with a call for a radical shift in the way Black people mold their identities, insisting that one develops a strong sense of place in this endeavor. In this chapter, I demonstrate how Lam's art reflects his belief that despite the histories of slavery, colonization, and European cultural imperialism the Caribbean has endured, the art and culture emerging from the region can help shape a new disposition. The compositions he created during this period masterfully eradicate reductive visual representations of Caribbean people and the land they inhabit in an effort to reclaim humanity and dignity. Lam referred to his art as an "art of decolonization" and urged all artists with a similar background to sever all ties with the colonial culture. With this in mind, I examine the ways in which Lam and his art encompass the proactive and transformative nature of Black modernism, emphasizing the fundamental purpose of the terrain in this venture.

To further underscore the immense potential of Black modernism in all its configurations, chapter 3 considers how performance can be recognized as a form of visual representation, given the primacy of the body as a medium of visual expression and an immediate means through which the body as a creative force can readily accomplish a direct connection with the terrain and thereby enact a *naming of place*. Through the examination of early to mid-twentieth-century performances of Trinidad Carnival, I interrogate the ways in which Trinidad Carnival of this period functioned as an articulation of Pan-Africanism. The chapter examines the emergence of the Jamette Carnival of the late nineteenth century that was a reflection of the members of the Black underclass who predominated the festivities. I explore the history of the term *jamette* and how it was first a descriptor for an entire class of people and eventually became a term that encompassed the debased traits of a certain type of woman in mid-twentieth-century Trinidad. I use feminist theory to discuss how during Carnival, jamettes defied Victorian principles that relegated women to subservience. The chapter also considers efforts by the colonial authorities to "clean up" the Carnival in an effort to institutionalize it in the early twentieth century and explores ways in which the Black working class and burgeoning Black middle class found ways to challenge these efforts through Carnival performances, costuming, and music. Despite the predicament of antidemocratic colonial policies, many Black Trinidadians found resolve in the proliferation of Ethiopianism and Garveyism, the labor movement that dealt specifically with issues that working men and women faced, as well as the anticolonialism movement. All of this provided much fodder for Carnival celebrations during this era and made possible a carnivalesque yet subversive performance of Black modernism. I also explicate how the festival engendered a type of corporeal expression that on the one hand is creatively oriented and on the other is political in its affect as a strategy of space-making. Carnival provided a visceral means of performatively reclaiming the land belonging to the colonizer while also engaging with the tropical terrain.

The realms of music and theater provide noteworthy examples of how Black bodily articulations can be powerful and effective means of making space, even if the tropical landscape is simulated and tropicalized Black subjectivities are performed. In chapter 4, I examine the ways in which the stage and screen performances of Josephine Baker and Maya Angelou highlight the internationalist ethos of Pan-Africanism through their corporeal venerations of tropicality. Through song and dance, Baker and

Angelou practiced an imperative of the modern era by transforming their predicament not only through self-reinvention but also through reorienting their relationship with the physical world. During the early twentieth century, Black performers such as Baker migrated from the United States, the Caribbean, Latin America, and Africa to the major European metropolises in order to capitalize on the negrophilia of the time. And in the same way Black Atlantic peoples in Paris vehemently took on structures of cultural power with the narratives they performed that explored the dimensions of these structures and sought opportunities for manipulation and reshaping them, they also defied notions of cartographic reason through their reification of Black people's geography within these geographies of domination.[73] Similarly, during the calypso craze that took America by storm in the 1950s, attempts by Black American calypso performers to mimic the Black primitive other symbolize a need to affiliate themselves with diasporic Black peoples. I explore key performances by Angelou and Baker that exemplify tropical aesthetics.

The book's conclusion encourages a consideration of contemporary iterations of tropicality evident in art and visual culture. This chapter first acknowledges the significance of the Tropicalismo movement of Brazil, spearheaded by artist Hélio Oiticica in the 1960s, which aimed to "cannibalize" foreign modern and contemporary artistic styles and, in turn, redeploy this power of the colonizers in an effort to create a new art of exotic Brazil. While this movement is particular to the idiosyncrasies of the Brazilian art world of the mid-twentieth century, it does serve as an example of a larger cultural effort to challenge the reductive connotations of cultural forms imposed by the West and redefine these meanings to create a new signification. Continuing in this trajectory, this chapter aims to examine works by contemporary artists Wangechi Mutu and Edouard Duval-Carrié. I also consider the Black speculative reaches of tropical aesthetics as they manifest in Mutu's works, which situate tropical aesthetics within a larger artistic and political practice that speculates on Black Atlantic pasts, presents, and futures.[74]

The imagined geographies investigated in *Tropical Aesthetics of Black Modernism* are urgent calls to inquire into the extent to which the discipline of art history can be pushed when geography comes into play. How can an attuned awareness of geography inform one's reading of art that ponders the Black experience? In addition, this book tackles the following question: How can the portrayal of the natural be constituted so that it functions as a counterdiscourse to the claim that only Europe is the domain of culture and therefore superior to non-Western parts of the world?[75] This book seeks to illuminate how artists and performers conjure the tropical landscape in order to delineate the various experiences, complexities, and affectations ever present in the terrain, thereby not reducing its value to mere physical properties that can be exploited for monetary gain.

In early twentieth-century art, the representation of tall buildings and urbanity was tantamount to the idea of modernity. Many of Aaron Douglas's
works from the 1920s to the 1940s prioritized such representations in an effort to emphasize African Americans' participation in American modernist enterprise. However, the compositions in which the natural landscapes
predominate should not be viewed as a visual rebuttal of modernism. The
artworks function as Black modernist re-presentations that envisage
tropicalia as monumental and integral to early twentieth-century Black
self-definition. These stylized tropical landscapes call for a more comprehensive understanding of early twentieth-century Black identity. Douglas
masterfully re-presents tropical terrains in a radical way. He employs *tropical aesthetics* in an effort to enact the *naming of place*, which is an assertion
of one's geopolitical prerogative.[1] Through the use of a tropical aesthetic,
Douglas enacts the humanization of space and makes visible and perceptible the complicated relationship that members of the Black Atlantic have
with their environment, one that can be empowering despite history and
integral to their self-making.

A number of scholars have noted the parallels that exist between Douglas's murals and the writing of Jean Toomer. In particular, Toomer's 1923
novel *Cane* bears a striking similarity to Douglas's art with its experimental fusion of fiction, poetry, and drama. This complex aesthetic structure
has visual congruity with the multifaceted imagery found in Douglas's
paintings.[2] *Cane* was inspired by Toomer's teaching job at an agricultural
college in Sparta, Georgia, as well as his exposure to Black folk culture.[3]
Set in rural Georgia and the urban centers of Washington, DC, and Chicago, the book was written in the early years of the Great Migration when
millions of African Americans were leaving rural communities in the
South for the industrialized cities of the North in search of economic opportunities and a less repressive racial climate.[4]

While *Cane* is often recognized as a premier example of modernist literature, Toomer's novel is often interpreted as a rebuttal of modernization, since it champions the fecundity of the farm in addition to its promise of economic and political autonomy for the African American southerner, despite the eventual overthrow by development.[5] The increasingly destitute African American sharecroppers in states such as Georgia emerged as a result of the collapse of the Black Belt plantation system, and this soon propelled their exodus to the North. Despite the southern terrain's misfortune, there are moments in the novel that exalt the splendor of the landscape and incite a nostalgic longing for agrarian life.[6] Such is the case in the chapter titled "Bona and Paul." Paul is a southern migrant in Chicago who, while looking out his window, embarks on a mind's excursion back to Georgia.

> Gray slanting roofs of houses are tinted lavender in the setting sun. Paul follows the sun, over the stock-yards where a fresh stench is just arising, across wheat lands that are still waving above their stubble, into the sun. Paul follows the sun to a pine-matted hillock in Georgia. He sees the slanting roofs of gray unpainted cabins tinted lavender. A Negress chants a lullaby beneath the mate-eyes of a southern planter. Her breasts are ample for the suckling of a song. She weans it, and sends it, curiously weaving, among lush melodies of cane and corn. Paul follows the sun into himself in Chicago.[7]

Here, Paul is able to transcend time and space via the sun in an effort to return to his idyllic southern terrain. This return is speculative though, since, as W. E. B. Du Bois cautioned in *The Souls of Black Folk*, the social and economic perils of the Black race seemed to have been centered in the state of Georgia.[8] For the challenges Black people faced were being overlooked, such as the issues of serfdom, poverty, and subordination. And at the core of this predicament was the creation of two separate worlds that the color line demarcated. Du Bois's notion of the color line was an "adjustment of relations in economic and political affairs . . . an adjustment subtle and difficult to grasp, yet singularly ingenious."[9]

Like Douglas's art, Toomer's *Cane* celebrates a kind of "tropical" modernism in an American context. On account of the inclusion of the tropical cane crop throughout the text, *Cane* occupies a similar space as Douglas's art, given its exploration of the natural landscape as well as modernity in its dealings with the American South. Inherent in both works by Douglas and Toomer is a celebration of the land and the benefits it has for Black people, not to mention the thematic resonance of a speculative return. More important, the diasporic potential of both Douglas's and Toomer's work is explicit.[10] With this in mind, a significant enterprise that must be considered is aptly queried by McKittrick: "How do geography and blackness work together to advance a different way of knowing and imagining the world[?]"[11] The art of Aaron Douglas offers a convincing means of exploring this phenomenon. Douglas's application of tropical aesthetics actualizes Ménil's conceptualization of the land of the marvelous through which one can defy spatial boundaries and even cross infinite distances.[12] In his art, Douglas reimagined the American landscape with the Black American in mind. He also connected it with other lands that members of the Black Atlantic occupied, in addition to establishing a vegetal connection with the tropical terrain of sub-Saharan Africa. In essence, Douglas created a Pan-Africanist visual aesthetic that was crucial to early twentieth-century Black self-definition. Even though the idea of belonging to a real/imagined Africa could never be fully realized, Douglas's works reify social geographies by offering a different sense of place that was indeed marvelous and a stunning revenge.[13] Undoubtedly, Douglas's renderings of the marvelous real offer a liberating regeneration of life so necessary for early twentieth-century Black folk.

This chapter examines the emergence of tropicalia in Douglas's art, taking into consideration the pivotal role his mentor Winold Reiss, a German-born artist and graphic designer, played in this aesthetic trajectory. More important, it situates Douglas among the pantheon of American artists who have celebrated the terrain as an endemic part of American identity. It particularly highlights the contributions of African American nineteenth-century landscape artists such as Robert S. Duncanson, whose compositions memorialize the complexities prevalent in the interactions between Black bodies and the American landscape. In so doing, this chapter acknowledges the works of Aaron Douglas that serve to continue this enterprise in American landscape painting. Another point of inquiry is the multivalent associations of the Black body and tropicalia, specifically the ways in which historical legacies of slavery and colonialism have rendered Black people as ungeographic subjectivities in tropical regions of the world. Despite this, Douglas's art proves that this fleeting sensibility that makes one feel out of place is empowering, thereby reflecting a counterideology to conventional understandings of modernity.[14] Also of significance are the iterations of Africanity that are so prevalent in Douglas's art. This chapter seeks to interrogate how Douglas's art implicates not only tropicality in the articulation of modernism but also visual narratives of Africanity that are often viewed as antithetical to the notion of modernity. Very timely in this intersection of Africanism and modernism in Douglas's art and the overall cultural oeuvre of the period is the crucial Pan-Africanism movement that gained momentum in the early twentieth century; the visual manifestation of this phenomenon in his art is also examined here.

This chapter explores numerous works that characterize the evolution of Douglas's oeuvre, including experimentation with stylized Africanisms in earlier pieces, such as Reiss's *Interpretation of Harlem Jazz I* (1925), as well as iconic works that focus on the American terrain and capture the imaginings of expansion and possibility for the Black working class, such as Douglas's *From Slavery to Reconstruction*, the second panel from the *Aspects of Negro Life* series (1934). *An Idyll of the Deep South*, the third panel from this series, offers an opportunity to interrogate the ways in which the natural environment was associated with provisions for survival on a number of levels. Douglas's *Haitian Mural* (1942) is a staunch tribute to Haiti's terrain but also to Haiti's significance as the first Black republic and thereby symbolic of Black political autonomy. Along these lines, works such as *Building More Stately Mansions* (1944) show how Douglas generates an empowering narrative of Africanity in his art that connects Black people to ancient African civilizations.

THE LEGACY OF LANDSCAPE PAINTING

Recognized as the premier artist of the Harlem Renaissance, Douglas created works that reflected the African American experience and highlighted the contributions made by Black Americans to American modernity. Leaders of the movement such as James Weldon Johnson used African American arts and culture to place African American social issues at the forefront of the national agenda.[15] Alain Locke, another prominent figure of the New Negro movement, believed that it was important for Black artists to create an artistic legacy and stop mimicking Western art, and to be engaged in artistic innovation.[16] More than any other artist of the Harlem Renaissance, Douglas was able to capture the "early-twentieth-century spirit of velocity and animation: the pulse of cities and their inhabitants, regardless of race, ethnicity and nationality."[17] Furthermore, Douglas was able to achieve this by portraying modernity in a way that was specific in its signification of African American history and culture, thereby creating modernist forms that were ultramodern and progressive.[18] In his art, Douglas conveyed symbolic allegories that reflected the complexities and contradictions of African American modernism—the urban skyscraper adjacent to the rural scene—via the clever combination of African motifs with European aesthetic approaches such as cubism and constructivism.[19]

While the portrayal of urbanity was intrinsic to his creative mission, the depiction of foliage seems to also bear the same weight, given its abundance in much of his works. Art historians have noted Douglas's rendering of tropical foliage in a number of his paintings.[20] However, very little attention has been given to the purpose and significance of the vegetation that proliferates these compositions. Works from the advent of his career such as *The Emperor Jones* series of 1926 to later pieces such as *Lagos, Nigeria* of 1956 feature stylistic and graphically rendered depictions of greenery. While it is debatable whether *all* the foliage represented in each work is tropical—since the paintings are often set in the United States, Africa, or the Caribbean—what is certain is that tropical flora such as banana trees are identifiable in some.

Even though Douglas did not spend considerable time in the tropics beyond his visits to the Caribbean in 1938 and Africa in 1956, it would be historically short-sighted to not consider the innumerable meditations on tropicalia in the arts that he would have been privy to while living in Harlem in the 1920s and 1930s. Given his broad intellect and cosmopolitan worldview, Douglas would have had a great appreciation and intellectual purview of much of the art, literature, music, theater, dance, and cinema that the Harlem Renaissance had to offer.[21] And many works in these various disciplines featured ruminations of tropicalia. Tropicality was evident in the novels *Cane* by Jean Toomer, *Tropic Death* by Eric Walrond, *Banana Bottom* by Claude McKay, and *Porgy* by DuBose Heyward. Douglas was also very close to McKay, who was originally from Jamaica, and from whom he would have garnered accounts of the Black experience in this tropical region of the Black Atlantic.[22] There were also the theater productions of *Voodoo Macbeth* (1936) and *Haiti* (1938) in New York, as well as early-twentieth century performances in Paris by Josephine Baker, who evoked tropicality. Douglas would have most likely seen her while studying in Paris in the early 1930s.[23] Like these aforementioned creative endeavors, the tropical landscape in Douglas's work made possible a geological conduit that linked the diaspora to Africa, effecting the possibilities and promise of Pan-Africanism. As a geological conduit, these evocations of tropicalia also make an aesthetic leap across centuries, underscoring Douglas's conviction that his "task was to fabricate such patterns as might have been conceived by Negro artists of ante-bellum days."[24] His tropical landscapes thus serve as reminders of the importance of African Americans to American progress over time.

With this in mind, Douglas's inclusion of banana trees in his stylized landscapes should not be seen as a far-fetched, imaginative leap. Some of his terrains were not geographically specific and can be perceived as not depicting a particular place/space but conveying a broader view of geography that even surpassed the boundaries of African America.[25] To say that tropical flora is intrinsically un-American is to not consider the many depictions of tropical landscapes by American painters beginning in the nineteenth century. While tropical topographies are not often associated with the United States, American subtropical environments do in fact exist, and Americans became very preoccupied with them by the mid-nineteenth century. In fact, Americans looked to the swamps, jungles, and marshes of the rural South as alternatives to the high romantic iconography of the Hudson River School.[26]

The incorporation of such lush tropical landscapes into his compositions leads one to question why the artist would even find it necessary to situate so many of his paintings in the outdoors. Douglas's midwestern upbringing may have contributed to such a discernment for the terrain. Born in Topeka, Kansas, on May 26, 1899, Douglas grew up in a politically astute Black community that valued cultural literacy and social uplift while also placing the self-help creed of Booker T. Washington in high regard. Topeka was among the first U.S. cities where Black institutions were established and where African Americans had great access to elective and appointive offices. Furthermore, it was one of the few metropolitan centers where Black people had less restricted interactions with white people.[27] As art historian Susan Earle notes, compared to regions like the Deep South and the East, midwestern states like Kansas had less institutionalized race consciousness and, coupled with the glorification of open spaces and the associations made between these spaces and freedom, this must have engendered in Douglas a desire to visually register this sensibility as coinciding with the aspirations of early twentieth-century African Americans.[28]

This sentiment is evident in Douglas's dust jacket design for Arthur Huff Fauset's book *For Freedom: A Biographical Story of the American Negro*, a work that he did early in his career (figure 1.1). The graphic-oriented composition presents three figures fashioned in Douglas's signature sil-

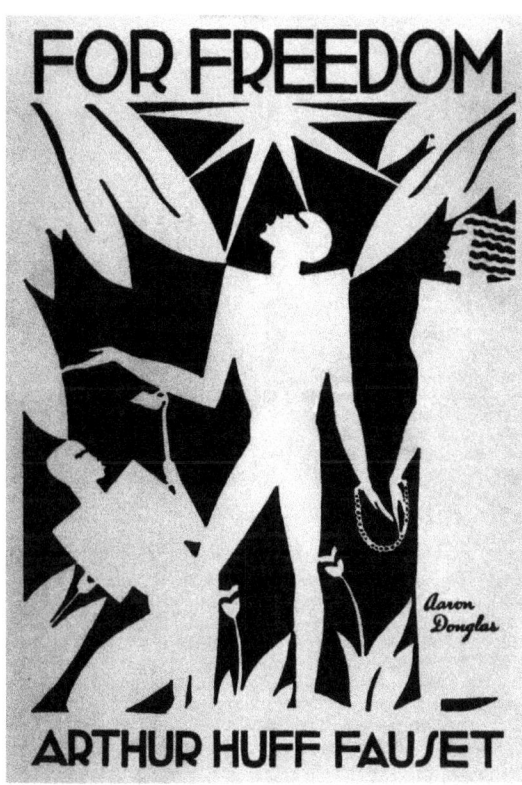

1.1 Arthur Huff Fauset, *For Freedom: A Biographical Story of the American Negro*, 1927. Dust jacket design by Aaron Douglas. Collection of Thomas H. Wirth.

houetted style who are positioned in a blossoming landscape filled with trees and flowers. The central figure's left hand is shackled to a figure on the right while a third figure kneels as if toiling the land. They all look up at a glaring sun, above which are the words of the book's title, *For Freedom*. With the central figure's arm gesturing upward, and all their mouths agape, this pictorial configuration conveys the spirit of eagerness enslaved Africans in the United States must have felt in the years leading up to the abolition of slavery.

Douglas created this work during his two-year fellowship at the Winold Reiss School of Art, and it is clear that Reiss had a tremendous impact on Douglas during this period. Reiss was a German modernist who, like his counterparts, was avidly interested in ethnography as well as documenting various racial groups. By the time Reiss immigrated to the United States

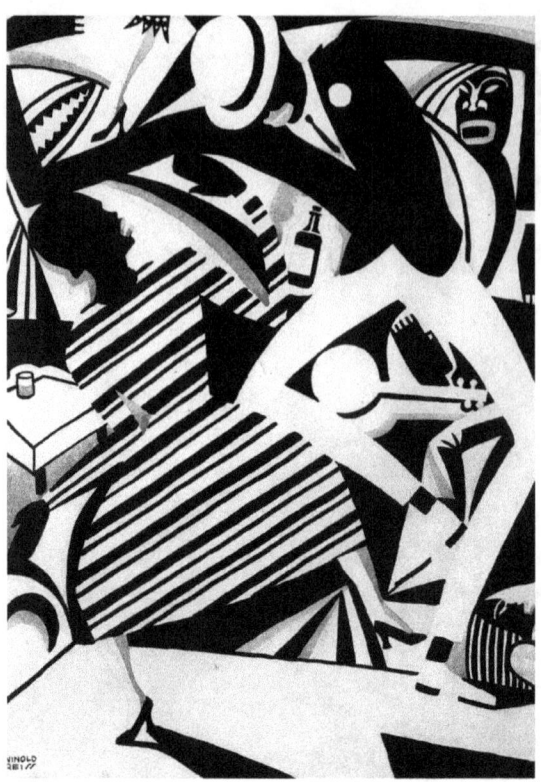

1.2 Winold Reiss, *Interpretation of Harlem Jazz I,*
1925. Collection of Henry S. Field.

and settled in New York City in 1913, he had turned his focus to the Black
subject in an effort to create his graphic and stylized Africanisms. Take,
for instance, *Interpretation of Harlem Jazz I* (1925) (figure 1.2), created the
year Douglas began his studies at Reiss's school. Using geometric shapes,
bold lines, and stylized African motifs, Reiss portrays a lively scene with a
couple dancing in one of many cabarets in Jazz Age Harlem. Their bodies
are rendered as flat silhouettes, with accentuated lips highlighting their
faces. This accent visually connects them to the African mask on the right
of the picture plane, examples of the Egyptian art and Art Deco intona-
tions of Reiss's oeuvre. The precarious posturing of the two bodies and
various objects in the work reflect Reiss's penchant for cubism. Another
work of the same year, simply titled *Illustration*, shows a monumental
Black silhouetted subject reclining on a stylized tropical landscape. This
piece once again reflects Reiss's aesthetic trajectory, which certainly had

an impact on Douglas, whom he encouraged to paint African-inspired imagery in an effort to find his own artistic voice.[29]

Reiss's aesthetic epitomizes the Jugendstil style of art, the German counterpart of the Art Nouveau philosophy of art and design that predominated Europe from the late nineteenth to early twentieth centuries. With the visual beckoning to tropical flora evident in many works of art, architecture, and design, this aesthetic of the Jugendstil oeuvre clearly characterizes the imagery of colonial empire that was prevalent in early twentieth-century Europe.[30] While this imagery may have served a particular purpose in Reiss's work, these same conceptions in Douglas's art express a signification that was absolutely distinct. As is evident in *For Freedom*, Douglas re-presents the tropicalist scenery in a new and radical way, employing tropical aesthetics that makes possible a visual articulation that reflects a different way of knowing and imagining the world. Unlike the subject in Reiss's *Illustration*, Douglas's Black figures express through their gestures a desire to identify with their environment in an effort to assert themselves and have their humanity be recognized with the promise of freedom.

Such an impassioned sense of obligation to convey these sentiments in his art is evident in the early stages of his career. Recalling this time in his life, Douglas explained:

> I took the beginning steps toward this fairly complete visual statement as far back as 1925. At that time, pleas could be heard on all sides for a visual pattern comparable to or rather suggestive of the uniqueness found in the gestures and bodily movements of the Negro dance, and the sounds and vocal patterns as found in the Negro song. I finally undertook the task simply because there was no one else to do so.
>
> Under the guidance, inspiration and encouragement of my teacher, Winold Reiss, I ventured forth. The results are these: Drawing for the *New Negro* book (1925), [and] Illustrations for *Emperor Jones* (1926).[31]

Douglas recognized the social importance of what he was about to embark upon. Over time, his art successfully reflected the pontifications of Black leaders of the day such as James Weldon Johnson and W. E. B. Du Bois. Very noticeable is Douglas's desire to create a quintessential artistic oeuvre that was uniquely African American, and thus the visual counterpart of the contributions African Americans made to American modernism. African American musical and performance forms such as jazz, the cakewalk, and the Charleston transformed American culture so that it no longer imitated older European models but was instead recognized as the epitome of modernity.[32] Douglas's artistic aspirations take heed of Locke's appeal that Black American artists could create a new American art, thereby continuing the spirit of innovation evident in the Black vernacular into the arena of fine art.[33] Douglas's comments quoted here undoubtedly capture the aspirations of an artist who wanted his art to embody this Black modernism.

As tantamount as modernism was in his endeavors, Douglas's stylized actualizations of the American landscape in his many noted works, with their silhouetted subjects interspersed throughout, are also wholly strategic in relaying the crucial role African Americans played in the nurturing and the development of "God's nature." This artistic celebration of the American terrain has its roots in the Hudson River School, the group of New York City–based landscape painters whose works characterized a quintessential American artistry in the mid-nineteenth century. Their compositions conveyed a reverence of nature, which was a reaction to the destruction of the wilderness for capitalist enterprise in early nineteenth-century America. Philosophers such as Ralph Waldo Emerson privileged nature and believed it to be synonymous with God. Transcending theological parameters that separated God and nature, this kind of Christianized naturalism replaced the Bible with nature. The dissemination of the idea of God's nature and God in nature was so widespread that even the orthodoxly religious opined that "if nature was God's Holy Book, it *was* God."[34] Many stakeholders of the Hudson River School, including Thomas Cole, no doubt an influential figure among the group, believed that God extended to artists the powers of revelation and creation. Asher B. Durand, another leading figure in the group, asserted that "art is in fact man's lowly imitation of the creative power of the Almighty."[35] Certainly, members of the Hudson River School contributed to a nationalistic project that identified America's destiny with the American landscape.[36]

This terrain, however, was considered the birthright to only the Anglo-Saxon portion of the American populace. Mid-nineteenth-century Black American political figures such as Martin Robison Delany recognized this predicament that all members of the Black race faced, enslaved and free alike. An abolitionist, physician, scientist, and inventor, among many other titles, Delany became devoted to the cause of African American emigration in the 1850s, particularly when political developments of this period curtailed his integrationist aspirations. While his political ideology shifted from Pan-African nationalism prior to the Civil War to universalist motivations that were void of race consciousness in the period after the Civil War and the Reconstruction, his writing from 1852 to 1862 is worth consideration. In his 1852 publication, *The Condition, Elevation, Emigration, and Destiny of the Colored People of the United States,* Delany discusses his travels to Africa as well as Central and South America in hopes of determining the most opportune location for an African American colony. When considering the prospects of immigrating to Central and South America, Delany writes:

> Will we go? Go we must, and go we will, as there is no alternative. To remain here in North America, and be crushed to the earth in vassalage and degradation, we never will. . . .
>
> Shall we be told that we can live nowhere, but under the will of our North American oppressors; that this (the United States,) is the country most favorable to our improvement and progress? Are we incapable of self-government, and making such improvements for ourselves as we delight to enjoy after American white men have made them for themselves?[37]

This bold language is written with the passion of a manifesto and reflects the sense of urgency Black Americans must have felt at this time. That living in North America in the middle of the nineteenth century was like living "nowhere" speaks to the insecurity Black people experienced in their relationship with the nation-state. Still, there were Black Americans who dared to imagine some level of affinity with the land of the United States. And among artist circles, this was expressed in the creative manifestations of the Hudson River School.

With so much emphasis on the rhetoric of Manifest Destiny, which was no doubt reflected in the Hudson River School paintings, it is clear that not only American artists of European descent were preoccupied with territorial expansion and its correlating ideals of freedom and upward social mobility. African American artists also responded to this glorification of the American landscape. One such artist was Robert S. Duncanson, whose *Blue Hole, Flood Waters, Little Miami River* (1851) (figure 1.3) provides an alternative meditation of the American terrain. Ten years prior to creating this painting, Duncanson settled in Cincinnati, long acclaimed for its considerable "free colored" population and abolitionist sentiment. The city was also recognized as a center for the Ohio River valley landscape tradition, and Duncanson soon became an acknowledged part of this school of painting. While it was not an organized group, the artists un-

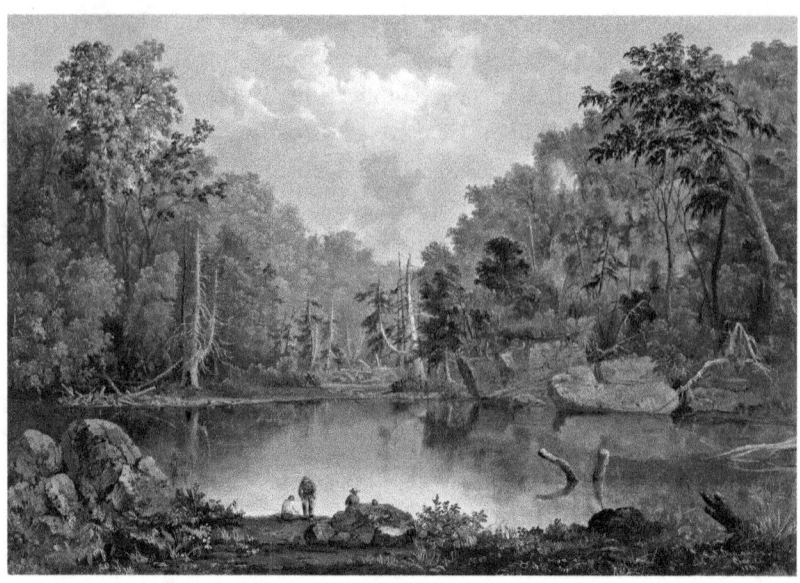

1.3 Robert S. Duncanson, *Blue Hole, Flood Waters, Little Miami River*, 1851. Oil on canvas, 28.5 × 41½ in. Cincinnati Art Museum; gift of Norbert Heermann and Arthur Helbig, 1926.18.

doubtedly aspired to paint in the style popularized by the Hudson River School of the Northeast.[38]

Duncanson was a self-taught artist who eventually gained tremendous esteem for his artistry. In fact, he was the first African American artist to receive international recognition.[39] A tributary of the Ohio River, Little Miami River was a popular site for many regional artists. The setting of the painting was also a preferred escape route for fugitive slaves.[40] Duncanson would have no doubt been aware of the historical significance of this location. His portrayal of the Little Miami River not only offers the viewer a picturesque perspective of this beloved destination; it also bears sociopolitical commentary. The towering trees on the upper left and right regions of the picture plane create a downward slope to the center of the painting. This feature produces a triangular-shaped sky, a shape that is somewhat echoed in the lake just below it. With this body of water rendered in the middle ground, the lush foliage embanking it creates a sort of haven for the three men seen in the foreground holding fishing rods. The diagonal formation of the foliage purposefully leads the eye to what appear to be long pieces of lumber as well as some driftwood, emblematic of efforts to pursue industrialization in newly acquired annexations on the continent. This idea does seem to go against the celebration of nature that was pervasive in the art of the Hudson River School, particularly since these landscape painters often aspired to capture a terrain in its purest form. However, the threat of annihilation was always seen as an eventual occurrence. In an 1847 review of Hudson River artist J. E. Cropsey, the writer proclaims: "The axe of civilization is busy with our old forests, and artisan ingenuity is fast sweeping away the relics of our national infancy. . . . Yankee enterprise has little sympathy with the picturesque, and it behooves our artists to rescue from its grasp the little that is left, before it is too late."[41] Entirely forthright in this warning is the unquestionable responsibility placed on the artists of the Hudson River School to simulate the grandeur of the untouched landscape on their canvases. And Duncanson also saw this as being his responsibility. However, it is these large logs and driftwood in *Blue Hole* that distinguish this landscape painting from others created around this time. Duncanson chose to capture evidence of the effects of the "axe of civilization," perhaps to acknowledge its inevitable arrival. Certainly, the early signs of industrialization on a site that was a popular escape route for fugitive slaves is an artistic beckoning for the geographic, and economic, reclamation for the centuries of toiling on land that enslaved Africans could never claim as their own. Du Bois's adept wording of this conundrum in the first decade of the twentieth century was "the problem of the color line," a geopolitical parameter that defined the relationship between the darker races and the lighter races. Du Bois firmly opined that "the Negro cannot stand the present reactionary tendencies and unreasoning drawing of the color-line indefinitely without discouragement and retrogression. And the condition of the Negro is ever the excuse for further discrimination. Only by a union of intelligence and sympathy across the color-line in this critical period of the Republic shall justice and right triumph."[42]

Despite Du Bois's supplication, this troubling predicament would continue to haunt the daily lives of Black people in decades to come. Certainly, one can interpret the racially ambiguous figures seen in the foreground as symbolic of the desire African Americans also had for the tenets of Manifest Destiny that was only seen as the unabashed entitlement of Anglo-Saxon Americans. While it is true that African Americans played an important role in the exploration and settlement of the American West, many Black people ventured to north central states such as Ohio where slavery was not permitted to escape living in bondage and seek opportunities for a new life. By 1830, more than sixteen thousand Black people were counted in Ohio, Indiana, Illinois, and Michigan at the time of the fifth census.[43] Cincinnati's Black population had more than doubled by 1850. Employment and education opportunities were not always available to African Americans in the city, and they probably could not proclaim an affinity to any institutions established there.[44] Yet, regardless of these tribulations, what Black people did do was create what McKittrick refers to as alternative geographic formulations, since "traditional geographies, and their attendant hierarchical categories of humanness, cannot do the emancipatory work some subjects demand."[45] Duncanson's *Blue Hole* begins the project of creating a different type of relationship with the terrain they now called home. Although they escaped the torment of slavery, the legislature in place still did not recognize them as deserving of the rights and privileges of a citizen, much less the land on which they now lived. Given the historical significance of the setting as a route for fugitive slaves, Duncanson's composition and its title make possible a renaming of place that is unique to the African American experience in nineteenth-century Ohio. For this renaming is a process of self-assertion and humanization that was lost in the efforts toward Black political and economic autonomy.[46]

Furthermore, Duncanson's *Blue Hole* offers an alternative geographical formulation by depicting a remapping of the space by Black Americans that incites a more just geographic construction.[47] The Little Miami River was in fact a popular site to portray among artists of southwestern Ohio. One's artistic interpretation of this locale would depend in large part on what vantage point one chose. As discussed in the introduction, European American photographers and painters would opt to capture a panoramic vista based on what was considered to be the best general view. Such an image would often consist of what was considered to be the idealized traits of the scenery, which included unique features of the region. Duncanson's composition is an explicit effort to challenge that predominant perception of nature. By creating a just geographic construction of this area, the artist and his work expressively go against the established European American value system of image-making.[48]

Just as Duncanson's art offered different means of relating to one's environment, Douglas's second panel of the *Aspects of Negro Life* series, *From Slavery to Reconstruction* (plate 1), featured imaginings of expansion and possibility for southern African Americans living in the years after slavery. This composition simultaneously conveys two pivotal events of African American history: slavery and the Reconstruction period. It features

Douglas's signature silhouetted human figures that recall ancient Egyptian wall paintings, the concentric circles that aid in highlighting focal points in his paintings, and the artist's monochromatic color palette. Read from right to left, the painting depicts an official reading of the Emancipation Proclamation to an elated group whose arms are outstretched above their heads. A trumpeter, who stands to the right of the official, provides musical accompaniment to the reading of the proclamation. Behind him a woman offers expressive corporeal movements that seem to echo the sentiments of the man to the left of the official with the broken chains still attached to his wrists. In the background stands a row of Union soldiers who symmetrically correspond to the second row of soldiers on the left side of the composition. They are less distinct than the first unit, yet their presence visually offsets the Ku Klux Klan (KKK) members depicted on horseback at the extreme left of the composition. The Klan members are positioned directly behind a group of sharecroppers, a primary occupation for many African Americans during the era of Reconstruction. Although a few sharecroppers take heed of their presence, the majority listen attentively to a Reconstruction leader telling the men of their right to vote as he points to the Capitol in the background.

Although not the main focus in the painting, the semitropical landscape of the American South is an important visual and aesthetic component of the composition. It may have informed Douglas's selections for the color palette, since the use of green hues is paramount in the organization of the work. The foliage provides a rich tapestry through which the viewer can further understand the painting's Black subjects. The off-white color of the cotton accenting the lower portion of the work serves as an iconic reminder of the significance of this crop in American history. One is also able to recall the predicament of cotton plantations being labored by enslaved Africans and later African American sharecroppers in the first half of the twentieth century. For Douglas, it was important to acknowledge the significance of African American labor in his art: "Labor of African Americans . . . one of the most important aspects of our development. We should be proud of it. That part of our lives has gone into the building of America, not only of ourselves."[49] Still, African Americans had a complex relationship with the land leading up to Reconstruction. Although they were forced to labor in plantations while in bondage, after the abolition of slavery, many of them chose to continue working on these plantations as sharecroppers, since it was often the only means of earning a living after the Civil War. However, due to the exorbitant prices charged by the landowners in this kind of subsistence farming, many sharecroppers often lived in abject poverty. Nonetheless, this means of living provided some sense of economic empowerment and hope for integrating into the American citizenry.[50]

The capitalist exploitation of the land by the plantation owners is situated in a strained opposition to the use of provisional land by the enslaved and now the subsistence farming of the Black peasantry. Literary scholar Sylvia Wynter recognized this power structure as being endemic in Caribbean literature and Caribbean culture at large.

> If the history of Caribbean society is that of a dual relation between planation and plot, the two poles which originate in a single historical process, the ambivalence between the two has been and is the distinguishing characteristic of the Caribbean response. This ambivalence is at once the root cause of our alienation; and the possibility of our salvation. . . . The planters gave the slaves plots of land on which to grow food to feed themselves in order to maximize profits. We suggest that this plot system was, like the novel form in literature terms, the focus of resistance to the market system and market values.[51]

Wynter's ideas can certainly be applied to the situation in the United States. One of the most significant qualities about *From Slavery to Reconstruction* is how Douglas is able to convey different historical moments on one pictorial plane yet connote an overlapping of these moments via the visual evocation of cotton. This crop is the means through which to comprehend the schism entrenched in the dual relation between plantation (servitude) and plot (non-ownership but some level of autonomy). It is the singular component in the painting that links the pivotal moments in the history of the African American experience from slavery to Reconstruction. In his unique pictorial style, Douglas's mural alters the best general view of the plantation predicated by the European American value system of image-making in an effort to reveal the sociopolitical and personal experiences of Black Americans across space and time.[52]

Although African American sharecroppers did contribute to the market system as employees of these plantation owners, their presence on the land as free people rather than enslaved people is significant. For the first time in American history, during the era of Reconstruction, African American men had the right to vote and to run for elected office. This was also a moment when pivotal African American institutions were established. These examples of political, cultural, and economic autonomy intimate a burgeoning yet steadfast identity forming among African Americans who collectively claimed their rightful space in the American landscape. However, the legacy of plantocratic power seems to be imbued in the daunting yet ghostlike presence of the KKK members as they enter the painting from the left with full force. Given the fact that the Ku Klux Klan was formed in 1866, the year after the end of the Civil War and a mere three years after the passing of the Emancipation Proclamation, their emergence onto the picture plane is a reminder of their resistance to Black empowerment and the integration of the newly emancipated population into the American citizenry and even the American terrain.[53]

Douglas's *From Slavery to Reconstruction* visually narrates the African American experience up to the late nineteenth century. Such potent imagery aids in the rewriting of American history, articulating the viable contributions of this sector of American society. Speaking of his artistic aspirations, Douglas asserted that "as an artist working in the second decade of the twentieth century, my task was to fabricate such visual patterns as might have been conceived by Negro artists of antebellum days and used to interpret the appearance and meaning of his limited environment and outlook."[54] It is clear that Douglas recognized the need to represent the plight of African Americans of the nineteenth century with a great sense of dignity, character, and urgency. Undoubtedly, *From Slavery to Reconstruction* calls attention to the significant role blacks played in the development of nineteenth-century America, despite their social and political predicament.

The narrative conveyed in Douglas's mural justified the migration of many African Americans to northern cities such as his hometown of Topeka after the Civil War once Kansas entered the Union in 1861. Institutionalized racism was not an intrinsic part of the social fabric in the state, particularly since New England abolitionists were among its founders. Planned communities such as Nicodemus served as safe havens for former slaves migrating from the South. Black people in Kansas had a higher probability of getting elected and being appointed to public offices, and their interactions with white people were less regulated. Also, high schools were integrated by law, although extracurricular activities often segregated African Americans. While Kansas was not void of racism, as was the case for Duncanson, the Black community there provided Douglas with a sense of support among the Black community and alerted him to the importance of social uplift.[55] Douglas also shared with Duncanson a midwestern heritage, and with that he possessed a particular kind of worldview that mused on a broader geographical landscape. While Douglas's landscapes in his compositions were less panoramic and had a greater human presence than those of Duncanson, they nonetheless reflected the intersectionalities of open spaces and a sense of freedom. Duncanson's legacy is evident in Douglas's work, and the latter continued the former's project of producing spaces that were not deemed as belonging to Black people, thereby producing their meaning and their significance. This creative production of space functions as a kind of process of reclamation, however imaginative it may appear to be.[56]

AMERICAN TROPICALITY AND THE BLACK BODY

Despite the value of "God's nature" in nineteenth-century America, the fact remains that most Black people did not always associate the land with opportunity and hope. For many Black Americans of the late nineteenth to early twentieth centuries, the natural environment was merely associated with provisions for survival that were useful on a number of levels: from providing employment through sharecropping or even offering sustenance through the cultivation of one's food, to more culturally significant associations such as recreational activities and social gatherings that served as a means of escape from their everyday lives. To a certain extent, Douglas's *An Idyll of the Deep South* (plate 2), the third panel from the *Aspects of Negro Life* series, speaks to this phenomenon. The scene may appear charming and idyllic at first glance. Yet upon closer reflection, it portrays imagery that is melancholic and burdensome. Read from right to left as in all his murals, each area of the composition is distinguished through the choice of colors for the three groups of figures, namely off-white, earthen browns, dark greens, and blues. The right section features Black laborers crouched over while toiling the land. The figures in the middle are accentuated by concentric circles and are depicted singing and dancing to the music provided by musicians, while on the left mourners are conveyed lamenting the death of a lynched man. The placid foliage in which the scene is situated augments the somber mood of the work; there is also a row of cabins clearly visible on elevated land on the upper-right area of the mural. All these elements provide context for the individuals depicted.

The set of concentric circles on the celebratory group in the middle appears to be illuminated by a ray of light beaming from a star at the top-left corner of the picture plane. This suggests that Douglas is portraying a night scene, given the darkened atmosphere in the remainder of the mural, particularly on the right side. The nighttime marked the end of the working day and offered an opportunity for relaxation or even escapist social gatherings such as what is represented here. However, despite this moment of fleeting leisure, there is the predicament of lynching that Black men and women had to deal with regularly. The light colors used to highlight members of the dancing and singing group in the middle is also applied to some of the bodies and the general area of the lynching scene on the left. This kind of visual interplay between these two areas offers two contrasting yet everyday realities in the lives of early twentieth-century African Americans of the South. Undoubtedly, Douglas felt compelled to portray such a scene in this mural despite objections from the Public Works Administration, which sponsored his library murals.[57] Like the contentious scene of the KKK members featured in the mural *From Slavery to Reconstruction*, this lynching scene provided further evidence of the refusal of many white Americans at the time to accept Black people into the American citizenry and in turn the American landscape. The site of lynching spectacles almost always took place on the natural landscape, with trees serving as the primary means of making this horrific act possible. As literary scholar Sandy Alexandre notes, this kind of imagery speaks to how "blacks are dispossessed: denied access to property and (by extension) to sanctuary on the American geographical landscape."[58] These two disparate scenes of pleasure and unspeakable violence show not only the harsh realities of Black life but also one of the ways in which blacks dealt with traumatic events. Moreover, these two juxtaposed sites in the composition function in tandem as they intimately communicate with and contradict each other, thereby affirming and denying Black life all at once.[59] Nonetheless, the natural setting in which Black southerners lived is a reminder of the reverence they had for the land that they toiled, celebrated, and were even murdered on, which ideologically signifies a different kind of relationship with nature that reflects Black people's unique way of experiencing their environment.

The way Douglas depicts the topography here is noteworthy. The land is flat and dark, providing a visual evocation of the wetlands so typical in southern landscapes. The semitropical environments of the rural South were characterized by swamps, jungles, and marshes. By the mid-nineteenth century, Americans looked to these new landscapes as antithetical to the iconographic imagery of the Hudson River School and the moral allegory and aesthetic criteria inscribed in its picturesque framing of the

American landscape. The nationalist romanticism once reserved for terrains of the North slowly attenuated and was eventually replaced by escapist connotations, most notably with the subtropical locales of the South. More than any other physical terrain, it was the imagery of the swamp that captivated people's interest, and it was most elusive. The American swamp was the domain of sin, death, and decay, the locale for witchcraft as well as ferocious creatures. Mostly located in the southern region of the United States, these terrains that were once perceived as wild and uninhabited soon came to be viewed as exotic and even fodder for exciting yet alien experiences. By the 1850s, many Americans became fixated with psychic fulfillment and self-discovery, and they believed that exploring these alien landscapes would contribute tremendously to their evolving worldview. Furthermore, the aestheticization of the swamp by artists and writers alike illuminated and made more palpable the emergent attitudes and insights of a changing American society and economy. It is worth noting that the American imaginary began its fascination with the imagistic features of the landscape during the age of Manifest Destiny. One can certainly see how the prevalent discourse of expanding the American nation-state through imperialism and conquest was a major preoccupation for many, engendering a desire to immerse oneself in an unknown place that could be potentially dangerous but also offer an invigorating experience.[60]

Such a desire for self-fulfillment definitely existed in the southern United States, and even the enslaved Africans who labored on the plantations recognized their right to pursue the same goals of development and expansionism. The traditional geographic arrangements of the antebellum South established unjust boundaries and other systems of suppression that made it impossible for Black people to lay claim to their lives, let alone to own any plot of land.[61] This "ungeographic" subjectivity is what motivated many enslaved individuals to escape the plantations and, in many instances, venture into the swamp. Historically, large numbers of enslaved Africans found sanctuary in the Dismal Swamp of Virginia and North Carolina, and creative interpretations of this began after the Nat Turner rebellion, which occurred in its vicinity.[62] The American landscape painter Thomas Moran captured this phenomenon in *Slave Hunt, Dismal Swamp* (1861–62) (figure 1.4). Set in Virginia, the painting features two escaped slaves wading through a swamp with the aim of fleeing the slave hunters emerging in the background at the far right. At closer proximity are the hunters' dogs, depicted jumping midair in an effort to get

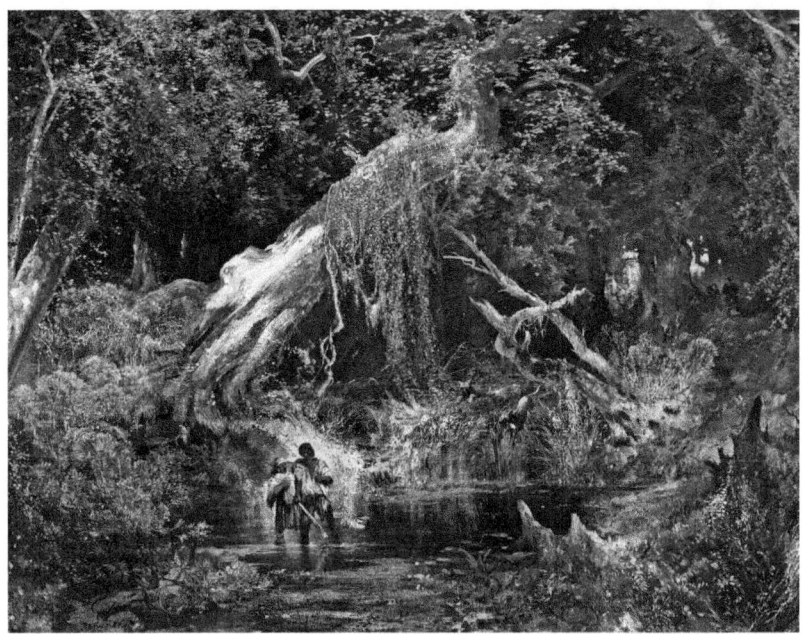

1.4 Thomas Moran, *Slave Hunt, Dismal Swamp, Virginia,* 1861–62. Oil on canvas, 34 × 44 in. Philbrook Museum of Art, Tulsa, OK; gift of Laura A. Clubb, 1947.8.44.

closer to their human targets. All this suspenseful drama is situated in the dark and impenetrable greenery of Moran's composition. The thick vegetation surrounding the enclosed swamp with its multicolored leafage, shrubbery, and vines is grandiose yet overpowering. An enormous tree trunk leans above the heads of the beleaguered escaped Africans, serving as yet another threat to their well-being. Undeniably, while the two runaway slaves perceive the slave hunters and their dogs as their adversaries, their minute dimensions in relation to the surrounding terrain reflects a fundamental concept of the sublime, namely "man's insignificance in the face of God's terrible power."[63]

The overwhelming fear of the slave hunters, their dogs, and the landscape that these two runaways possess reifies their ungeographic subjectivity. Their depiction in this painting makes palpable the assertion McKittrick offers: "If *who* we see is tied up with *where* we see through truthful, commonsensical narratives, then the placement of subaltern bodies deceptively hardens spatial binaries, in turn suggesting that some bodies belong, some bodies do not belong, and some bodies are out of place."[64]

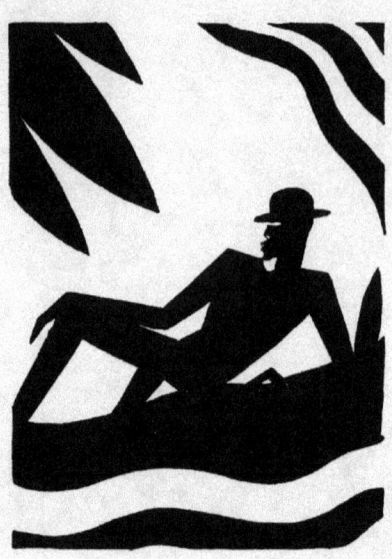

WEARY AS I CAN BE

1.5 Aaron Douglas, *Weary as I Can Be*, 1926. From
Opportunity Art Folio, 1926. Relief print, letterpress,
16 × 11½ in. Spencer Museum of Art, University
of Kansas, Lawrence.

The lone figure in a print created by Douglas in 1926 reflects this conundrum. Accompanying a poem, "Lonesome Place," by Langston
Hughes, *Weary as I Can Be* (figure 1.5) depicts a reclining figure near a
river. He looks into the distance, and veering in his direction are large, animated leaves of a tree. The sense of not belonging or of being simply out
of place is underlined by the subject's placement by the river, which, like
the swamp, provides him a means of escape from his weary life. Personi-
fying the voice of the protagonist in the poem, the subject's displacement
is captured in the included lines:

Got to leave this town cause
It's a lonesome place,
A po,' po' boy can't
Find a friendly face.

Goin' down to de river
Flowin' deep an' slow,
Goin' down to de river
Deep an' slow,—
Cause there ain't no worries
Where de waters go.[65]

The protagonist's unconcern for where the water may take him speaks to the unnerving displacement many African Americans experienced during (and even after) slavery. This sense of belonging to an ungeographic space, a place that was nowhere, was what one encountered when venturing into the swamp.

The swamp was such a dreaded entity in the American imaginary that it was inconceivable to think people would actually live in its vicinity. Indeed, enslaved Africans were well aware of European Americans' perceptions of the swamp, and this is precisely why many of them opted to maroon in these dreaded areas. The geographic arrangements of the antebellum South were dominated by European Americans, thereby displacing individuals who did not meet the racialized and gendered criteria for land ownership.[66] The swamp was their next best option, and transforming them into maroon spaces certainly challenged traditional geographic arrangements and served as the imagined Black nation fully realized.

For marronage was that liminal and transitional social space between slavery and freedom. Given that these societies existed outside standards of normativity, maroons cultivated freedom on their own terms. Political scientist Neil Roberts defines marronage as flight, with the concept of fleeing "denoting the intransitive act of marronage and its particular notion of flight. . . . Flight, therefore, is directional movement in the domain of physical environment, embodied cognition, and/or the metaphysical."[67] While movement has been fundamental to the attainment of freedom for enslaved Black people, it is fleeing that encapsulates the unorthodox nature of marronage, since this metaphysical existence is never fixed. Maroon spaces conceptually function as a type of land of the marvelous, given their liminality and the fact that it is, as Ménil declares, "situated vertiginously between nothingness and being."[68] The concept of fleeing is not unique to the experience of the escaped slaves in Moran's *The Slave Hunt, Dismal Swamp*; it is also palpable in Douglas's *Weary as I Can Be* and *An Idyll of the Deep South*, thereby compelling one to acknowledge the continuity of this disposition of Black people even after slavery. Despite these apparent parallels, Douglas's treatment of the landscapes and how the subjects relate to these spaces in both works is markedly distinct from that of Moran. While Moran conveys his Black subjects as being overpowered by "God's nature" that presumably belonged to Americans of European descent, Douglas seems to relate more to his subjects, making them as powerful and monumental as the terrain. Furthermore, Douglas's subjects have a more engaged and contemplative relationship with nature that surrounds them. Douglas's stylistic compositions characterize the sensibility of flight, a way of life that became synonymous with the Black experience for centuries, in a manner that is empowering. This unfixed existence reflects a counterideology to conventional understandings of modernity that makes palpable the unique yet complex relationship that Black people had with their natural surroundings in the early twentieth century.

AFRICANISMS AND BLACK MODERNISM

Given the Africanisms inherent in much of his early work, one can certainly associate Douglas's tropical landscapes as evocations of Africa. For him, Africa was the common thread that connected Black people of all nationalities. Douglas's interest in African art was closely linked to his desire to reach the common man and his belief that through art, Black people could begin the process of discovering their African roots. The African sculptures that he studied under the tutelage of Reiss provided him with the structural framework to pictorially render Black Atlantic social and cultural expression.[69] Apart from the hard-edged figures inspired by ancient Egyptian painted reliefs, slit-eyed masks from West and Central Africa also served as points of reference. Powell offers a semiotic reading of these ubiquitous slit-eyed profiles in Douglas's art. Noting that this pervasive element conveys a quality that is simultaneously linguistic and mute, Powell asserts that the slit eye does not necessarily represent unmediated vision but vision that is "almost closed, squinting, and under the influence of a shadowy but not dour ambience."[70] Such an interpretation highlights the existential attributes that Douglas's figures seem to possess, regardless of the time period being depicted. Moreover, it also recalls his belief that the spiritual essence of Black people was always hinged to an awareness of their African heritage.

This signification holds true in the first panel from the *Aspects of Negro Life* series, *The Negro in an African Setting* (1934) (figure 1.6). It depicts a celebratory scene in which two figures are dancing energetically in the

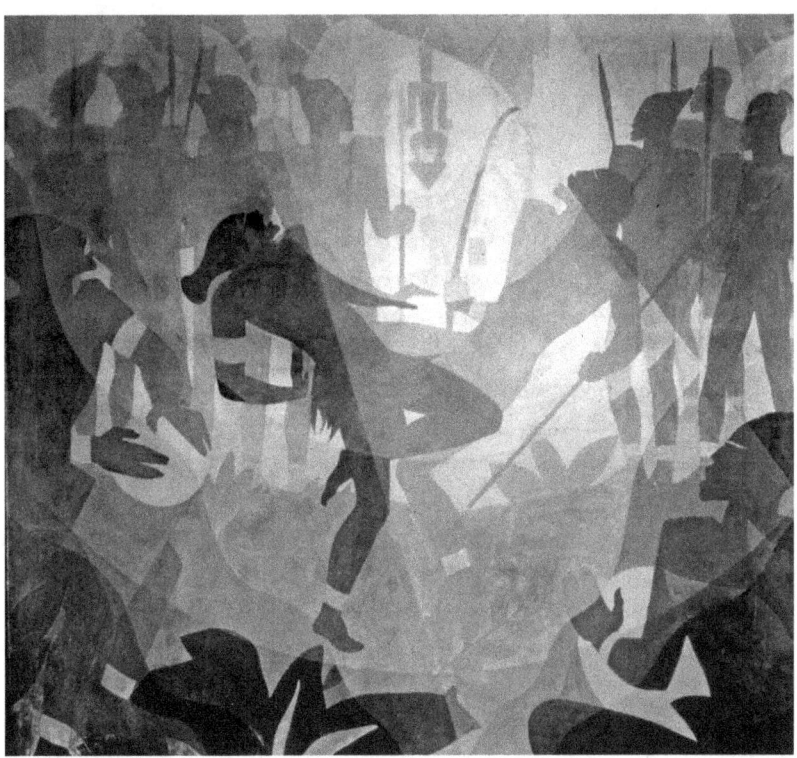

1.6 Aaron Douglas, *Aspects of Negro Life: The Negro in an African Setting*, 1934. Oil on canvas, 57¾ × 138¼ in. Schomburg Center for Research in Black Culture, New York Public Library, New York. VAGA at Artists Rights Society (ARS), New York.

center of the composition. Their devotion to the performance is visually registered in their arched backs and slightly open mouths. Two drummers positioned in the foreground provide musical accompaniment and, along with two rows of spear-wielding figures in the background, encircle the dancers. Some of the figures have similar cone-shaped head pieces or coiffures. While their bodies are silhouetted, Douglas makes their golden anklets and bracelets decidedly contrasting in color. This distinction is complimented by the slit eyes evident in the profiles. Also noticeable is the tropical vegetation, such as banana leaves, that the artist features in the upper and lower areas and uses to poetically frame the composition. Such greenery situates the scene in a tropical region of Africa, and the warm ochre hues used to convey much of the natural environment allude to these balmy temperatures. While the figures in the background are also depicted in these ochre colors, the dancers and the musicians are painted in shades of a grayish blue.

While Douglas's characteristic concentric circles are present in this work, their presence in the composition seems theatrical to effect the dynamism of the dancers and musicians in this performance-oriented imagery. However, it is the African woodcarving that is given the most illumination here, and all the heads of the figures are slanted toward its direction. Although the composition leans heavily on the archetypical association of Black people with music and dancing, this highlighted woodcarving is symbolic of how the subjects' performative acts resonate with Douglas's belief in the significance of an African heritage.

Undoubtedly, these stylistic elements reflect the penchant many early twentieth-century artists had for the movement of Africanism so inherent in modern art. Locke believed that Black American artists should look to African art for inspiration. The "father" of the New Negro movement purported that much could be yielded from the legacy of African art and that Black artists ought to learn about the mastery of African art, which was their own cultural and artistic heritage. Locke advised artists to emulate the classical background, discipline, and style of the arts of the forefathers, boldly asking, "If the forefathers could so adroitly master these mediums [of art], why not we?" That African art greatly influenced European modern art did not escape Locke, and he believed that this truth would serve as a catalyst in its possible influence on American Negro artists.[71]

However, for the European artists Locke mentioned in his essay, such as Henri Matisse and Pablo Picasso, African art had a completely different signification for them. They held a romanticist and reductive view of African cultures and envisioned the continent as being composed of primordial beings. There was a tendency to mystify rather than examine various cultural practices, and this was implicated in the evocations of scarified African masks featured in the works of European modernists. Artists and writers working in an anarchist vein in early twentieth-century Paris grew increasingly anticolonial as a result of the scandals surrounding French colonial policy in West and Central Africa. Nevertheless, the subversive revisions of colonial stereotypes featured in their modernist images were very similar to the racist caricatures they opposed. As art historian Patricia Leighten points out, "We must recognize how profoundly these artists misunderstood African art and how utterly Western and *moderniste* were the terms of their admiration."[72]

And indeed the admiration many Harlem Renaissance artists had for African art was also utterly *moderniste*. Yet for artists like Douglas, this veneration of precolonial African art fueled a creative impetus to existentially interrogate modern African American subjecthood with an African heritage in mind: "We can go to African life and get a certain amount of understanding, form and color and use this knowledge in development of an expression which interprets our life."[73] Given the predominance of primitivism in modern art, this was an aesthetic that Douglas chose to develop in his art. Locke even acknowledges Douglas's work as making substantial contributions to what he termed the "school of Negro art."[74]

However, sometimes these artistic innovations came at a cost. As was the case in early twentieth-century Paris, there was a demand among the vogue white enclaves who frequented the artistic and cultural hubs of Harlem for Black primitivism. Many white patrons were of the opinion that, by virtue of being African-descended, artists such as Douglas possessed the intuitions and rhythms of the primitive.[75] Despite the unavoidable connotations that came with an affinity with primitivism, Douglas's fabricated Africanism seems to be indelibly connected to a true understanding of Black modernism. This fiction is crucial, given its role in formulating Black Atlantic identity as well as a metaphysical unity throughout the diaspora in order to stake a claim at modernism.[76]

Undoubtedly, Douglas was deliberate in his efforts to create an empowering narrative of Africanity through his art. In so doing, he not only pictorially connects Black people to ancient African civilizations but also ties this legacy to modernity and future growth.[77] His painting *Building More Stately Mansions* (1944) (figure 1.7) serves as an apt example. Here, the artist amasses a collection of monumental sculptural and architectural forms in mirage-like imagery that dominates the setting. A pyramid, an Egyptian sphinx, a constructivist-like tower, and an arch are depicted, each structure seemingly superimposed on the adjacent one along a sloping landscape. While these forms appear a bit translucent or illusionary, other structures closer to the foreground—a few tall modern buildings to the left as well as a church spire and a construction crane suspended above the cityscape—are depicted more concretely. A swirling line of smoke oozes out of the most defined building to the left. At the very front, seven figures are positioned along a hilly terrain. Four of them are strapping men equipped with construction tools or parts, and the other three are a woman and two children who stand in front of a globe with a stand placed

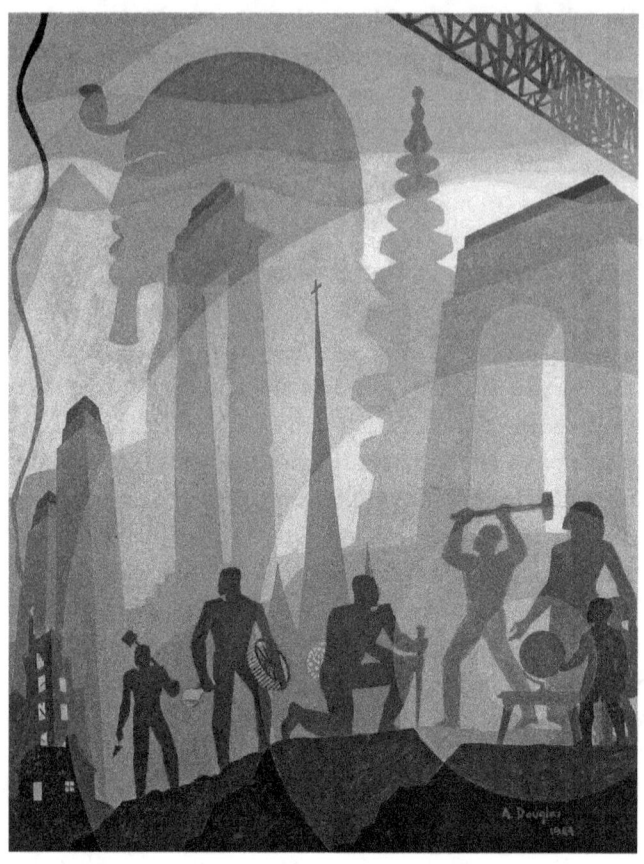

1.7 Aaron Douglas, *Building More Stately Mansions*, 1944. Oil on canvas, 54 × 42 in. Fisk University Galleries, Nashville, TN.

on a table. It is in this vicinity of the painting from which concentric circles emanate; the juxtaposition of the globe with the young children relays an idea of the global reaches of Black thought and enterprise in the future.

Reflecting on the intersection of Africanism and modernism, Douglas once wrote: "Our artistic contribution in ancient Egypt alone is enough to induce in us a great thrill of pride in our past as well as to inspire great hopes for the future."[78] Aesthetically registered in the neo-Egyptian human and architectural forms of *Building More Stately Mansions* is an implicit racial association. Douglas wanted to underscore the immeasurable contributions people of African descent made not only to the great civilizations of the past but also to modern life. The four stalwart men featured in the composition emblematize the enduring participation of African American muscle and imagination in the creation of modernity.[79] Although the artistic and cultural forms of Africa and its diaspora contributed significantly to the development of modern art, they were seldom seen as having a fundamental role in the shaping of modernity.

Given the positionality of Africa in the European imaginary as constitutive of barbarism, the role of African art and African-descended peoples in the making of modernism has always been minimized. Africa has always been acknowledged as a critical episode in the evolution of modern art. However, its presence was deemed momentary, only part of the narrative and not central enough to be considered as a fundamental influence in the shaping of modernism. As Simon Gikandi queries: "What threat does the acknowledgement of correlativity between the modern and its Others pose?"[80] Kobena Mercer justly characterizes modernism as global or cosmopolitan, given the interactive relationships that have always been present between the Western center and societies hitherto placed on the periphery.[81] In this vein, *Building More Stately Mansions* and other works challenge reductive views of Africanity and its affinity with modernity and exemplify an alternative modernism of the early twentieth century, which was particular to the diverse experiences of Black modernism. As Édouard Glissant explains, the human spirit yearns for a cross-cultural relationship without universalist transcendence, and diversity requires the presence of people with the intention of creating a new relationship.[82] This is precisely the project that Douglas sought to achieve in his art through his dynamic representations of the early twentieth-century Black cultural milieu. Lowery Stokes Sims explains that for Black artists, "modernism affirmed the notion that a modern individual could be an agent of change or transformation. [Modernism] represented a potential revolution in self-definition and self-image as they assumed the role of proactive rather than reactive agents in contemporary society."[83] This sense of ingenuity and ambition is reflected in Douglas's writing: "My goal . . . was to project through the processes of thought, certain forms that might be accepted as visual equivalents of such folk creations as the Pigeon Wing, the Cake Walk, the Charleston, the Lindbergh Hop, and all types of antebellum spirituals and songs."[84]

LANDSCAPE AND BELONGING

Building More Stately Mansions certainly conveys the epitome of modernity with its vast urban cityscape. Nonetheless, Aaron Douglas's panoramic landscapes problematize a constructed derivation of "the tropics," given his consideration of new iterations of modernity, particularly as it pertains to rural regions of the United States like the South. Early twentieth-century modernity was never associated with the natural landscape, and certainly not with the rural South. For Locke, the New Negro was undeniably from the North and possessed a new psychology in addition to "transforming what has been a perennial problem into the progressive phases of contemporary life." The Old Negro was antithetical to this idea, and this "stock figure" of historical fiction was always southern and associated with an old way of living.[85] Douglas's art amplifies the fictional resonance of this stereotype of regressive Black folk living in the South and permits a consideration of how geographical location and blackness work in concert to advance a different way one can come to know one's environment.[86]

Black people's relationship with the land in late nineteenth- to early twentieth-century America would have been characteristically different from the relationship people of European descent had with the terrain. It is inherently connected to the legacy of slavery and the still-prevalent pursuit of sharecropping. The connotations are clearly not romantic but are very much associated with trauma, violence, deprivation, and forced labor. However, there was still a willingness among Black people to transform this symbolism, particularly for a sense of belonging, a sense of "home."

It is possible to discern that Douglas wanted his natural landscapes to be reminiscent of not only the South but also tropical Africa as well as other tropical parts of the Black Atlantic. This is seen in his conveyance of the topography of the American landscape. In many of his compositions, they do not appear to be quintessentially American, particularly with the inclusion of banana leaves. As previously discussed, due to the relocation of tropical plants throughout various parts of the tropical world via colonialism, the presence of a banana tree in the southern United States proves how interconnected it is to the Caribbean archipelago. Inspired by Glissant's framing of the Caribbean Sea as the estuary of the Americas, literary scholar Michael Niblett astutely asserts that the Caribbean Sea encompasses not only the Caribbean but also "the surrounding rimlands from the Carolinas down to the Guyanas." The topography of these southern states clearly is in tandem geographically and geologically with the Caribbean.[87] Furthermore, the inclusion of the banana leaves is a reminder of the shared histories of slavery and the inevitable cross-cultural exchanges in the region. The iconographic banana tree in Douglas's art functions as a common thread that symbolically connects African America to the African Caribbean as well as the African continent.

The interconnectedness of the United States and the Caribbean is embedded in Douglas's *The Emperor Jones* series. In 1920 playwright Eugene O'Neill wrote *The Emperor Jones*, which told the story of an African American Pullman porter who deceptively ascends to the throne of a fictitious Caribbean island only to fall from power at the hands of his rebellious subjects. Although the reign of this fictional Black emperor was momentary, Douglas was very much inspired by O'Neill's play to create a series of prints of the same name. His depictions of the emperor feature the signature hard-edged silhouetted figures, yet his deportment is precariously balanced in the majority of the prints as if to hint at his eventual fall from power.[88] Two of the prints were featured in the February 1926 issue of *Theatre Arts Monthly*, in which Locke, an integral figure in the Harlem Renaissance, celebrated the series for encompassing "the dynamic quality of that tragedy of terror. There is an arbitrary contrast of Black masses and white spaces; and the clash of broken line becomes highly expressive in suggesting the proximate collapse of the Emperor's throne and the fear it inspires."[89]

But more pertinent is the fact that this is one of the first times we see a tropical landscape depicted in Douglas's art. Douglas incorporates various stylized iterations of tropical flora, including banana leaves, that engender their own animated and ominous presence in much of the prints. In the print titled *Defiance* (1926) (figure 1.8), Emperor Jones is encircled by a variety of lush greenery emanating from all angles of the picture frame. While some echo the curvature of small shrubbery, others that resemble banana leaves are angular and appear threatening. The hostile nature of this foliage is fully realized in *Flight* (1926) (figure 1.9), in which Jones seems virtually trapped by the leafage, particularly the large and jagged leaves targeting him from above. Such a symbolic characterization of the terrain in these compositions is reminiscent of how tropical regions of the world have historically been viewed by the West. Although the tropics was often perceived as Edenic, for many Europeans who ventured to these parts of the world as early as the fifteenth century, there was a less attractive side that was fearsome and dangerous. The Europeans perceived the vegetation of these locations as thick, uncultivated, and all-encompassing, and, combined with the rustling of the animals inhabiting these terrains, the tropics made for a potentially life-threatening existence.[90] At the same time, Douglas treats the foliage as the second subject/character in the se-

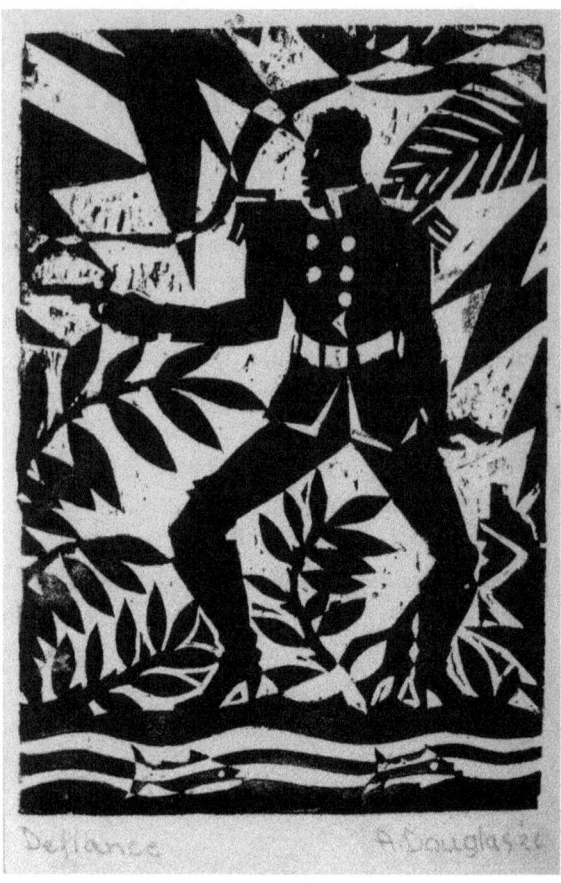

1.8 Aaron Douglas, *Defiance*, from *The Emperor Jones*
series, 1926. Woodblock print on paper, 8 × 5⅝ in.
Collection of Jason Schoen, Miami, FL.

ries that chooses to enact their moral compass. Although it is in fact, according to the play, the subjects of this kingdom who plan a rebellion to
dethrone the emperor, Douglas uses his creative license to make the landscape the retaliating protagonist.

Douglas would have been aware that the play was O'Neill's complicated commentary on the U.S. occupation of Haiti that began in 1915, and
perhaps he wanted to shed light on his opinions as well.[91] The Black republic gained independence from France in the early nineteenth century after the successful revolution led by Toussaint Louverture. Until the 1950s,
it was the only independent Black nation, and, for people who identified
with the ethos of Pan-Africanism, Haiti became somewhat of a central fo-

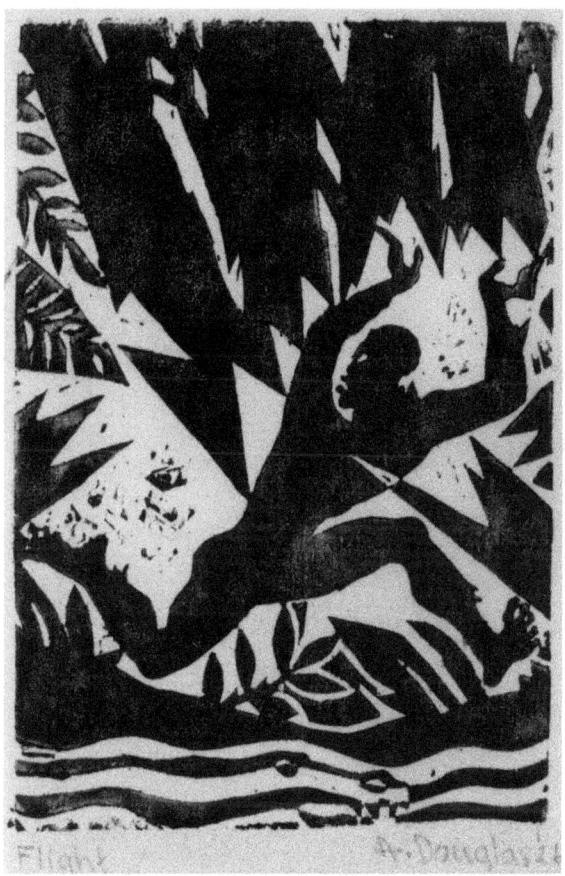

1.9 Aaron Douglas, *Flight*, from *The Emperor Jones* series, 1926. Woodblock print on paper, 8 × 5⅝ in. Collection of Jason Schoen, Miami, FL.

cus.[92] Here we see the land resisting the imperialist presence. What is also entirely apparent is an association of Black nationhood with the tropical terrain, and this makes sense, given that Haiti was the first such example in the Western Hemisphere.

Douglas proved how visual art gave African Americans the opportunity to imagine their worlds. Leaders of the Pan-Africanism movement championed the cause for improving the well-being of people of African descent around the world. The more radical thinkers of the movement imagined the possibilities of political autonomy and self-governance.[93] As mentioned earlier, since Haiti epitomized this ideal, the country became somewhat of a central focus in the early twentieth century.

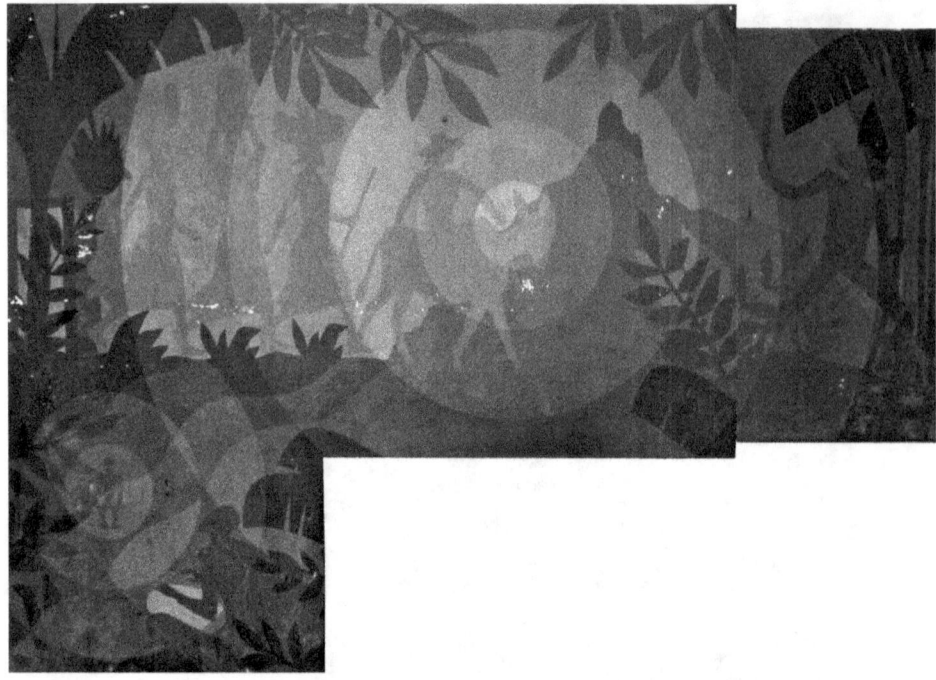

1.10 Aaron Douglas, *Haitian Mural* for the home
of Grace Goens in Wilmington, DE, 1942.

It thus comes as no surprise that Douglas would want to create a mural
commemorating the Haitian terrain. Douglas painted the *Haitian Mural*
(figure 1.10) for the home of Grace Goens in Wilmington, Delaware, in
1942.[94] The composition features a lush tropical landscape replete with a
variety of flora, including a number of banana trees. The artist's signature
concentric circles, along with five tree branches, lead the eye to a woman
sitting on the back of a donkey. Following her are three other women with
large baskets of produce on their heads. A man is a few steps ahead of all
four women and is using a machete to clear their path through the thick
vegetation. Douglas's inclusion of these Black market women is not unique
in the representation of Caribbean tropical landscapes, since, as Krista
Thompson notes, this figure has been the visual companion of tropical
nature as early as the late nineteenth century. Such depictions of Black
market women balancing fresh produce on the crowns of their heads completed the visualization of the tropically abundant environment.[95] While
there are also two men in the mural, their marginal positioning does not

grant them the same import that the women possess. In fact, they seem to serve supporting roles. The second man can be seen near the second set of concentric circles in the lower left region of the composition. Here, a sculptural form is highlighted with the man playing a large drum in its direction.

The sculptural figure is similar to the one seen in *The Negro in an African Setting* from the *Aspects of Negro Life* series. This dialogic gesture not only visually parallels the two compositions but also establishes Haiti as an extension of Africa that is in close proximity to the United States. Douglas's inclusion of the figure reflects a certain adherence to primitivism, which was the case for a number of visual artists of the New Negro movement. By subscribing to this discourse so prevalent in European modern art and culture, Douglas aims to highlight the cultural differences between Haitians and Black Americans.[96] At the same time, the presence of the sculptural figure serves as a symbolic register of Haiti's centrality in Pan-Africanist thought. Symbolism is also present in the architectural structure situated on a hill. The structure may reference La Citadelle, the mountaintop fortress built in the early nineteenth century by Henri Christophe, an important figure in the Haitian Revolution who eventually proclaimed himself king of Haiti. He built La Citadelle to serve as a stronghold against France if French forces attempted to reconquer Haiti. Earle affirms that buildings often depicted in Douglas's works are symbolic of the mind, of expansion and possibilities, notions not often associated with the Black race and certainly not with Haiti.[97] This is especially telling given that the year Douglas created the *Haitian Mural*, the U.S. government officially ended its supervision of Haiti's economy, which began in 1934. Prior to this period, Haiti had endured America's military occupation since 1915. By inserting this structure into the composition, an iconographic pronouncement of Haiti's transformation from a French plantocratic colony to an independent nation is established to reaffirm the possibility of Black sovereignty.[98]

This was not the first work of art pertaining to Haiti that the artist composed. Douglas visited Haiti in 1938 on a Julius Rosenwald Fellowship and created a number of paintings portraying the landscape and "Negro types."[99] In his review of these works, Locke was absolutely frank in his lack of regard for Douglas's "mild local color impressionism" evident in the compositions that was a departure from his established aesthetic.[100] Completed about four years after Douglas's sojourn to Haiti, this mural is distinct from his earlier Haitian paintings and in keeping with his modernist style; perhaps Douglas took Locke's critique into consideration here. Nonetheless, one can deduce that he would have used his sketches and memories from his residency to create this mural.

James Weldon Johnson visited Haiti in 1920 and witnessed atrocious acts of discrimination and brutality at the hands of the U.S. marines stationed there.[101] For him, these events were inextricably linked to the institutionalized racism that existed back home, and, as Thompson notes, "the same political rationalizations that fueled a long history of racism in the United States governed the official logic for the occupation of Haiti—that blacks, being racially inferior, were incapable of governing themselves."[102] Indeed, African American artists such as Jacob Lawrence, Richmond Barthé, and Aaron Douglas defied this logic by portraying historical Haitian leaders, and even fictitious ones as found in Douglas's *Emperor Jones* series, so as to visualize a historical narrative created by Black people for Black people.[103] Despite the pejorative view many held of Haiti because of its arduous political history and the many instances of African cultural retention, others recognized these qualities as evidence of the possibilities of Black political autonomy and cultural heritage. Large Black communities in America such as Harlem soon drew comparisons with legendary Black republics such as Haiti, Ethiopia, and Liberia since they were socially isolated and culturally independent. Recognized as a Black cultural mecca, Harlem was home to major cultural and political icons such as Duke Ellington and the Reverend Adam Clayton Powell as well as noted cultural institutions such as the Apollo Theater and the Savoy Ballroom. This insulated "city-state" had no doubt contributed to America's reputation of being the epitome of modernity.[104]

The works of Aaron Douglas undoubtedly express the notion that "landscape becomes a metaphor for cultural identity."[105] The landscapes in his works have a new signification, a different function. Historically, the Black community's relationship with the land was threatened as a result of alienation, yet at the same time, as Glissant asserts, this relationship "becomes so fundamental in this discourse that landscape in the work stops being merely decorative or supportive and emerges as a full character." The landscape is inseparable from the community and the individual in the process of creating history as well as the construction of identity.[106] One can certainly view the landscapes that Douglas created as spaces in which oppositions involving "the natural and the unnatural, the given and the made, the temperate and the tropical, the natural and the cultural," are complicated yet destabilized.[107] By proposing an alternative understanding of the tropics, Douglas effectively contributed to the development of modernism.[108] Tropicality can be helpful in allowing one to think beyond the stereotypical relationship often established between people and terrains. Tropicality also calls for a new understanding of the African diasporic experience, a unifying element connecting the Black Atlantic that is not generic but creates a linkage between this enclave and the land of origin: Africa. The notion of tropicality that Douglas conjured thus disrupts the construction of Africa as the antithesis of Europe and the embodiment of the past and renders the Pan-African world as a purposeful interlocutor of modern life.

As the next chapter demonstrates, the art of Wifredo Lam also elucidates the significance of the terrain in Black modernism. Like Douglas, Lam aspired to represent the land of Cuba, and the Caribbean by extension, as loci that could engender a new and self-possessed disposition for people of African descent despite the troubled histories of slavery, colonialism, and European cultural imperialism. In the pages that follow, Lam's adroit ability to convey the monumentality of the tropical terrain and its critical role in the sustenance of Black Cuban subjectivity and culture are examined. Indeed, this chapter shows that he did this to combat any pretense of Cuba being allegedly subordinate and inferior to industrialized countries of the West. Tropical aesthetics thus serves once again to reify the possibilities endemic in visually underscoring the complex yet fruitful relationship Black Atlantic peoples have with their natural environment.

Upon Wifredo Lam's return to Cuba in 1941, he became fully preoccupied with the "dense, natural wildlife of his country."[1] Undoubtedly, it was
the natural terrain that prevailed in much of the art he created while on
the island. Lam's reinvention of the landscape in his compositions is part
of a tradition of self-invention in the Caribbean and is central to a New
World aesthetic.[2] Ultimately, this propensity to invent a new landscape
is in line with creating an empowering historical narrative. Through his
art, Lam is re-signifying the tropical landscape as indicative of modernity
while also commemorating the connection that Black Cubans had with
the land. Art historian Gerardo Mosquera posits that during his post-European Cuban period, Lam transforms the Western pictorial tradition to
represent the Cuban landscape in an innovative way.[3] This, along with
the visual language of surrealism, contributed to Lam's ground-breaking
aesthetic that was brazenly avant-garde.[4] He successfully depicted the Cuban terrain from the perspective of a Black Cuban worldview that could
easily be applied to a pan-Caribbean context. Through his disruption and
transformation of Western modernism, his art truly reflected his propagation for an art of decolonization and thereby challenged wide-held notions of originality. Indeed, as J. Michael Dash notes, it is the poetics of
invention and reinvention, which are so central to a New World aesthetic,
that make literature (and visual art) "so modern . . . in its impulse toward
self-invention."[5]

The artistic continuities between Aaron Douglas and Wifredo Lam
are undoubtedly explicit, particularly in the Pan-African reaches of their
works. Lam's art indicates the invaluable recognition of a Pan-Africanist
longing among Cuba's Black population that undeniably speaks to the vital role of ancestry in aspirations for times ahead.[6] Like Douglas, whose
art venerates the subtropical landscapes of the United States, Lam abun-
dantly celebrates the terrain in his art but with Black Cuban subjectivity

in mind. His art conveys the land as the locus for self-determination and affirmation for them in the midst of social, political, and economic disenfranchisement. This chapter interrogates, as in the previous chapter, the significance of celebrating Africanity but with the cultural specificity of the Caribbean in mind. Lam's paintings privilege the African continuums endemic in Cuban culture as well as the important role of nature in this regard, and how all of this ultimately contributes to Black modernism.

In addition, I focus on the political dimensions of the landscapes that are prevalent in Lam's paintings in the years after his return to Cuba. Through his art, Lam transformed the Cuban landscape as well as the way Black Cubans are symbolically registered in these portrayals. More importantly, his art allowed for a reimagining of the latter's relationship with the environment that they occupied, given the preeminence of nature in Black Cuban religious and cultural practices. This chapter reveals how Lam's reinvention of the landscape was ultimately a prelude to the self-definition Black Cubans and ultimately all Black Atlantic peoples aspired to have. Using Afrocubanismo as a point of departure, this chapter considers how the Black Cuban subject was at the core of Lam's creative endeavors. This is significant since he was the first artist whose art featured Black Cuban culture as a decisive factor of expression.[7] A number of scholars have explored Lam's conveyance of the landscape and his incorporation of the human form. Art historian Julia P. Herzberg, for example, has noted that after his return to Cuba, a noticeable change became evident in Lam's art; his aesthetic trajectory transformed and he began to create these fascinating hybrid figures that integrate with the landscape.[8] The merging of human and plant forms in his paintings hints at the urgent plight of Black Cubans whose socioeconomic situation had not progressed and whose relationship with the land was complicated by established geographic arrangements brought on by slavery and colonialism. More than anything, these hybrid figures signify the reality that, as McKittrick declares, geography is not secure yet people produce the meaning of space and make geography what it is.[9] This chapter thus considers what these creative transformations suggest about Lam and his reaction to what he sees upon his return to Cuba.

It also takes into consideration the various experiences and new friendships he developed, which altered his "style and worldview."[10] The writers associated with the negritude movement contributed tremendously to the evolution of his aesthetic trajectory. Aimé Césaire's negritude movement championed African civilizations prior to contact with European culture and reflected the reality that, after contact, Black people truly participated in and influenced modernism. Much of the work produced by Aimé and his wife, Suzanne Césaire, was heavily informed by the geography of their native Martinique, and Suzanne even propagated that one's Antillean identity could be empowered if it is situated in the soil, the nucleus of the landscape. This chapter thus examines the ways in which Lam's dense topographies not only reference Cuba but are also indelibly linked to the tropical terrains of ancestral Africa.

Historically, the terrains of the Caribbean archipelago have been constructed in particular ways in the Western imaginary. Much of Lam's art challenges these constructs and tackles the extent to which such a conceptualization of the Cuban environment is connected to the touristic exoticization of Cuban people and the landscape they inhabit. In this chapter, I consider how tropical aesthetics can be a useful strategy employed by Lam to disrupt this touristic gaze, given its potential for inducing agency and imagining new possibilities for one's natural surroundings. Given that the land is exploited by those in power and seen as sacred by the oppressed, a galvanizing effort to subvert the hegemonic order is closely hinged on Lam's artistic endeavor. The concept of cannibalism developed by Martinican writer Suzanne Césaire and Brazilian modernist poet Oswald de Andrade further elucidates the tropical aesthetics Lam incorporates in his art, especially in the way his compositions devour Western-imposed ideas that Cuba and other Caribbean islands became susceptible to due to colonial conquest. In addition, as I explore in this chapter, the important work of the negritude writers Aimé Césaire, Suzanne Césaire, and René Ménil of Martinique proved to be crucial in the development of Lam's artistic methodology and is deeply embedded in the tropical aesthetics that I argue he employs. Indeed, Lam's art manifests Ménil's claim that "the land of marvelous is most stunning revenge . . . against a life that . . . depresses us."[11] Lam's art masterfully eradicates reductive visual representations of Caribbean people and the land they inhabit in an effort to reclaim humanity and dignity. This reclamation aids in the generation of a new representation of Cubans and Black Atlantic peoples alike as well as their alternative geographic formulations, and this effort at redefinition affirms the persistence of Black modernity.[12]

I examine key works Wifredo Lam created during his return to Cuba. The most celebrated of this period is *The Jungle* (1943), a signature painting that reflects a desire to reclaim Cuba's landscape in the early twentieth century in an effort to attain a level of political autonomy, particularly for the Black masses of the island. *La Sombre Malembo, Dieu du Carrefour* (Malembo, God of the Crossroads) (1943) is a work that demonstrates the dynamic way in which the artist visualizes tropicality to emphasize the spirituality inherent in one's interaction with nature. Similarly, *Autel pour Elegua* (Altar for Elegua) (1944) conveys a domestic altar set in a garden and captures the sacredness with which Black Cubans viewed the land due to an African-derived worldview. The influences of negritude and surrealism are explicit in *Harpe Astrale* (The Astral Harp) (1944), a composition that asserts a Black Cuban imperative onto the Cuban terrain despite the legacies of slavery, colonialism, and the engulfing American neocolonialism of that period. Finally, I explore Lam's *El Tercer Mundo* (The Third World) (1965–66) and its symbolic intimation of cannibalism; moreover, the piece is global in its call for oppressed nations to reclaim and assert their power.

The art Lam created after returning to his homeland is not limited to the Cuban sociopolitical paradigm but defies a nationalistic conception.[13] Given his leanings with the negritude movement and its Pan-Africanist implications, this chapter acknowledges the possibilities of viewing his post-European Cuban artwork as a metanarrative of the Black Atlantic world of the early to mid-twentieth century.

✳

Much of the landscape in parts of the Caribbean was fabricated with a particular goal in mind. As Thompson explains in *An Eye for the Tropics*, in an effort to develop the budding tourism industries of the late nineteenth century in the Anglophone Caribbean, hoteliers, members of the white elite, and colonial administrators went to great lengths to tropicalize the landscape. They initiated cleanliness drives and imported "tropical" trees from other equatorial territories to (re)create a visual ideal of the tropical Caribbean landscape. Not only did tourism promoters use photographs to project a new vision of the islands, they also marketed the landscapes and inhabitants as picturesque, orderly, and tropical, or, more specifically, like photographs.[14]

Given the extent to which particular conceptions of the tropics informed the creation of place-images of some of the Caribbean islands, it is clear that the tourism promoters perpetuated a framing of the Caribbean as a fictive space, a terra firma that was subject to reinvention.[15] Dash reminds us that the unstable nature of meaning leads to reinvention in the New World so much so that "geographical space, landscape, and human communities are inscribed with the rhetoric and images of given discursive practices."[16] For him, the fragility and openness of the broken chain of islands that make up the Caribbean archipelago make it susceptible to control. As a result, there is no consideration of the histories and societies that existed before colonialism; such an absence of this conceptualization for Caribbean space is directly linked to a lack of an indigenous population in many of the islands.[17]

Apart from recognizing how the landscape is inscribed so that it becomes something else, what is crucial in Dash's assessment of the reinvention of the New World is the acknowledgment that even Caribbean people are implicated in this invented rendering. With the majority of the Caribbean's population being of African descent and whose ancestors came from tropical Africa, a prevailing view that the Black population of the Caribbean should be deemed inherently primitive was established during slavery. Emerging as an ideological construct of colonial conquest and exploitation, Black people were represented as the primitive racial other who lived in a state of timelessness, not evolving or changing but existing in an inferior culture. As a result, the people are viewed in close relation with the scenery that surrounds them and, as Ménil attests, they eventually are viewed as "part of the scenery, as objects and as décor." What transpires is a construction of the "native" as "picturesque," as exotic. This is because the "natural tendency in exoticism is to miss the 'seriousness' and authenticity of the drama (of the other) and to confine oneself to an idyllic and superficial vision." There is a negation of individual characteristics since the Caribbean person becomes "exotic-to-myself. . . . My view of myself is the view of the white person having become mine after three centuries of colonial conditioning."[18] Exoticism, like tropicality, is a form of human relations in which the non-Western racial group is viewed as alien and opposite to what is deemed normal. And, in the colonies, such as what existed in most of the early twentieth-century Caribbean, there exists a unique conundrum in which the people have an exotic vision of themselves. When the Caribbean individual describes herself from a distance, rather superficially, without divulging any personal circumstances, it is often in an attempt to satisfy the Western desire for exoticism.[19]

Wifredo Lam was one such individual who was rendered the exotic other in Europe, given his birthplace and ethnic makeup. Born in Cuba in 1902 to a Chinese father and a mother of African and Spanish descent, Lam migrated to Europe in 1923 to further his artistic education. During this period, his work was palpably influenced by Matisse and Picasso, two major figures in European modern art. Lam was readily accepted into a number of artist circles in Spain and France, and one can ascertain that his being viewed as a quintessential "primitive" was the primary reason for this.[20] Picasso, for instance, took a keen interest in Lam's artistic development and, as Sims notes, this coincided with an ardent fascination for precolonial African art among the Parisian avant-garde.[21] Notwithstanding, it would take another two decades before Lam conveyed any kinship to Africanity in his art. For Lam, African sculpture became a source of formations and structures that he reused in different contexts and for distinct purposes. Picasso and his European counterparts appropriated African art in a similar way, taking advantage of the geometrical forms that they synthesized with the human image. There is no denying that Lam's desire to connect with his African roots is problematic since his experience of Africanity is mediated by Western culture. However, the Baule Goli masks as well as the Gouro masks of the Ivory Coast of Lam's own collection were significant for the Cuban artist since these art forms gave him a means of creating a truly modern Black art. More than anything, Lam responded most to the literalness of this non-Western, nonacademic art, and it contributed to his creation of an art that served a distinct political purpose.[22]

NEGRITUDE AND THE RETURN TO CUBA

In 1941 Lam began a journey that would eventually take him back to Cuba. When he was finally able to escape war-torn France with his then companion, Helena Holzer, along with the surrealist André Breton and his family as well as Claude Lévi-Strauss, they boarded a ship bound for Martinique. It was during their six-week stay there that Lam and Breton befriended Aimé and Suzanne Césaire and René Ménil, who had just begun publishing the journal *Tropiques*, and their influence should not be overlooked.

Aimé Césaire, a poet and writer, coined the term *negritude* while pursuing his tertiary education in Paris in the 1930s. Soon, it emerged as a literary movement that he developed with Senegal's Léopold Sédar Senghor. Césaire, who immersed himself in reading about Africa, articulated the importance of refusing cultural assimilation in his defining negritude and called for a resurrection of Black values.[23] For him, anything that was inherent to the Black experience prior to contact with European culture ought to be prized since the subjugation of the idea of the "barbaric Negro" was integral for the movement.[24] Césaire's conceptualization of negritude reflected the obvious reality that Black people truly participated in and influenced modernism. Certainly, one can thus define negritude as blacks proclaiming their "blackness as constitutive of their relation to the world around them."[25] Césaire returned to Martinique with Suzanne in 1939, and they later launched the journal *Tropiques* along with other Martinican intellectuals. The periodical often published articles on natural history and the intention was to stimulate Antilleans to revere their natural environment. It also featured poetry, criticism, and articles that reflected the tenets of surrealism and radical politics. No doubt the literature reflected the Césaires' avid interest in plant life, and Lam would have been deeply affected by these ideas during the six weeks he stayed in Martinique.[26] Ménil acknowledged Lam's "solidarity with Césaire's poetry and the aesthetic of *Tropiques*."[27] What was even more significant about the journal was the fact that it attempted to define an Antillean identity as a mode of cultural liberation. This was critical in the first half of the journal's existence, when it was subject to censorship by the island's Vichy government. This period of political conservatism played a significant part in radicalizing Black Martinicans.[28]

Just as surrealism provided Lam the tools necessary to visually articulate the psychic state of Afro-Cubans, it was through surrealism that Césaire recognized the "strategy of revolution of the mind."[29] Through discourses Breton and his colleagues developed about "exotic" cultures that they associated with the mythical, the magical, and the fantastic, the surrealists became preoccupied with using the "primitive" not to solve Western aesthetic problems but to disrupt Western solutions.[30] Given their disdain for their own society following the atrocities they witnessed during World War I, the art and culture of the non-West was a welcomed point of departure as well as a threshold onto a new world of creative expression. Undoubtedly, the Caribbean was no exception. The surrealists immediately took to the Caribbean, given the region's history of slavery and colonialism at the hands of Europe's powerful monarchies. They openly expressed aversion toward the imposition of imperialism, capitalism, and Christendom onto all colonized peoples. In response to Europe's control over the colonized, the surrealists sought not only to invert existing hierarchies of power but also to spread their movement in these parts of the world, since they believed themselves to be champions of the downtrodden.[31]

Yet surrealism served different purposes for each of the editors of *Tropiques*. For Aimé Césaire, it was a poetic tool as well as a moral sensibility. Contrastingly, surrealism was a means of reflection for Suzanne Césaire and Ménil that provided them with a critical foundation from which to explore the cultural politics of Martinique and the wider Caribbean.[32] As Suzanne Césaire boldly stated, "We know our situation here in Martinique. . . . And from among the powerful machines of war, the bombs and explosives, the modern world places at our disposal, our audacity chooses surrealism which currently offers it the best chance of success."[33] Despite their disparate incentives, the writings of both Aimé and Suzanne Césaire venerate the terrain of Martinique and exclaim the innate connection Black Martinicans have with it while also tackling the history of slavery and predicament of colonialism. In his book-length poem *Cahier d'un Retour au Pays Natal* (*Notebook of a Return to the Native Land*), Aimé Césaire writes:

> To go away . . . I would arrive sleek and young in this land of mine and I would say to this land whose loam is part of my flesh: "I have wandered for a long time and I am coming back to the deserted hideousness of your sores." . . .
>
> My negritude is not a stone, its deafness hurled against the clamor of the day
> my negritude is not a leukemia of dead liquid over the earth's dead eye
> my negritude is neither tower nor cathedral
> it takes root in the red flesh of the soil
> it takes root in the ardent flesh of the sky
> it breaks through opaque prostration with its upright patience[34]

In a similar vein, Suzanne Césaire defines the Martinican sensibility as it relates to one's environment:

> What, at root, intimately, immutably, is the Martiniquan, and how does he live?
>
> In response to these questions we see an astonishing contradiction appear between his deepest being, desires, impulses and unconscious powers and the life he lives, with its necessities, urgent demands and heavy burdens. This is a phenomenon of decisive importance for the future of this land.
>
> What is the Martiniquan?
>
> He is the plant-man.
>
> Like the plant, he abandons himself to the rhythm of universal life. He makes no effort to dominate nature. He is a poor farmer. Perhaps. I'm not saying that he makes the plants grow; I'm saying that he grows, that he lives like a plant. . . .

It is inspiring to imagine these tropical lands being restored at last to their inner truth, the lasting and fertile accord of man and the land. Under the sign of the plant.[35]

The writings of the Césaires confirm the debilitating effects slavery and colonialism have on both flora and human beings alike. Undoubtedly, the foundation of a newly defined Black Caribbean subjectivity or, as Aimé Césaire defines it, an Antillean identity, is situated in the soil, the nucleus of the landscape. And the political, cultural, and spiritual identity of modern Black people is inherently connected to vegetation. For Suzanne Césaire, the plant is the means through which humanity can be redeemed and empowered. In the Césairian ethos, the plant connotes an Africa-derived worldview in which man does not dominate nature but "abandons himself to the rhythm of universal life." In tandem with this counter-ideology, the plant can be recognized as a symbol of slave insurrection, since the plant-man has no desire to dominate and exploit nature for the sake of capitalist expansion.[36] But it is also symbolic of anticolonialism and the advent of a cultural and political nationalism in the Caribbean region.

This ethos finds parallels in the writings of Alejo Carpentier, particularly his reflections on the marvelous real and how it can be used to enrich one's experience of the physical realm. For Carpentier, the marvelous is invoked "when it arises from an unexpected alteration of reality (the miracle), from a privileged revelation of reality."[37] The history of the Americas was, according to Carpentier, a chronicle of the marvelous real, and he recognized Lam's art for making visible the magic of tropical vegetation.[38] Carpentier believed that the artist trained the viewer to see "the unbridled creativity of our natural forms with all their metamorphoses and symbioses on monumental canvases in an expressive mode that is unique in contemporary art."[39] The philosophical dimensions of the negritude movement, along with the Césaires' call for Black empowerment via the terrain and its vegetation as well as the dynamic ideas of Carpentier, inarguably provided a necessary foundation for Lam to embark on this new artistic path.

THE JUNGLE

Lam's friend the folklorist and ethnographer Lydia Cabrera and her partner, María Teresa Rojas, helped Lam and Helena Holzer establish themselves in Havana. Lam encountered a lot of hostility as a poor, racially mixed man living with a white woman in a common-law marriage, and this was extremely isolating for him. In Cabrera he found a kindred spirit as she too was marginalized—although she was a white woman, her relationship with María was unacceptable for a woman of her class. Also, both Lam and Cabrera shared a deep interest in the cultural forms of the Cuban Black masses.[40] It was in his homeland where he reconnected with his African ancestry, and his friendship with Cabrera was very instrumental in this.[41] Cuban society, though, was generally dismissive of Black Cuban culture, and Black Cubans rarely spoke openly with white Cubans about their African cultural heritage.[42] In fact, since the dawn of Cuban independence, many Black Cubans of privileged socioeconomic standing believed that the island's African legacy served as a hindrance toward any efforts Black people had to improve their overall status in the nation. For them, it was imperative to dissociate themselves "from the cultural backwardness embodied by Africanist practices."[43] Yet by the 1920s, the cultural sphere became exemplified by a group of Cuban intellectuals who promoted Afrocubanismo as a defining force for Cuban national identity. Cuban modernists championed the Black Cuban masses as well as their creative forms that lay outside the usual academic and elitist purview. However, their affirming ideologies did not overshadow the social, political, and economic predicament Black Cubans experienced in their everyday lives, and this reality was troubling to Lam and gave him much fodder for his artistic mission.

> When I returned to Havana [my first impression] was one of profound sadness. The whole colonial drama of my youth seemed to be reborn in me. . . . What I saw on my return was like some sort of hell. For me, trafficking in the dignity of a people is just that, hell. Poetry in Cuba was either political and committed . . . or else written for tourists. The latter I rejected, for it had nothing to do with an exploited people, with a society that crushed and humiliated its slaves. No, I decided that my painting would never be the equivalent of that pseudo Cuban music for nightclubs. I refused to paint cha-cha-cha. I wanted with all my heart to paint the drama of my country.[44]

For Lam, returning to Cuba was like returning to his beginnings. By the time he left for Europe in the early 1920s, Cuba was already considered a U.S. territory due to its overwhelming control of the island's sugar industry. American corporations owned 75 percent of the sugar production, and due to the centralization of the mills in major cities like Havana, many rural Cubans migrated to urban centers to find work. When Lam returned to Cuba in 1941, Cuba went from producing 20 percent of the world's sugar

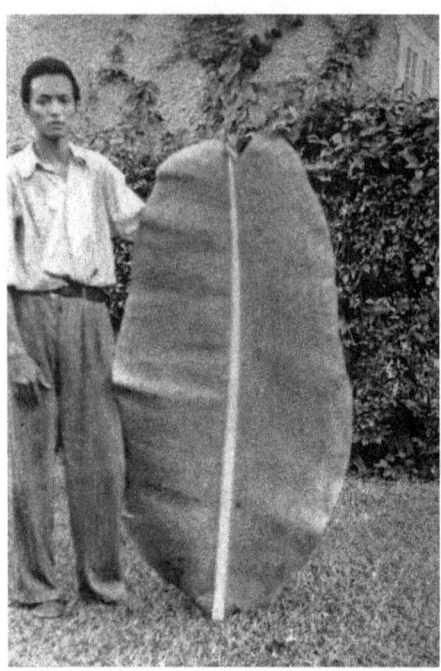
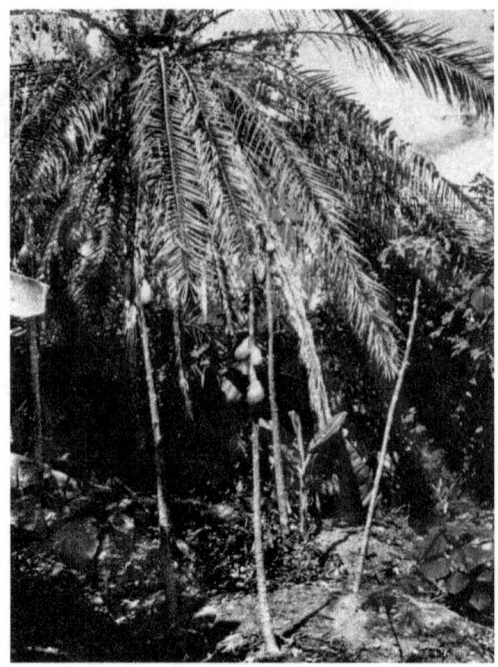

2.1 Wifredo Lam in his garden, Havana, Cuba, 1942. From Max-Pol Fouchet, *Wifredo Lam* (Barcelona: Ediciones Poligrafa, 1976).

2.2 Wifredo Lam's garden, Havana, Cuba, 1942. From Max-Pol Fouchet, *Wifredo Lam* (Barcelona: Ediciones Poligrafa, 1976).

to having a mere 10 percent share in the world's supply. In addition, the island's economy had to contend with the collapse of world sugar prices. A rapid increase in Cuba's population also had a devastating effect on its citizens, who had to contend with the uncertainty of unemployment and underemployment. As a Cuban of African descent, the debilitating poverty of Black Cubans most certainly was of major significance to Lam.[45]

It was therefore imperative that his art become a political weapon that visualized the plight of a subaltern people. Exploring the synthesis of various cultures that occurred in Cuba and, more than anything else, the Black Cuban spirit were key in his new approach to art-making. The emergence of Afrocubanismo is proof of how intrinsic African-derived cultural forms were to the evolution of Cuban identity, and Lam was the first artist whose art featured Black Cuban culture as a decisive factor of expression.[46] And just as crucial to his oeuvre were the intercultural relationships among the various racial groups that are inherent in a creolized society like Cuba. In his definition of creolization, Edward Kamau Brathwaite defined interculturation as an unplanned, unstructured but osmotic relationship proceeding from the yoking of a powerful culture over a dominated culture.[47] This definition holds true for many Caribbean societies, as it acknowledges the complexities and challenges endemic in these countries that emerged due to the histories of slavery and colonialism. In his articulation of his aesthetic imperatives, Lam created art that signified these realities, imaginatively portraying the multilayered Cuban sensibility.

Lam's art also "creolized" different styles of modern Western painting, using aspects of surrealism and cubism that inevitably freed him from traditional representation, allowing him to invent a cohesive visual language that communicated the intricacies of the Caribbean.[48] A significant aspect of Lam's stylistic and conceptual shift was the reconfiguration of the human form that was now in hybrid form and often situated in a lush tropical landscape.[49] Perhaps through surrealist means of creativity such as automatic drawing or simply spontaneity, Lam created human forms that blended with plant and animal forms, a technique he more than likely absorbed from the French surrealist painter André Masson.[50] What is significant about this hybrid is that it establishes a link between the body and the landscape and suggests a desire on the part of the artist to reconnect with the tropical terrain of his homeland. Lam's arrival in Cuba must have unearthed in him a feeling of belonging, recalling the sentiments his friend Aimé Césaire expressed in his epic poem *Notebook of a Return to the Native Land*.

Yet what distinguished the art Lam created from those of surrealist artists is what curators Holliday T. Day and Hollister Sturges call fantastic imagery. For much of the twentieth century, Latin American writers and artists have extracted from this imagery to convey cultural forces that have shaped their identities. Indeed, fantasy is endemic in the art of Latin American artists and their surrealist counterparts, as their works privilege both intuition and imagination. However, while "Surrealism was a consciously intellectual movement first articulated in the manifesto by André Breton [who] reacted against the limits of Western rationalism . . . artists in Latin America drew from their own cultural history."[51] Latin American artists looked to their distinct cultural elements rather than intellectual theory in order to create an art that was more spontaneous and direct. Art of the fantastic is exemplified by "the juxtaposition, distortion, or amalgamation of images and/or materials that extend experiences by contradicting our normal expectations formally or iconographically."[52] One can certainly situate the incredible landscapes that Lam created within a specific cultural-political framework unique to Latin America and the Caribbean.

Taken in the garden of a house he rented in the outskirts of Havana in 1942, a photograph features Lam holding a gigantic banana leaf reaching just above his shoulders (figure 2.1). It is a testament to the lush tropical flora found in his garden, which is typical in Cuba. Lam appears picturesque in this image since he is adjacent to the leaf. Such a configuration reflects an ethos the artist referred to as the "tourist frivolity" of the island in which people of African descent are degraded.[53] In fact, the photograph is very reminiscent of early twentieth-century ethnographic photography, which sought to scrutinize non-Western people's biology and sexuality by scrupulously capturing as many details of the sitter as possible.[54] This photograph seems to go a step further by situating Lam in the natural landscape while being juxtaposed with a leaf, not only objectifying him but also rendering him the exotic other. Despite this, the photograph captures Lam's connectedness to his homeland, which he had only returned to a year earlier, having been away for eighteen years. Lam spent a lot of time in this garden and even painted many of his landscape compositions there. Lam's garden contained crops like bananas, oranges, avocados, and papayas as well as different types of flowers and shrubs (figure 2.2). A number of these fruits appeared in his paintings, converging with human and animal forms.[55]

For him, the garden was a microcosm of the flora that was indigenous to Cuba. Perhaps being immersed in that garden and studying the colors, shapes, and textures of the various flora it contained allowed Lam to have an awareness of the Cuban landscape. As a result, he was now able to develop a visual language through which he could conceptually reinvent the Cuban terrain, making more tangible for the viewer the notion of what McKittrick refers to as a different sense of place, even if it was a place that was already familiar.[56] Given his disdain for the unchanged dilemma of many Black Cubans upon his return, it is clear that Lam's new style of art conveys a geographical yearning that attempts to unfix the Black masses from their "natural" place.[57] Speaking of his aesthetic approach after moving back to Cuba, Lam expressed: "I knew I was running the risk of not being understood by the man in the street or by the others. But a true picture has the power to set the imagination to work, even if it takes time."[58] Recognizing the crucial role of art in envisioning a new sense of place, Lam thereby employed tropical aesthetics that put into effect a grammar of liberation, a "sayability" of geography. This assertive mode allowed the artist to create a poetics of landscape as a way of responding to spatial and thus socioeconomic inequities.[59] His painting The Jungle (1942–43) truly encapsulates this unique articulation of geography.

The Jungle (plate 3) is a visually rich composition featuring a tapestry of thick tropical foliage, notably sugar cane stalks, tobacco leaves, and palm leaves. The greenery depicted by Lam has a striking and animated presence, and its depth and varying textures clearly parallel the imagery seen in the photographs of Lam's garden, which was a major source of inspiration.[60] The composition defies the Renaissance notion of linear perspective, offering a visual realm that, according to Sims, parallels the "all-over" paintings of 1950s New York where "the sense of a centralized focus was eliminated in favor of an 'equal' distribution of parts to the overall whole."[61] Emanating from the foliage are four anthropomorphic beings. Their linear frames echo the verticality of the cane stalks, and their coloring allows for a camouflage effect. Yet their masklike faces, large bulbous breasts and buttocks, which resemble fruits like papaya, not to mention their large feet and hands render them as distinct. Some arms are outstretched, others akimbo, while the arm of the second figure from the left reaches down to the ground like a foot. The overlapping forms and amalgams of body parts are configured via cubist pictorial arrangements of multiple viewpoints, while the transgression against naturalist representations is certainly an adherence to the surrealist liberties that Lam employed. Herzberg notes that Lam began merging the figure with the landscape just before he painted *The Jungle*. Prior to that, there was a fusing of the human form with an array of zoological elements, most notably parts of the horse's body. By 1942 there was a rapid progression in unifying his anthropomorphic forms with leaves and eventually with dense vegetation.[62]

Such glorification of the landscape in tandem with the human figure was not atypical in Cuban art during this period. Members of the Cuban *vanguardia* of the early twentieth century were champions of modernism and strongly rebelled against academicism, and their art featured archetypal representations of the quintessential Cuban as well as the physical environment. These romanticized depictions of the rural peasantry and their surroundings were a nostalgic reaction against urbanization and the ever-present U.S. interventionism pervading the country. Artists such as Víctor Manuel García and Antonio Gattorno created works that featured exotic interpretations of the *mulata* archetype, a Creole archetype of femininity—who came to embody Cuba's multiracial, multicultural identity—set in a landscape highlighted by palm trees, sugar cane, and banana trees, which became an emblematic motif in nationalist Caribbean art.[63] On a fundamental level, Lam's *The Jungle* abides by this formula and thereby participates in this nationalist tradition of art-making. However, Lam also engages in the practice of eroticizing the female form in the natural landscape, particularly through his renderings of the bosoms and derrieres of the figures. The breasts resemble papayas; this visual reference is indelibly linked to associations made between the tropical fruit and female genitalia in many parts of Cuba. As a result, the papaya is often called *fruta-bomba* to avoid such connotations.[64] These instances echo the sexualized depictions of mulatas by other Cuban artists such as Carlos Enríquez, whose *The Abduction of the Mulatas* (1938) portrays voluptuous mulatas being abducted by macho *mambises*, the peasant outlaws of the Independence Wars.[65] Works such as this and Gattorno's *Women by the River* (1927) perpetuate the myth of the sexual availability of the racially mixed woman. In spite of these similarities, Lam's work is not as one-dimensional in its symbolism, given its multivalent references, not to mention his complicated visual language that is thoroughly engaged with cubism as well as the surrealist delight for the visual surprise.[66] In addition, it is important to remember that Lam remained an outsider to the Cuban modernism enclave and was very critical of the bourgeois disposition of some of his contemporaries, such as Amelia Peláez del Castal and René Portocarrero.[67]

One of the many references inherent in *The Jungle* that makes it distinct from other Cuban works is the veneration of Afro-Cuban religion. The figures in the painting can be interpreted as what art historian Edward Lucie-Smith describes as a Santeria procession. Santeria is the syncretic religion of Cuba that combines both Yoruba religious ideologies and Roman Catholicism. In *The Jungle*, Santeria deities meander through and blend with the tall stalks of sugar cane and tobacco leaves. In fact, Lam was the first modern artist in Cuba to visually explore African-derived religion in art.[68] While Lam was exposed to the religion during his childhood due in large part to his godmother, Mantonica Wilson, who was a priestess, he also had a keen interest in Vodou, the African-derived religion of Haiti. Though spiritual traditions, these were not explicit points of departure for the imagistic direction of the painting. Still, the Black religious forms of Cuba like Santeria and Palo Monte are thematically relevant to the composition. Dense untilled botanical areas, the *monte*, where religious ceremonies take place, are often considered to be sacred. In *El Monte*, Cabrera states that the Spanish words *jungla* (jungle) and *selva* (forest) are not appropriate to describe the characteristics of a natural forest area as they do not connote a sacred terrain. Only *monte* or its synonym *la manigua* are appropriate in this context.[69] It is believed that orishas (the Yoruba deities of the Santeria religion) are invoked in these spaces, thereby allowing the sacred to come into the space. This is also the site where the priests and priestesses gather necessary plants for rites that support the well-being of their devotees.[70] Palo Monte is even more significant here, particularly since the word *monte* is included in its name and monte is the sacred space. Related to religious practices from the precolonial kingdom of Kongo in central Africa, the word *palo* means a segment of wood, while *monte* refers to a forested area that is sacred as well as a rural stronghold. Thus the name of the religion reflects the geography of the people of Kongolese descent in Cuba.[71] Acknowledging the reverence of nature as well as the Afro-Caribbean religious ideology that nature is humanity's point of contact with the transcendental, Cabrera asserts, "Creator of life, we are the children of the woods because life began there; the saints are born of the woods, and our religion is also born of the woods."[72] Lam astutely captured the sacredness of the landscape with his rich and selective color palette. In addition, with the limbs of the figures firmly rooted on the natural terrain, the anthropomorphic bodies produce a semicircle, which is reminiscent of the circle or ring formation integral in many African-derived religious ceremonies.[73] *The Jungle* can thus be recognized as a tribute to this fundamental aspect of Afro-Cuban religious heritage.

Another characteristic that makes *The Jungle* viscerally in tandem with the African continuum that exists in Cuba is the masquerade-like qualities endemic in the anthropomorphic forms. Their bodies seem to slither through the cane- and tobacco-filled terrain, and their placement in the foreground is commanding in such a way that recalls revelers asserting themselves in the public sphere during one of Cuba's festivals. Structurally, *The Jungle* echoes Federico Mialhe's *Day of the Magi* (1853) (figure 2.3) with its vibrant and masquerading figures occupying the foreground, most notably the six figures at the very front. Day of the Magi is a festival celebration that commemorates the day when the three kings arrived to worship and bring gifts to baby Jesus in Bethlehem. In nineteenth-century Cuba, Black Cubans were the majority of the participants in the festival, so much so that it was soon referred to as Carnaval de los Negros (Black Carnival). During slavery, which ended in 1886, enslaved Africans usually had "freedom" during the Day of the Magi, and it was thus a period when they could escape enslavement and colonial power through carnivalesque revelry and role reversal.[74] The humanlike figures in *The Jungle* signify the Black bodies that would be laboring the sugar cane and to-

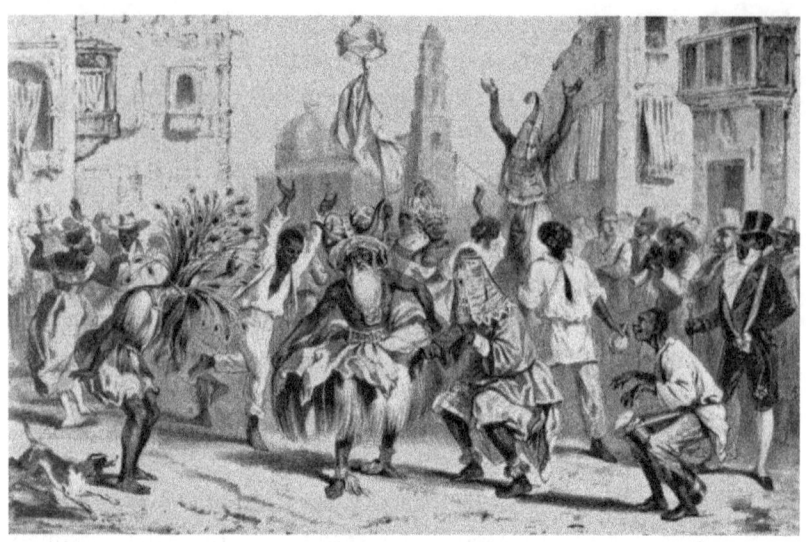

2.3 Federico Mialhe, *Day of the Magi*, 1853. From *Album Pintoresco de la Isla de Cuba* (Havana[?]: May, 1851[?]).

bacco plantations in Cuba during and even after slavery, who, on the Day of the Magi, would be immersed in gaiety much like the subjects in Mi-ahle's painting. At best, the collective emergence of Lam's figures from the vegetation encourages one to think of the transgressive possibilities of the carnivalesque and the eminence of this cultural form to people of African descent in Cuba.[75] This transgression permeates the monumental anthropomorphic figures that crowd the foreground, creating spatial tension. There is also a great sense of dynamism in the push-and-pull effect of the large forms, given the large feet and hands that press downward and push upward, generating a sense of movement in different directions that is pervasive in the gaiety of Carnival.[76] Such spatial tension generated from every section of the composition, along with the representation of crops associated with slavery and colonialism, signifies a horrid legacy of exploitation and oppression. Yet it also highlights the counterhistories of resistance and revival embedded in the counterideologies of Black Cuban culture. Through the use of tropical aesthetics, Lam's *The Jungle* effectively functions through this legacy of insurrection with its hybridization of animals, tropical plants, and people whom he once referred to as monsters, and thus continues the practice of subversion so inherent in his culture.[77] Indeed, the notion of a marvelous land becomes plausible in the dynamic interplay between the figures and terrain, particularly given the assertive stances the anthropomorphic forms possess.

In keeping with this idea of subversion, *The Jungle* articulates a political imperative. Lam is clearly making a choice to feature the landscape rather than the urbanity found in many of Cuba's metropolitan centers. He explained the painting "was intended to communicate a psychic state." Lam also expressed that he wanted to "represent the spirit of the negroes in the situation in which they were then. I have used poetry to show the reality of acceptance and protest."[78] For him, the word *jungle* aptly captured this reality. Etymologically, the word *jungle* was adapted from the Sanskrit word *jangala* in an effort to convey environmental differences between Europe and tropical localities. *Jangala*, which is translated to mean tangled thicket, was gradually distorted from its original, culturally specific meaning. By 1813 it became *jangle*, which was defined as "a wood or thicket, a country overrun with wood or long grass, in a rude and uncultivated state."[79] Eventually *jangle* became *jungle*, which denoted the dense, tangled, and menacing vegetation representative of tropical nature that stood in stark contrast to the orderliness of temperate woodlands.[80] Jungle, as a construct, thus became universalized to signify all dense forests of the tropical world and augmented the established notion that a lack of organization and coherence in the physical environment is directly connected to a lack of organization and coherence among its inhabitants. Lam was keenly aware of this signification and of how the word connoted "a place of threats, of aggressions, of perils known and unknown."[81] He also recognized how relevant this word was during this historical moment when Cuban artists and writers acknowledged the landscape, along with the mulata, as a symbol of cultural nationalism.[82] Yet, although there is no jungle in Cuba—as Lam rightly stated, the terrain consists of woods, hills, and open country—the artist's decision to use the word *jungle* to epitomize the current state of affairs for Afro-Cubans is clever, since he is usurping a Western construct of the tropics in a satirical way to visually convey a socioeconomic predicament of Black Cubans that was the result of Western institutions of slavery and colonialism.[83] Such an employment of the term is astute, as it also provides complex commentary on the Western construct of the tropicality and its association with the Black body.

Using what Dash refers to as a New World aesthetic, Lam is reinventing the Cuban terrain in his art, discounting and demystifying the legacy of the European presence in the Caribbean, particularly in terms of how the Europeans characterized the landscape and in turn the people of the

Caribbean. In addition, Lam is also transforming how Black Cubans are represented and, more important, reimagining their world and their relationship with the environment that they occupy.[84] In his composition, the Cuban landscape now has a new signification, a different function. Historically, the Black community's relationship with the land was threatened as a result of systemic alienation, yet at the same time, as Glissant asserts, this relationship "becomes so fundamental in this discourse that landscape in the work stops being merely decorative or supportive and emerges as a full character." The landscape is inseparable from the community and the individual in the process of creating history.[85] Using the aesthetic rubric of modernism, Lam's art makes it possible for the viewer to recognize the ways in which the Black masses relate to their environment. By converging the human form with plant life as well as the terrain, Lam activates tropical aesthetics and thereby demonstrates an imaginative reclaiming of the land. This claim is not a capitalist effort to assume ownership of a predetermined property. Through the practice of a grammar of liberation, Lam's art allows for the naming of place that makes self-assertion and self-definition possible.[86]

One can certainly interpret many of Lam's works after 1942 as taking issue with the institutionalized racism experienced by Black Cubans as well as the U.S. presence in postcolonial Cuba. Lam had articulated that his first impression of Havana upon his return was one of terrible sadness, given that there was still that same level of poverty as when he left, the same discrimination between the races who were fully exploited by the rich. But particularly close to his heart was the state of Cubans of African descent.[87] Black Cubans had been systematically marginalized since Cuba gained independence in 1898. Yet with the increasing presence of American corporations and citizens on Cuban soil since the late nineteenth century, Cubans were subjected to North American hegemony. By 1940 America had replaced Spain, the former colonizer, as the key exploiter of Cuba's sugar industry, since it owned the majority of the mills. And the Americans brought their explicit racial delineations with them, normalizing practices of discrimination on the island that greatly affected the Cuban social sphere.[88] While there was no institutionalized racial oppression like what existed in the southern United States, a type of debilitating discrimination became the norm for Black Cubans. Commercial and social establishments that Americans frequented in the cities refused to hire any person of color unless it was for the basest of occupations. As a result, Black people comprised the majority of the poor and the majority of the unemployed in Cuba, and their socioeconomic situation was tied to the sugar industry and its incumbent American presence.[89]

While Black Cubans were foremost in Lam's mind when creating *The Jungle*, the work also examines the subject of sex work. Lam's eroticized female forms in *The Jungle* are in conversation not only with other Cuban works that feature the mulata but also with Picasso's *Demoiselles d'Avignon*, given the similar structures of both compositions. Lam even described the figure on the right as being "obscene as a whore," and most likely he did so to illuminate the prevalence of sex work in Cuba at this historical moment.[90] When Lam returned to Cuba, sex work flourished, since sex workers were a key attraction for male tourists. Havana alone had about 270 brothels as well as sex shows and live pornographic theaters. It is estimated that more than 11,500 women were employed as sex workers in Havana, with mulatto women often being favored in large part due to the sexual neuroses of colonialism.[91]

Lam's signature piece commemorates the many challenges Black Cubans endured up until the artist's return. *The Jungle* celebrates their perseverance while simultaneously rejecting any pretense as to who the land belongs to, serving as a gesture of reclamation for land that was mostly owned by American companies and used for the capitalist prosperity of the United States. Undoubtedly, this painting encompasses the revolutionary spirit of Black modernism, given Lam's bold reinterpretation of the Cuban landscape, while also emphasizing the resolute character of the Black masses.

INVOKING SPIRITUALITY

Another painting that explores the masses' relationship with the land is *La Sombre Malembo, Dieu du Carrefour* (Malembo, God of the Crossroads) (1943) (plate 4). Given the "pointillist" style that Lam uses to create this composition, there is an amalgamating effect that is visible between the anthropomorphic figures and the scenery that surrounds them.[92] While the color palette here is similar to that used in *The Jungle*, the painterly gestures are noticeably different. Whereas attention is given to defining the shapes and colors of the flora in *The Jungle*, in *Malembo* Lam chooses to execute blotches and slight strokes to denote the vegetation with only a number of leaf and stalk forms interspersed throughout the top half of the picture plane that would indicate the type of crop being conveyed. His decision to use the technique of pointillism to convey the landscape in this painting suggests an eagerness to explore different ways of portraying the Cuban terrain. Pointillism is a painting technique, developed by the Neo-Impressionists Georges Seurat and Paul Signac in the late nineteenth century, in which small and distinct dots of color are arranged in patterns to create a composition. Believing that colors had a more intense visual effect when mixed optically rather than on the palette, these artists created mechanical-like imagery that seemed to record both color and light.[93] Perhaps this is precisely what Lam wanted to record in *Malembo*, as it is known that he would often paint in his light-filled garden. For him, the garden was a microcosm of Cuba's marvelous landscape.[94] The environment conveyed in *Malembo* features not only shades of green, yellow, and blue but also speckling of white throughout to express the reflective quality of light in the Caribbean.[95]

The large hybrid figures in the middle of the composition take up much of the picture plane. They appear to emanate from the surroundings, since much of their surfaces are identical to the pointillist flora in the vicinity. These anthropomorphic figures fuse human, animal, and vegetal elements and also include circular-shaped heads that recall African-like masks. There seems to be a continuous line used to contour the forms, so much so that the two predominant figures appear to be conjoined: the male on the left and the female on the right. Their bodies are oblong, with the male figure appearing four-limbed and having a goliath presence while the female figure stands upright with disproportionately long arms. Emanating from her torso are other hybrid forms that are depicted as morphing into their own respective beings. Still connected to each other, they stream from right to left and echo the direction of the male figure's hair. These tresses begin at the base of his head and flow along the frame of his elephant-like torso, almost touching the ground. The last of the three has strands of new growth that mirror the mane of the male figure. Lam seems to be presenting a kind of family portrait that is symbolic of the collective history of his people.[96]

It was Lam's friend Lydia Cabrera who created the title of this painting and several others. Like Lam, Cabrera lived in Paris, where she studied art before pursuing her writing career. It was in Paris that she developed an interest in Afro-Cuban culture and started writing about myths, religious beliefs, and practices as well as folklore. Cabrera returned to Cuba in 1938 and met Lam there three years later. According to Herzberg, it was Lam's friendship with Cabrera as well as Alejo Carpentier that propelled the aesthetic direction of his work.[97] Black Cubans had always endured institutionalized racism, but this was because of a predominant view that rejected Africa's legacy in the formulation of a civilized and modern Cuba. Black Cuban cultural forms like Santeria and rumba were seen as culturally backward and antithetical to any kind of national progress.[98] It is therefore understandable why the word *Malembo* was included in the title, since it reinserts Africa back into Cuba.

In addition, *Malembo* also reflects Cabrera's interest in the Kongo.[99] When translated from the French, the title of the painting means "Dark Malembo, God of the Crossroads." Herzberg articulates that *Malembo* in the Kongo region of sub-Saharan Africa refers to the evil found at the crossroads. While the word *God* is in the title, Malembo is not a deity but an evil force that should be avoided at the crossroads.[100] However, it should also be noted that Malembo is the name of a slave port in northern Angola that thrived from the eighteenth to the nineteenth centuries. First controlled by the Dutch and then later by the French, this slave port supplied a large portion of the slave population in the Dutch Guianas.[101]

Whether Lam or Cabrera was aware of the slave port is unclear. Nonetheless, *La Sombre Malembo, Dieu du Carrefour* is explicit in its resonance with the Palo Monte religion and the primacy of the land in Afro-Cuban religion. In light of this, Sims encourages a reading of Lam's dense topographies as referencing both Cuba and the tropical terrains of ancestral Africa.[102] Furthermore, Lam is creating a world that is fantastic and therefore metaphorical "for a worldview intimately tied both to Africa, through his Cuban heritage and to his own inventive imagination."[103] The work makes a marvelous imaging of a transnational existence plausible through Pan-Africanist longing, which acknowledges the vital role of ancestry in the quest for a hopeful future.

Lam's *Malembo* is an iconographic conveyance of a refusal to subscribe to the racist notion that de-Africanizing the populace would benefit Cuba. By reinventing the landscape, Lam's art renders a new kind of modernity that privileges nature and man's relationship with it. Given Lam's preoccupation with the land of Cuba and with Black Cuban culture, it is not far-fetched to construe Lam's effort to insightfully represent the environment as an alternative repository of memory that fosters a sense of rootedness, a sense of place with the terrain for Black Cubans, many of whom were diminished by poverty and exploitation.[104] The inclusion of the word *Malembo* in the title underscores the importance of coming to terms with iniquities that can plague a land's character, given the troubled histories of Black Cuban folk and their desire to seek a spiritual means of coming to terms with this past.

Undoubtedly, Africanisms are pervasive in Lam's oeuvre. Lucie-Smith claimed that the masks from New Guinea, not Africa, were the visual references used to convey the masklike faces seen in many of Lam's works.[105] However, a number of other art historians acknowledge the influence African art had on Lam's art. Sims asserts that Lam would have been exposed to African art when first moving to Europe and settling in Spain. He would have been able to see the collection of the Museo Antropológico that was a section of the Museo Nacional de Ciencias Naturales. Evidence of this is reflected in early works such as *Sans titre* (1937).[106] Even Herzberg discusses the conceivable influence of the Dogon-lidded box that was housed in the Musée de l'Homme at the time Lam lived in Paris.[107] Mosquera notes that African art inspired Lam to create more abstract-oriented works. Lam's African art collection gave him a means of creating a truly modern Black art. On the one hand, European artists had embraced African and Oceanic sculptures, which they deemed to be "primitive" art, for the purpose of transforming Western art and making it modern; this was Europe being colonized in reverse. On the other hand, Third World artists such as Lam entered these societies and participated in a cross-cultural exchange in which they usurped African art traditions as a creative method to express their own voice. While Lam gained much from studying the works of prolific European artists such as Picasso, his fascination with the dimensions of African sculpture provided much fodder for his creative direction, manifesting in a kind of Africanization of Western art.[108]

The African-based religions of Cuba proved to be another source of creativity for the artist, particularly throughout the years 1943 to 1945. During this period, Lam did a series of landscapes featuring anthropomorphic manifestations of orishas and, to a lesser extent, still life compositions that presented objects used to honor these orishas. In compositions such as *Autel pour Elegua* (Altar for Elegua) (1944) (figure 2.4), Lam presents the home altar as still life. These domestic altars could be situated in the home or in the outdoors in one's yard and were made to honor the orishas that are deities or gods associated with the Santeria religion. These orishas are spiritual beings that are thought to possess different aspects of the Supreme God.[109] *Autel pour Elegua* represents an altar honoring the deity Elegua, the messenger god who facilitates communication between the deities and their devotees but who is also associated with the crossroads and is recognized as a custodian during pivotal moments of transition in one's life.

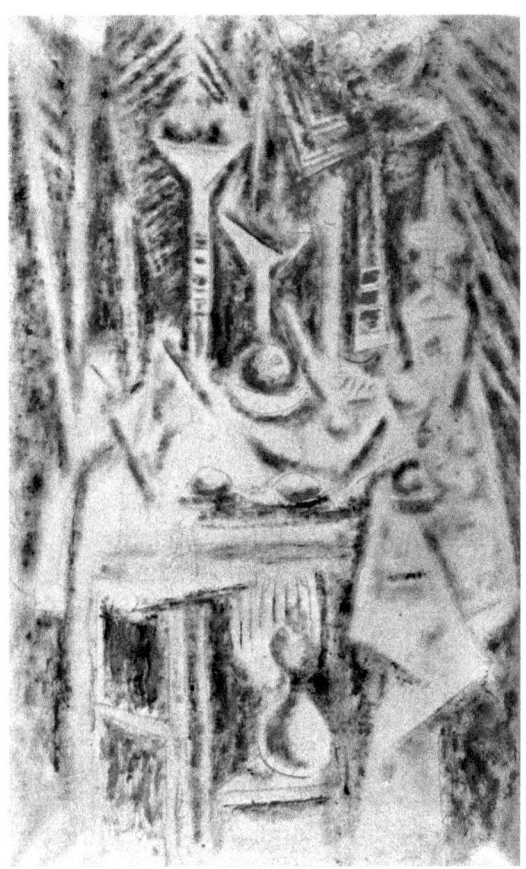

2.4 Wifredo Lam, *Autel pour Elegua* (Altar for Elegua), 1944. Private Collection—Paris. © Artists Rights Society (ARS), New York / ADAGP, Paris.

This altar created for Elegua seems to be situated in a lush garden of someone's home, and the setting is apropos since orishas are believed to dwell in the monte, which is a sacred area for prayer and supplication.[110] Lam's still life includes objects like candles, egg-like forms, horseshoes (symbol of another orisha called Ogun), double-headed axes, (symbol of Chango), and double bull horns (symbol of Oya).[111] In his conveyance of the altar and its many sacred objects, very light applications of brushstrokes are used and in some areas only faint lines are created to suggest form. Even the palm fronds in the background are intimately represented and, along with the altar and its contents, emit a very spiritual character. Sims interprets Lam's painterly gestures as pointillist stippling that represent the impression of sunlight on reflective glass and metal surfaces.[112] As in *La Sombre Malembo, Dieu du Carrefour*, Lam succeeds in conveying the reflective quality of light in the Caribbean in *Autel pour Elegua*, not to mention how it aids the artist in venerating the landscape through art. *Autel pour Elegua* highlights the primacy of the natural terrain as a sacred space. Many believe that orishas are born in the forest, thereby allowing religion to come into existence. By establishing an altar in one's garden, a Santeria devotee is consecrating the environment in which orishas live. This land can thus be seen as physically yet spiritually yoked with el monte. Herzberg aptly points out that the altar-cum-still life is another example of Lam's penchant for using a traditional genre of Western art in a very untraditional way. Despite using an aesthetic language informed by a contemporary modernist ethos, the artist is still able to articulate a personal and collective Cuban subjectivity that is inherent in a Santeria worldview.[113] Here, Afrocubanismo is infused with a surrealist aesthetic, yet it imparts "a significance that is greater than that connected with Surrealist ideas through their allusion to traditional Afro-Cuban celebrations."[114] The tropical aesthetics that Lam uses in this work highlights the relationship many Black Cubans had with the land, which was characterized by religious expression. Although this cultural practice was disparaged, it was nonetheless a manifestation of self-definition that Black Cubans asserted along with other members of the Black Atlantic in the early twentieth century.

These works are imbued with a call to acknowledge the radical way in which Black people mold their identities via a strong sense of place. These paintings reflect Lam's belief that despite the histories of slavery, colonization, and European cultural imperialism that the Caribbean has endured, the art and culture emerging from the region can help shape a new disposition. He referred to his art as an "art of decolonization" and urged all artists with a similar background to sever all ties with the colonial culture.[115] In so doing, Lam and his art encompass the proactive and transformative nature of Black modernism while emphasizing the fundamental purpose of the terrain in this venture.

In most of the compositions Lam created from 1941 to 1945, the infinite foliage is an exemplary symbol of power. His tropical terrains seem impenetrable, with the figures that interlock with the vegetation keeping guard, making it impossible for any trespasser to infiltrate. As Lam himself attested, "In these works . . . we can see . . . beings in their passage from vegetal state to that of an animal and still charged with vestiges of the forest."[116] His polymorphic beings take it upon themselves to go against the Western prerogative of private property by recognizing what Glissant refers to as the indivisibility of the land, which makes the dignity of the community possible.[117] Such a purposeful relationship between the community and the landscape is what grants the land its full character.[118] Art historian Suzanne Garrigues Daniel recognizes the vibrant presence and function of the terrain that Lam creates when she affirms that "color ignites the painting, activates the rhythm of the linear grid and the entire surface pulsates, in and out, back and forth, up and down. It is a jungle that attracts and repels. A jungle that lives, breathes, grows. A jungle that is infinitely alive and in process."[119] Indeed, Lam's lush foliage embodies that sayability of geography that is empowering and enriching. Although the subjects of this art are left with the vestiges of the forest, these remnants exist as an alternative institution to any capitalist enterprise.

THE CONVERGENCE OF NEGRITUDE AND SURREALISM

Negritude's call for the veneration of Black values in the age of modernism did not go unnoticed for Lam during his stay in Martinique en route to his native Cuba; neither did the radical ideas proliferated by Aimé and Suzanne Césaire and René Ménil within the pages of the journal *Tropiques*, where the Antillean identity was declared to be a mode of cultural liberation. The profound effect that these ideologies had on Lam is very evident when considering the work *Harpe Astrale* [*Harpe Cardinale*] (The Astral Harp) (1944) (figure 2.5). Painted the year after Lam created *The Jungle*, *Harpe Astrale* is one such painting in which land is commemorated as a source of empowerment and invigoration. Four major hybrids dominate the composition, and their forms appear to be slightly translucent. The figure on the left bears a masklike face and pronounced neck. Stemming from under its head is what seems to be a slender trunk reminiscent of a tree; three roots form a tripod on the ground, and a head is clearly visible on one of them. Given the structure of the tree trunk, it is reminiscent of the trunk of the human form and it epitomizes Suzanne Césaire's notion of the "plant-man."[120] A limb conjoins the first hybrid figure with the third one, whose face is more visually complex than that of the first, yet its body is indistinguishable from the landscape. The last hybrid is mounted atop an array of leaves and has limbs that are long and stalklike, the two in the front echoing the shape and structure of the trunk to the left.

Like *Autel pour Elegua* (Altar for Elegua), which he also painted in 1944, brushstrokes are applied lightly onto the canvas. Yet the forms are more

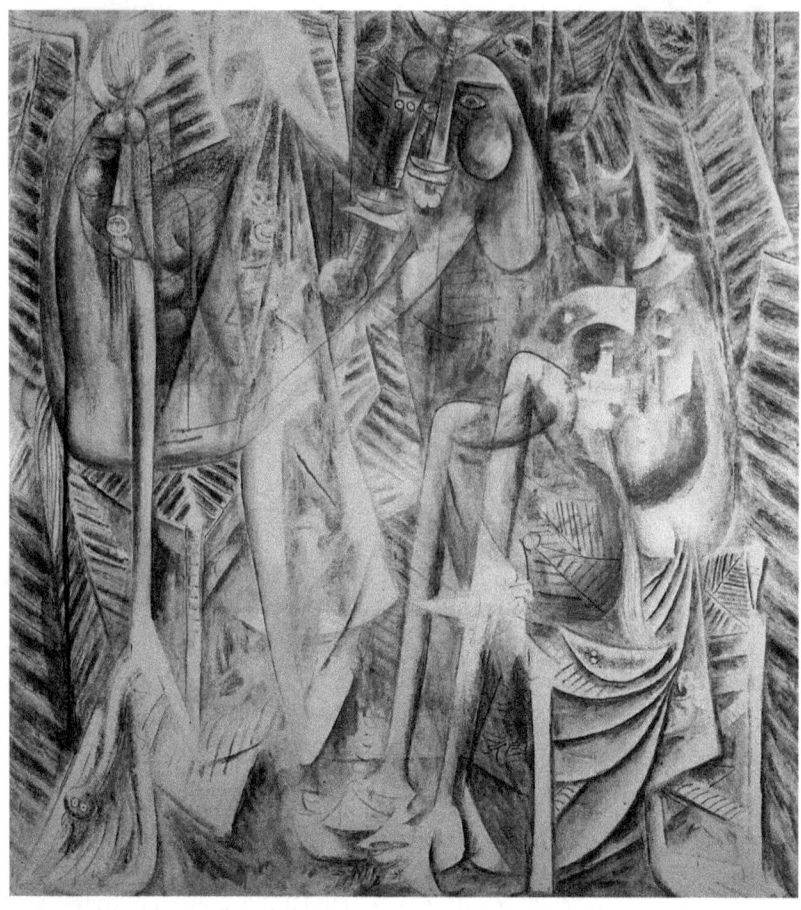

2.5 Wifredo Lam, *Harpe Astrale* [*Harpe Cardinale*] (The Astral Harp), 1944. Collection of Baron B. Urvater, Paris. © Artists Rights Society (ARS), New York / ADAGP, Paris.

definitive, while the textures and dimensions of the various elements in the composition are more overt. In the foreground, Lam portrays banana leaves as if they are individual entities. These sculptural representations are a departure from previous iterations of the plant in older paintings and reflect an evolution of his aesthetic. The leaves have a prevailing character and they envelop the figures, even intertwining with their bodies in certain areas. These leaves visually link the hybrid figures to the thick foliage in the background. The tropical terrain here seems impenetrable as the figures interlock with the vegetation in a mutual gesture of protection for the sanctity of the landscape.

Through his inventive imagery, Lam does not copy nature here but, like the surrealists, uses painting as a visual language to communicate a truth that is particular to the Black Cuban outlook, one that is not dependent on naturalist representations that merely copy the environment.[121] Furthermore, surrealism offered Lam a creative yet dynamic way to tackle racial politics in Cuba and its intersectionality with the complexities of sovereignty and land ownership. Aimé Césaire spoke candidly of this power in Lam's art.

> In a society where money and the machine have immeasurably increased the distance between Man and things, Wifredo Lam fixes on canvas the ceremony through which everything exists; the ceremony of the physical union of Man and the world. . . . Painting is one of the few weapons left to us against the sordidness of history. Wifredo Lam is there to prove it. And this is one of the meanings of this richest of all paintings: that it stops the *Conquistador* in his tracks; that is demonstrates to this bloody epoch of bastardization its own failure by the insolent affirmation that something is happening in the Antilles. Something that has nothing to do with quotas in sugar and rum, with military bases, with constitutional amendments, something unusual, something eminently disturbing to economic agreements and political plans, and that threatens to upset any regime that ignores it. . . . Wifredo Lam doesn't hesitate to take the part of a great disturber. . . . Wifredo Lam gives the boot to academies and conformities.[122]

Césaire proclaims art to be as powerful as a weapon; he argues it can be a meaningful defense mechanism in the face of systemic oppression. One can discern from his words that art can contribute substantially to what McKittrick calls the "struggle toward some kind of sociospatial liberation," which can only fortify Antillean identity.[123] Césaire also seems to be highlighting the U.S. presence in Cuba, referring to them as the conquistador. While this is the Spanish word for "conqueror" and alludes to the legacy of colonialism in Cuba and the wider Caribbean, it also signifies the ongoing neocolonialist tendencies of the American government and corporations that began on the island of Cuba in 1906.[124]

Indeed, Césaire not only recognized Lam's transgression over the political and social establishment but also conveyed how Lam transgresses the academy in his art so that he could more effectively challenge Cuban and American hegemonies. Through "infusing a Surrealist aesthetic with references to Afro-Cubanism, Lam established a special territory for himself" in the Western art world.[125] And this domain paralleled that of Aimé Césaire in the realm of literature; Lam's key works such as *The Jungle* and *Harpe Astrale* can be seen as visual companion pieces to Césaire's *Cahier d'un Retour au Pays Natal* (*Notebook of a Return to the Native Land*).[126]

In 1943 Cabrera embarked on a project with Lam and Césaire: they published a Spanish translation of *Cahier d'un Retour au Pays Natal*, with Cabrera taking charge of the translation and Lam providing the illustrations. The publication also included an introduction by French surrealist poet Benjamin Péret.[127] As literary scholar Emily A. Maguire points out, this project was the only collaboration between Césaire, Lam, and Cabrera, and it was significant since it "connects . . . a Pan-Caribbean avant-garde spirit" of three Caribbean artists who served "important roles . . . in shaping ideas of blackness and racial identity in the region."[128] Moreover, in keeping with the idea of a special territory, it is plausible to view these three individuals not as secondary inheritors of surrealism but as engaging in a contact zone, which Mary Louise Pratt defines as "social spaces where disparate cultures meet, clash, and grapple with each other, often in highly asymmetrical relations of domination and subordination."[129] Through their ground-breaking work, created both individually and collectively, Césaire, Lam, and Cabrera used surrealism as a means to critically engage in an inter-American discourse. Doing so challenges the predominant way in which the flow of knowledge production and innovation is often framed—between Europe and the Caribbean, the center and the periphery.[130]

No doubt, the works of Lam and Césaire are testaments to the aesthetic freedom and creative vicissitude that surrealism encouraged. However, the movement was not without its shortcomings. While its members disavowed the discourses of evolutionism and also used the "primitive" artifact to transgress the European image of the world, they substituted reductive ideologies about "exotic" cultures with those of the fantastic, the magical, and the mythical. And despite their efforts to challenge the dominant bourgeois ideologies of Western modernity, "they never totally broke free of the boundaries of their own (largely French) race, language and culture."[131] Furthermore, the artistic traditions as well as the idea of a symbolic return to Africa that were crucial to the development of Lam's art and Césaire's development of negritude, respectively, were not held in high esteem by Breton. The founder of surrealism believed that Africa had no place in his aesthetic vision for the movement and occupied a small space in the 1929 surrealist map; this estimation ironically mirrored the same cultural imperialism the movement vehemently denounced.[132]

But negritude proved to be problematic as well. The literary movement also perceived African cultures as "primitive" and looked to them for fodder to counteract European cultural imperialism.[133] Ménil, who cofounded *Tropiques* and eventually parted ways with Césaire, became a scathing critic of the movement. As Michael Richardson elucidates: "For Ménil, negritude came to stand for a political doctrine whose apparent ideological credentials were a mask by which European imperialism used the native petty bourgeoisie to ensure the continuance of a neo-colonialist mentality following independence that would ensure continuing European dominance."[134] Ménil was well aware of the high probability for the European colonizer to maintain a strategic kind of power dynamic. This issue was never fully addressed in the movement since it never questioned these relations. The consequence of this inadequacy in any colonial society is what Ménil refers to as "separation from oneself, exile from oneself. . . . I am 'exotic-to-myself' because my view of myself is the view of the white person having become mine."[135]

Despite these inadequacies of the negritude movement, what surrealism lost among the avant-garde of radical Europe, it gained in the Americas. After all, Breton considered the tropics to be the quintessential terrain since he affirmed that the surrealist landscape was embodied in tropical regions such as the Caribbean.[136] Although Jean-Paul Sartre romanticized Black culture just as much as the surrealists, he too acknowledged that the surrealist movement is transformed into another iteration of the "Universal Revolution" in the Caribbean.[137] The movement was able to resuscitate its revolutionary and political dimensions in regions such as the Caribbean.[138] Given its liberationist ideology, Antillean surrealists such as Aimé and Suzanne Césaire, as well as René Ménil, fashioned a surrealism that was particular to the Martinican context. They were able to articulate this through poetry, which for them epitomized "a grasping of reality in its pure state."[139] This poetry does not simply accept the parameters established by the movement per se but cannibalizes it. As Suzanne Césaire affirmed, "Martiniquan poetry will be cannibal or will not be."[140]

Literary scholar Valérie Loichot defines this historical practice of Caribbean writers engaging in literary cannibalism to refer to the conscious effort "to devour fragments of texts written mostly, but not only, by European or colonial writers. This act of ingestion . . . is driven by a violence that responds to revenge or of justice."[141] Therefore, it does not allude to notions of originality but engages in a mode of devouring the other that has no beginning or end. Literary cannibalism, in fact, questions the validity of the widely held claim that Europe is the custodian of originality, which is dependent on the precept that writers of the colonies are mere imitators, cannibals of these texts.[142] Literary scholar Peter Stallybrass rightfully reminds us of the importance of questioning "our relation to the ownership of knowledge," since, for example, "Shakespeare deliberately and shamelessly . . . appropriated for his own use what he read or heard."[143] Without the awareness of this historical yet common practice, it was commonplace to view the writers of the colonies as those who devour the ideas coming from the metropole. Such a rendering of Caribbean knowledge production hinges on the epistemological signification of the word *cannibalism* as it relates to the Caribbean. The region's discursive relationship with cannibalism began with Columbus's misinterpretation of the word *Cariba* screamed by the Carib Amerindians during that first encounter. Instead of hearing *cari*, he heard *cani*, which he associated with the Latin *canis*. Thus this initial meeting, Loichot asserts, "marks the simultaneous birth of the cannibal and the Caribbean in European lexicons and in European fantasies."[144]

The Caribbean was not the only region in the world where this bold form of creative production referred to as cannibalism emerged. Almost two decades prior to Suzanne Césaire's daring assertion, Oswald de Andrade published his "Manifesto Antropófago" (Cannibalist Manifesto). In it, he disputed the "dualities civilization/barbarism, modern/primitive, and original/derivative, which had informed the construction of Brazilian culture since the days of the colony."[145] Andrade's cannibal metaphor allowed the modern Brazilian subject to "devour" his colonial identity in order to construct a native culture that was original in its own way.[146] Pronouncing the immense benefits of anthropophagism, Andrade states: "Everyday love and the capitalist way of life. Cannibalism. Absorption of the sacred enemy. Even so, only the pure elites managed to realize carnal cannibalism, which carries within itself the highest meaning of life and avoids all the ills identified by Freud—catechist ills. What results is not a sublimation of the sexual instinct. It is the thermometrical scale of the cannibal instinct. Carnal at first, this instinct becomes elective, and creates friendship. When it is affective, it creates love. When it is speculative, it creates science."[147] For Andrade, cannibalism is a life-affirming endeavor that devours the enemy. At the same time, this carnal cannibalism is revitalizing and liberates the mind in an effort to spawn creativity. In an emphatic attempt to problematize the binary oppositions that rendered Brazil as the antithesis of Europe, the poet situates cannibalism in the limitless bounds

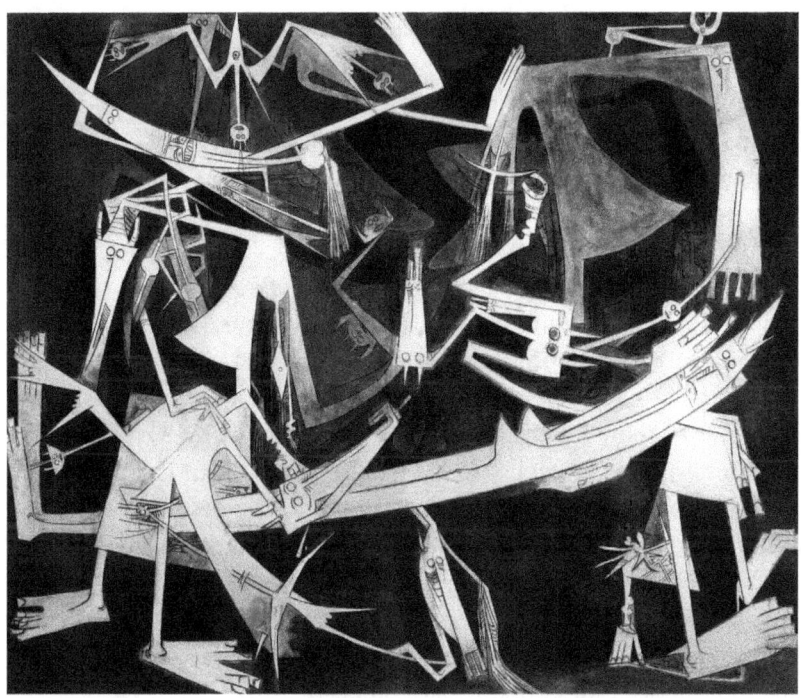

2.6 Wifredo Lam, *El Tercer Mundo* (The Third World), 1965–66.
Museo Nacional de Bellas Artes, Havana, Cuba.

of sentiment that effectively counter the rigidity of academic conformity. But more fundamentally, the text questions the very notion of originality.

Lam and other visual artists engaged in a type of "artistic cannibalism."[148] Like his counterparts in the literary realm, his art aims to consume reductive visual representations of the people and the land they occupy in an effort to reclaim humanity and dignity. This bearing very much parallels his belief that his art is an art of decolonization, and he even called "on all artists like himself to sever all ties with the colonial culture."[149]

While this ideology of decolonization is reflected in much of his art after returning to Cuba, *El Tercer Mundo* (The Third World) (1965–66) (figure 2.6) seems to epitomize this artistic cannibalism in very striking ways. By the time Lam created this work, he had returned to Europe, opting to settle in Albisola, Italy, rather than Paris. At this moment in his career, there is a profound evolution in his signature imagery. No longer situated in a robust landscape, the compositions of this period are largely figurative. *El Tercer Mundo* features a limited color palette, with the background consisting of shades of brown and black, with mostly white and beige figures. Sims explains that the dynamic interaction between the figures is in tandem with the relationship portrayed in *The Jungle*.[150] The bodies in the foreground superimpose receding figures that appear to fade into the dark background. As Sims remarks, "Lam creates a complex interplay and interpenetration between line and color, void and mass, frontality and background. . . . While the forms meander around the composition, they come full circle to grasp themselves or grip the random diagonal lines to anchor themselves and the whole visually as well as structurally."[151] Although *El Tercer Mundo* veers into abstraction, Lam's surrealist sensibility is still evident with the innovative linearity used to create the angular figures. There is a sense of spontaneity and swift movement in the interactions of the silhouettes. The biggest figure spans the breadth of the composition in the lower foreground, and the limbs of proximate bodies touch and sometimes merge with it. One figure pierces through another to establish contact with the largest body, adding to the overall sense of "visual energy" and interconnectedness.[152] Overall, there is a sense of balance in the structure of the composition, and it is evident that the work is visually exploring the concept of entities working harmoniously with each other.

The term *Third World* emerged in the 1950s and referred to countries that were not affiliated with the powerful countries that were members of the North Atlantic Treaty Organization (NATO) and the communist bloc during the Cold War era. Members of NATO consisted of First World nations—the United States, some Western European countries—while communist nations such as the former USSR, China, and Cuba were considered Second World countries. The remaining nonaligned nations were relegated to a Third World identity. Given the hierarchical nature of these categories, the explicit peripheralization of these nations meant that proactive steps had to be taken for them to withstand any vulnerability to the oppositional policies of the United States and the USSR. The Non-Aligned Movement (NAM) was one such gesture and was composed of many nation-states that shared histories of colonialism. Efforts were made to promote economic and cultural cooperation and to collectively work against colonialism, neocolonialism, and any form of hegemony exercised by aligned nations.[153] Soon, Third-Worldism became a term that characterized new social and political movements emerging in regions such as Asia and Africa, and it "was based on an anti-imperialist ideology of national self-determination."[154] The term *Third World* eventually became a great source of pride for people of the Global South and came to encapsulate a collective identity that distinguished these people from those of the East-West entities of the Cold War period. It is this very sentiment that is encoded in the dynamic imagery of Lam's *El Tercer Mundo*.

El Tercer Mundo champions the Global South and is artistic cannibalism fully realized. This notion of cannibalism, through its denouncement of colonialism and imperialism, also challenges the "civilization/barbarism . . . originators/imitators" oppositional binaries.[155] The spirit of the composition parallels Andrade's affront to Enlightenment discourses of natural right when he proclaims, "We want the Carib Revolution. Greater than the French Revolution. The unification of all productive revolts for the progress of humanity. Without us, Europe wouldn't even have its meager declaration of the rights of man."[156] Lam's *El Tercer Mundo* augments the call for justice as well as the redistribution of global power and wealth that largely benefited First World nations. As is conveyed in other works such as *The Jungle*, *El Tercer Mundo* asserts an imperative of reclamation by the people and their ancestors who have inhabited and/or toiled the land. The work is artistically emblematic of Third-Worldism, rendering the possibility that comes with the galvanizing efforts of various nations joining forces. While this ideological stance is explicit, it is important to consider that Lam's devouring of a surrealist visual language not only engages in the act of cannibalizing an artistic tradition but also acknowledges the history of mutual or cross-cultural exchange that has always existed between the First, Second, and Third Worlds. The surrealists looked to art of the Third World for artistic inspiration and were being, as artist Robert Linsley explained, "colonized in reverse," since "Third World artists were themselves entering [European] culture and twisting it to their own purposes, effecting a more complete Africanization of western art."[157]

Surrealism, though, ought not to be viewed as European thought, and figures such as the Césaires should be recognized as innovators of the movement. Both of them encouraged an embracing of the marvelous that would bring forth the freed image, a call to Africa.[158] In this sense, negritude becomes inextricably linked to surrealism and the most apt ideological posturing through which Lam could convey the collective psyche of Black Cubans. While they existed in a society that Lam thought to be oppressive, his art nonetheless seems to commemorate the cultural, economic, spiritual, and social impact that African-descended peoples have had on Cuba, a summoning of an African heritage that has contributed tirelessly to a modern Cuba.

On a more literal sense, Lam's art conveys a natural world that is revered not with any intention to transform the environment but as a way to accept the idiosyncrasies of the terrain. By not changing or "improving" the land, this act (or lack thereof) becomes an articulation of resistance, a resistance to the historical rhetoric of the "Conquest of the Tropics."[159] To this end, works such as *Autel pour Elegua* (Altar for Elegua) and *The Jungle* unabashedly recall Fernando Ortiz's propagation in his infamous text *Contrapunteo cubano del tobacco y el azucar* (*Cuban Counterpoint: Tobacco and Sugar*) that sugar was more associated with Spanish absolutism. Ortiz tellingly conjures an image that likens sugar to the horrific system of slavery and to foreign intervention as a whole. Alternatively, tobacco represented national independence since it is a crop that is indigenous to Cuba. However, given that their historical and economic qualities are so intertwined, Ortiz astutely points out that "capitalism . . . is reducing everything to the same denominator."[160] Perhaps this is why Lam portrays both crops throughout the entire picture plane of *The Jungle*, with tobacco leaves seemingly growing out of cane stalks in some areas. This surely reflects the ways in which tobacco and sugar incorporate multiple meanings, given their shifting histories in Cuba.[161] Certainly, many of Lam's artworks depict landscapes that are symbolic of that dual relation between plantation (servitude) and plot (nonownership but some level of autonomy).[162] While much of his art visually commemorates the significance of the history of slavery and its relevance in the present moment, they still articulate a desire for the empowerment and assertion of a subjugated people. Lam successfully communicates a pronouncement of social and political autonomy against external domination, conveying a collective Black subjectivity's relationship to modernity that is not passive but, as Glissant asserted, irruptive.[163]

Through his restructuring of modernist aesthetics in his own terms, Lam became an insistent and persevering force within the Western art world, thereby transforming the cannon into one that is global.[164] His art conjured a world that was decidedly Caribbean, using the Western pictorial tradition as a point of departure. Surrealism provided the means for his reinvention of the Cuban landscape and the depiction of the Cuban worldview in general. Like the surrealists, Lam uses painting as a visual language to communicate a truth that is particular to the Black Cuban outlook, one that is in no way dependent on naturalist representations.[165] Quintessentially a fantastic art, Lam's work possesses "utopian elements [that] contain essential universal truths," which ultimately teach us that by "transcending the norms of perceived reality, the fantastic transports the viewer into a world where the implausible becomes plausible."[166] Indeed, surrealism as well as the incorporation of fantasy offered Lam creative yet dynamic ways to tackle racial politics in Cuba and how it is deeply connected to sovereignty and a right to claim the land as one's own.

Prior to the emergence of Afrocubanismo as a defining force for Cuban national identity, a predominant school of thought upheld the belief that the island's African legacy served as a hindrance toward any efforts Black Cubans had to improve their socioeconomic status in the nation, let alone the overall advancement of the nation-state. This all changed by the 1920s when Cuban modernists championed the Black Cuban masses as well as their creative forms that lay outside the usual academic and elitist purview. Lam was the first artist whose art featured Black Cuban culture as a decisive factor of expression, and visually exploring the Black Cuban spirit was a vital part of his oeuvre.[167] Furthermore, negritude provided an ideological framework through which he could develop the art he created in Cuba, particularly since for Aimé and Suzanne Césaire, the political, cultural and spiritual identity of modern Black people is inherently connected to the terrain.[168] This herculean endeavor of galvanizing the Black masses of the Caribbean toward the idea of belonging to a place is based on a struggle for sociospatial liberation.[169] The pursuit of this venture is often never fully realized. Yet Lam's art offers "alternative geographic formulations," a particular rendering of a "different sense of place."[170] His art makes it possible to experience a different way of knowing and imagining the world.

In a similar way, festival traditions allow for the full realization of the struggle for sociospatial liberation through the reveling, and sometimes contentious, encounters of masqueraders in real time and space. Indeed, the dynamic and vibrant paintings Lam constructed offered imaginative meditations of Black Cubans asserting their connectedness to Cuba's natural environment. Yet in another part of the Caribbean, the unruly Black female body of late nineteenth- to early twentieth-century Trinidad contributed to unparalleled moments of freedom that brought to life the land of the marvelous. As the following chapter explores, their unruly bodies ignored colonially mandated modes of behavior, and the numerous costumed Black bodies in motion that meandered the public sphere in the tropics assertively challenged the geographic domination of the colonial order.

On Saturday, February 2, 1991, the semifinal round of the Calypso Monarch competition was in full swing at Skinner Park in San Fernando, Trinidad. The calypsonian Super Blue was a contender that day and was expected to perform his popular, and now classic, soca song "Get Something and Wave."[1] Without question, his act was one of the most anticipated. Many spectators found things to wave by the time he got on stage, including one schoolteacher who brandished a pair of red underwear (figure 3.1). She would have been seen on the nationally owned television network, Trinidad and Tobago Television, which broadcast the competition live.[2] However, an image of her on the front page of the newspaper the next day did a better job of archiving her act.

In the picture, she is elevated slightly above those around her and is immersed in the excitement of the moment as she grips the red panties with both hands. This image triggered a huge backlash against the woman as well as the *Trinidad Express* newspaper for publishing the photograph. Many people condemned the Catholic schoolteacher for setting a poor example for her students and their peers.[3] Two pastors of St. John's Baptist Church commented that "a possible image conveyed to the world is that the stereotypes of Carnival, Black people and sex, are synonymous."[4] Despite such criticism, the Catholic Board of Education did not enforce any disciplinary measures against the teacher, particularly since many of her peers agreed that she was dedicated to her profession.[5]

Perhaps the board was well aware of the satire embedded in the teacher's act, a key aspect of the pre-Lenten Catholic festival that is Carnival. While the red of her undergarment is one of Trinidad and Tobago's national colors, it also symbolizes blood, which directly references the *pisse-en-lit* costume that nineteenth-century *jamette* women masqueraded during Carnival. The costume, composed of a white chemise or nightgown and a red-stained menstrual cloth, caused tremendous uproar

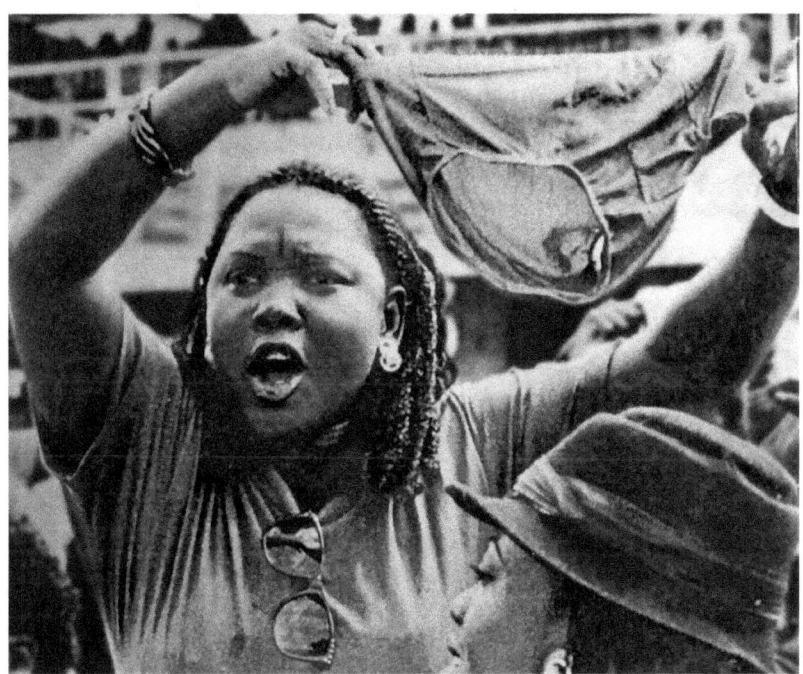

3.1 Teacher waving a piece of red underwear at Skinner Park. From *Sunday Express* (Port of Spain, Trinidad), February 3, 1991, 1.

among the nineteenth-century elites, who saw it as offensive and tactless.[6] Since governmental authorities did not recognize the jametre women's civil rights, these women used their deeds to speak to their social, political, economic, and cultural oppression. The act of the Catholic schoolteacher at the Calypso Monarch competition undeniably recalls and parallels the pisse-en-lit masquerade.[7] Without question, *jamettes* began a legacy of performance-based bravado and social critique that continues today.

Although the jamette is no longer a symbol of disorder and licentiousness in Trinidad, her impact on the corporeal expression of the contemporary woman is unmistakable. From the late nineteenth century until the mid-twentieth century, the poor Black woman who defied standards of propriety and retaliated against her dehumanizing position in society was referred to as the jamette. When jamettes violated the conservative rules of etiquette in everyday life and during Carnival, they prompted a reevaluation in Trinidadian society of the ways in which women appeared and behaved in public, thereby challenging colonialism's control of their bodies. These working-class women of African descent were historically seen as abominations by the authorities and members of the elite during the colonial period because the writhing of their frames was viewed as inde-cent.[8] As a participant in Carnival in the mid-twentieth century, jamettes saw how their unruly behavior could be used for both revelry and political purposes.[9]

This chapter examines the ways in which women and men of the ja-metre class defined the Carnival of the late nineteenth century, so much so that Carnival was referred to as Jametre (Jamette) Carnival. At this important juncture in the festival's evolution, jametre women created thought-provoking costumes, composed and sang *kalinda* songs that were the source of calypso, and had a significant influence on the formation of "bands," the formal groupings of costumed masqueraders in Carnival. I also trace the evolution of the term *jamette* from a word used to describe a class of poor, underprivileged, and formerly enslaved people to become a strategically gendered descriptor for women of a certain race, class, and deportment. Integral to understanding the shift of the classification's use is the recognition of the efforts made by the colonial order to "improve" Carnival in the early twentieth century so that it would be continental, that is, on par with the Carnivals of Europe. It became taboo for women of the jametre class to be *chantuelles* (the lead singers of costumed bands), since this did not reflect respectability.[10] This is an important juncture in the shift from vocal to corporeal expression in women's participation in Carnival, and encouraged a further discovery of the potential for the phys-icality to be effectively provocative in its articulation.

Although the social classification of jamette was oppressive, it nonethe-less empowered these women by prompting the jamettes to be more defi-ant than ever. Despite the oppressive tactics of the police and ultimately the colonial authorities, jamettes developed a different sense of place that allowed them to discover possibilities in the existing landscape that would counter geographic domination.[11] In the early to mid- twentieth century, jamettes were instrumental in the development of many urban, working-class, cultural practices. They were pivotal in their contributions to cor-poreal expression in Carnival, especially the development of the steel band procession and the sailor masquerade. From the 1940s, this move-ment provided the jamettes a space for innovation and creative freedom in their roles as flag women for the steel bands and masqueraders in sailor mas bands. Their actions, gestures, and provocative movements on the streets of major towns and cities as flag women prove to be instances of the jamettes creating meaning for these spaces in the tropical landscape, thereby enacting a naming of place.[12]

Despite the predicament of antidemocratic colonial policies, jamettes and their working-class counterparts found resolve in the proliferation of Ethiopianism and Garveyism, the labor movement that dealt specifically with issues that working men and women faced, as well as the anticolonialism movement. All provided much fodder for Carnival celebrations during this era and made possible a carnivalesque yet subversive performance of Black modernism. This chapter thus explicates how the festival engendered a type of corporeal expression that is creatively oriented yet also political in its affect as a strategy of space-making. Carnival provided a visceral means of enacting tropical modernism by performatively reclaiming the land belonging to the colonizer while also engaging directly with the tropical terrain. In addition, these subversive bodily movements are akin to how RoseLee Goldberg defines performance art's unabashed "refusal to separate art activities from everyday life and the subsequent incorporation of everyday action . . . as performance material."[13]

While the visual art of Aaron Douglas and Wifredo Lam beautifully and hauntingly captures how Black Atlantic peoples reimagined their natural environments as being a crucial part of their self-definition in the overall articulation of modernism, Black performance traditions such as Carnival offer immediate means to creatively envision the land of the marvelous in real time and space. Although rendered ungeographic, Black colonial subjects can nonetheless effect a collective transformation of the dominant geographic order, if only for a few moments. This chapter continues the exploration of how Black Atlantic peoples creatively assert their humanity and their unabashed right to land—with which they are very familiar. Through performance, they disengage with the reductive rhetoric of Western thought that views their corporeal expression as degenerate and ceremoniously acknowledge the ways in which a Pan-Africanist ethos unites them with disparate lands occupied by other members of the Black Atlantic.

Indeed, the idiosyncrasies of Carnival in early twentieth-century Trinidad emphasize the uneven geographies endemic in colonial territories. Yet they also reveal the ways in which these uneven geographies can be reconfigured by the moving, carnivalesque body of a dissident, Black working-class woman.[14] The geographic domination of the colonial hegemonic order was always reconstituted during the Carnival season, a period during which the sentiment that "you don't give a damn" is kinetically articulated by theorist and poet M. NourbeSe Philip as follows:

> sweat and jostle and
> jostle and push
> jostle and jostle
> push and jostle and
> and shove and move
> to the pulse
> riddim pan
> riddim and beat
> the beat
> sweat like a ram goat
> sweat for so[15]

In such ostensibly simple prose, Philip captures the collective movement of revelers who literally take over the public sphere during the festival, something that the carnivalesque moment makes possible. The idea of the freedom of the carnival spirit that is oriented toward the future serves to fertilize various areas of life and culture for Black Atlantic peoples.[16] Indeed, the subversive performances of these jamette women epitomize the true spirit of Black modernism, in which the modern individual becomes the agent of change against a regime that relegates them and the tropical environment as degenerate and menacing.[17]

Etymologically, the word *Carnival* is derived from the Italian *carnevale*, an alteration of the earlier Latin word *carnelevare* that literally means the removal of meat. Originating in medieval Europe, Carnival was a Roman Catholic festival that promoted and celebrated physical abandonment (including unlimited eating and drinking, and the rejection of societal codes of conduct) before the religious observation of Lent: the forty-day period leading up to Easter Sunday when Catholics fast to strengthen their spirituality and relationship with God, just as Jesus Christ did in the wilderness.[18]

This festival was such an important part of European culture that, rather than being mere spectacle or an extension of the performing arts, it belonged to the borderline between art and life. The cultural historian Mikhail Bakhtin argues that Carnival was a special condition of the world's revival and renewal in which all take part. Life was subject to the laws of its own freedom with the suspension of all hierarchical rank being key, and the spirit of the festival was universal.[19] This definition of Carnival leads one to the understanding that the rules that govern society are completely overlooked. In Bakhtin's Carnival, what actually occurs is an inversion of the hierarchical structure on which society is based. In the establishment of this upside-down world, people essentially feel free because they are liberated from the fear imposed by the existence of the rule.[20] With Carnival there is the suspended disbelief of all established rules. Also, the collapse of society is more ritual than actual.[21] Marking the suspension of all hierarchical rank, privileges, norms, and prohibitions, everyone is considered equal.[22] The "festive laughter" inherent in the ritual is gay yet mocking and universal in scope, reflecting the ideal and real type of communication that is impossible in ordinary life.

An important concept that Bakhtin sees as central in Carnival is "grotesque realism." This concept emphasizes the centrality of physicality during the carnivalesque moment. In this utopian realm of human relation, the fusion of bodies regardless of social standing sway, twist, bend, and touch in seemingly psychical syncopation with each other on the market square. Such an awareness of the anatomical principle is extended to the earthly terrain that complements this experience and echoes the universality inherent in Carnival. There is the degradation of everything high, spiritual, ideal, and abstract to the material level or, more plainly, to the sphere of Earth and physicality that engenders this universality. And the grotesque body is connected to the rest of world through the openings of the body—mouth, genitalia, and anus—along with other anatomical parts such as the breasts and the potbelly.[23]

Yet, while the figure's carnality is key in conceptualizing its relation to the tangibleness of the world, there is also a spiritual element present. The possibility of growth and abundance is seen and felt in the countless bodies who, as a collective entity, actually serve the role as giver of life. This tendency for abundance is echoed in the fundamental attribute of exaggeration and excessiveness in the collective grotesque body. It is constantly immersed in the act of becoming; "it is continually built, created, and builds and creates another body."[24] This powerful trait is crucial and it seems that Bakhtin placed great value in this element of "grotesque realism." With these qualities, the grotesque physicality has immense potential to incite change in a people's social and political reality. Grotesque realism's possibility for abundance and change resonates with the surrealist concept of the marvelous real, which emerges due to the reality that human desires encounter severe prohibitions and obstacles in the physical world. The land of the marvelous therefore provides a magnificent solution to the limitations of the real world by assuring the satisfaction of living desires.[25] For Carpentier, the marvelous offers an unaccustomed insight into the "unexpected richness of reality" that can be recognized with great intensity "by virtue of an exaltation of the spirit that leads to a kind of extreme state."[26] The collective experience entrenched in grotesque realism thereby finds its regenerative tendencies strengthened by the deeply spiritual state of being of the marvelous real.

But for scholars such as Umberto Eco, the utopian model of Carnival that Bakhtin elucidates as revolutionary is misleading, since for him Carnival can only be enjoyed if rules and rituals are parodied, with the assumption that these rules and rituals are already respected and recognized.[27] The insubordination embedded in the carnivalesque moment, which is constricted through time and space, is for Eco a reaction to the knowledge of the degree to which certain behaviors are forbidden. For this scholar, Carnival represents paramount examples of law enforcement and is thus an authorized unruliness without any possibility for spontaneous uprisings, out of which will result a permanent social and political transformation.[28] Eco deems that cosmic carnivalization should not be seen as global liberation since "revolutions produce a restoration of their own in order to install their new social model," otherwise they are not effective.[29]

At the same time, intricate demonstrations of rebellion should be envisioned, as Peter Stallybrass and Allon White suggest, as part of a wider phenomenon of recklessness; they reveal how "the underlying structural features of Carnival operate far beyond the strict confines of popular festivity and are intrinsic to the dialectics of social classification as such."[30] Carnival, as it evolved from Dionysian rites to the cyclical rituals appropriated by the Catholic Church of sixteenth-century Europe, may not have had radical consequences for the political and social fabric of these societies, given the level of antagonism felt toward the powers that were, yet Carnival effectively served as "catalyst and site of actual and symbolic struggle."[31]

Moreover, when examining Carnival practices, one should discern that the potential for seditious activities to erupt and the consequences that such actions may have are inevitable and should not be overlooked. The distinctive milieu that is Carnival is one that crafts, as scholar Keith Nurse states, a "reflection of the configuration of social forces and the conflict that arises from them as well as the submerged aspirations and tensions of the respective societies."[32] Furthermore, while official power has capitalized on exploiting Carnival as a site to channel energies that may have otherwise been used for revolt, it still remains that the artistic and performative practices in Carnival cannot be possessed and controlled.[33]

Nevertheless, it is clear that the undeniable transgression endemic in the realm of the carnivalesque makes it possible for the marvelous real to be invoked. The carnivalesque realm augments the embodiment and a momentary lived experience of the marvelous real. Ménil is astute in his assertion that "the marvelous is the image of our absolute liberty." Although he admits that the imagined marvelous occupies the mind, it is still "inseparable from the human body which *actualizes* it in time and space."[34] And this can be actualized amid the revelry of Carnival, since not only do people become aware of their immortality, but there is also the realization that established authority and truth are relative.[35] As I show in this chapter, the jamettes of early to mid-twentieth-century Trinidad exemplified how the marvelous real could be actualized during Carnival. In addition, their immersion in transgression within the carnivalesque domain was in fact an immersive embodiment of tropical aesthetics, given the myriad ways in which jamettes claimed public territories as their own during Carnival, which, although only momentary, was in the direction of reality.[36]

And although they masqueraded in the colony and not in the metropole, their performances were just as significant, if not more. The momentary freedom to traverse the land during Carnival is especially connected to the freedom experienced once slavery was abolished. The pretty mas and Jouvay festivities seen on the streets during the formal parades, and even the steel bands that dominated as the source of musical entertainment as early as the 1940s, are all symbolic of this sense of freedom.[37] The very act of covering the body with mud or oil, both of which are sourced from the earth, during Jouvay ritualizes the literal connection these masquerading bodies desired to have with the land.[38] It serves to ritualize the self-assertion Black people expressed in order to situate themselves as heritors of the public sphere despite being relegated to an ungeographic status. During this era of Ethiopianism, the tropical terrain of Trinidad would function as an extension of Africa and immediately link the revelers to the Pan-African universe in the carnivalesque moment. In the midst of these moving bodies, it is in fact "the sound of Africa cutting loose and moving across the Atlantic" and "turning and turning around and across the Atlantic."[39]

In order to explore the figure of the jamette in Trinidad Carnival, it is necessary to first understand the historical context from which she emerges. During the period of the transatlantic slave trade until emancipation, enslaved African women were, like their male counterparts, the property of the plantation owner. The women's bodies were integral to the continued prosperity that the sugar cane crop brought to the British monarchy. Women played a key role in the production of sugar, since they outnumbered men in the execution of cultivation tasks, which included hoeing and reaping, the two most physically demanding jobs on the plantation.[40] Their reproductive capabilities were not overlooked and, with the abolition of the slave trade, planters sought them out to increase the slave population of the colony. Like their male counterparts, enslaved African women endured a horrific existence under slavery, and, with its abolition in 1838, they entered a colonial society to which they had to acclimatize themselves even though they were relegated to its periphery.

Former slaves sought ways of surviving in a social structure that did not provide any mechanisms to support their transition to freedom. Members of the elite, including the already free Black and colored middle class, opposed the entry of women into the workforce. Still, formerly enslaved men and women sought out employment in order to survive.[41] Baptist missionaries were integral in the introduction of new gender ideologies among the Black working poor, and this was part of an effort to reorganize their postemancipation existence socially, economically, and politically.[42] Black men, they argued, should serve as productive and responsible Christians who contributed to society and provided for their families, while Black women, now freed from the burden of being the sexual property of the plantation owner, should be loyal wives who remained dependent on their husbands.[43] Many of the African-descended masses squatted on land privately owned or owned by the Crown, or founded settlements on the outskirts of plantations; such villages numbered more than five thousand by 1846.[44] Others succumbed to the efforts of the planters to make them into semiserfs, tied to the estates through arrangements that obliged them to work for minimal wages.[45]

The formerly enslaved Africans who migrated to urban areas were greeted by extreme poverty. Employment opportunities were scarce due to the arrival of immigrants from other colonies in the region and from other continents. In an effort to compensate for the loss of free labor on the plantations, the British authorities began to import Chinese workers as early as 1806.[46] By the late nineteenth century, there were just over 2,500 Chinese immigrants in Trinidad.[47] However, because these men were generally tradesmen rather than rural farmworkers, they tended to leave the plantations, eventually to establish their own shops.[48] Authorities then set their hopes on the Portuguese peasants of Madeira, Fayal, and the Azores islands off the coast of Africa. About 41,000 Portuguese were brought in to work on the plantations of British Guiana, Jamaica, Trinidad, St. Vincent, and Grenada.[49] This experiment also failed, since not only were the Portuguese grape vine rather than sugar cane cultivators, but many of them died in the humid swamps and lowlands of the Caribbean.[50] After these failed attempts, India became the next source of cheap immigrant labor. The first Indian indentured workers came to Trinidad in 1842, and by 1916 nearly 30,000 of them had arrived to work on the rural plantations.[51] At least 9,000 Africans had come to Trinidad as indentured laborers by 1867.[52] About 10,000 migrants from other colonies in the West Indies arrived between 1839 and 1849.[53] All these people flocked to Port of Spain, the urban center of Trinidad, hoping to find work.

Carnival proved to be a useful coping mechanism that enabled the formerly enslaved Africans to deal with their past and current conditions. Charles Day, an English visitor who chronicled his Caribbean travels, gave a detailed account of the Carnival he witnessed in Trinidad in 1848. He wrote of young girls dressed in *á la jupe*, the attire of the French Black women from Martinique and Guadeloupe who introduced it to Trinidad in the late eighteenth century through their drum dances.[54] Based on the early eighteenth-century French woman's open gown that included an open skirt that revealed an underskirt, *á la jupe* or *chemisette et jupe* differed as it included a detached skirt and bodice, with the hem of the full floor-length skirt draped, slightly rolled and tucked into the waist, which effected folds while simultaneously revealing a decorated underskirt; the look was completed with a large scarf draped around the neck and shoulders, a turban decorated with brooches on the head, along with earrings, bracelets, and necklaces. The overall presentation created a powerful effect, since a major part of the dress aesthetic involved juxtaposing highly contrasted fabric of varying colors and designs. Along with the extensive application of jewelry, the colors women wore were determined by their skin complexions, thereby creating a dynamic visual impact. The

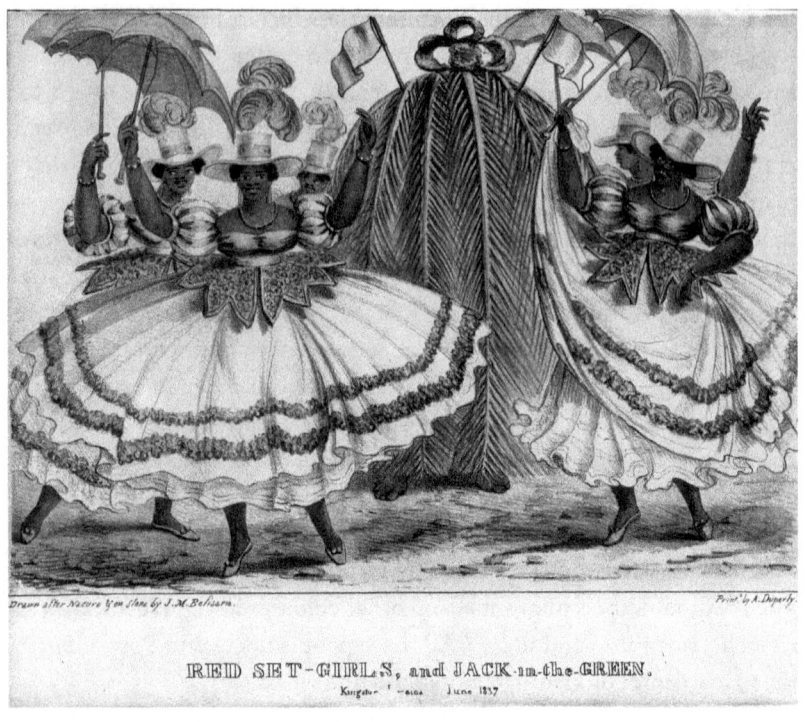

RED SET-GIRLS, and JACK-in-the-GREEN.

Kingston Jamaica June 1837

3.2 Isaac Mendes Belisario, *The Red Set Girls and Jack-in-the-Green*, 1836. Courtesy of National Library of Jamaica.

women who dressed á la jupe throughout the Francophone Caribbean demonstrated attempts to create an alternative social order for themselves through bourgeois-like attire.

Another of the many masquerades Day observed in his chronicle were "parties of negro ladies [who] danced through the streets, each *clique* distinguished by boddices of the same colour."[55] These parties were similar to what was seen in Jonkonnu, the festival that occurred in postemancipation Jamaica during the Christmas season, and illustrated by Creole artist Isaac Mendes Belisario in an 1836 drawing, *The Red Set Girls and Jack-in-the-Green* (figure 3.2). Belisario reported that the colors each group wore represented the nationality with which they culturally identified, such as the English, the Scots, and the French, with the French comprising immigrants from Haiti.[56] The dresses these women wore were elaborate, the wide skirts detailed with colored frills. The bodice was the central part of the overall design and was the same color as the frills on the skirt. Expensive fabrics were obviously used here, not to mention the umbrellas and the wide-brimmed hats adorned with plumes. This drawing provides us with an idea of what the cliques of women dancing in the streets of Port of Spain may have looked like. The practice appears to have been the predominant model that Black women used to organize themselves for masquerading in Carnival. While these women may have been ridiculing women of the upper class, their motions are also suffused with self-assertion and boldness. The women's masquerades that Belisario portrays recall the performance practices and costumed bands that jametre women developed, which, in turn, influenced the woman-dominated costumed bands of today.

The various iterations of the Creole term *jametre* first came into usage in the second half of the nineteenth century, a few decades after enslaved Africans were emancipated.[57] The newly emancipated now used a public sphere that had previously been the domain of the European elite and the small Black and colored middle class. In the late nineteenth century, as the economic and sociopolitical situation for the formerly enslaved became especially dire, their masquerade illuminated their conditions. They created what became known as the Jametre Carnival, the term referring to their subaltern status.[58]

In most scholarly texts, the word *jamette* is often used to describe both the Carnival of the late nineteenth century and the licentious twentieth-century working-class women.[59] I have chosen to use the term *jametre* to refer to the class of people that characterized Carnival of the aforesaid period and the designation *jamette* for the women of this class of the twentieth century. The term *jamette* clearly feminizes the cultural practices of a certain class of people and, in turn, is used by society to regulate and scrutinize the sexuality of Black women. The Creole word *jamette* was derived from the French *diametre*, which translates into "diameter," referring to the imaginary line that divided society into two sectors, the respectable and the criminal.[60] Some scholars have interpreted *diametre* to figuratively mean "border" because it relegated the Black working class to a debased position in society.[61] Others have deconstructed it to mean a class of people who fall below the limits of morality, into the "underworld."[62] The use of *underworld* to describe the locus of these people helps one understand the worldview the jametres self-imposed. The term undoubtedly reflects the inferior position African people held in society. Oral historian Mitto Sampson best encapsulated how the Black masses in Trinidad associated Europe with good and Africa with evil when he quipped: "Since God is a white man and the devil is a Negro, every negro has that devilish ferocious quality in him."[63] This ideology was such a significant part of the jametre class's worldview that Trinidad's stickmen often used it when preparing for battle with other street gangs.[64]

Still, the literal meaning of *diameter* begs for more analysis. According to the *Oxford English Dictionary*, *diameter* is a straight line passing through the center of a circle (or sphere), and terminated at each end by its circumference (or surface). It also means the length of a straight line passing from side to side of any body through the center. Taking these literal meanings into account, one can say that the members of the jametre class, like these demarcated figures, were inextricably marked so that they were easily identified in society. The jametre class was not only demarcated to accord with the geopolitical and social strata reserved for them in society, but they also functioned as the periphery of society's hierarchical structure. However, despite its marginal position in society at large, the jametre class was still central in defining colonial Trinidad: its infrastructure and its most important cultural events.

In the Jametre Carnival, the social, economic, and political predicament of the same-named class was manifest, both physically and vocally. Their bands, consisting of adults and children alike, were a combination of various social groups created in the barrack yards where they resided.[65] While masquerading, they "boasted their skill and bravery, verbal wit, talent in song, dance, and drumming, their indifference to the law, their sexual prowess, their familiarity with jail, and sometimes their contempt for the church."[66] Women more often than not were the chantuelles who sang praises of male stick fighters and impromptu lyrics meant to shock and entertain.[67] These women wore masks and traditional Martinican dress and sometimes exposed their breasts.[68] The elite complained incessantly about the transvestism they witnessed in the Jametre Carnival.[69] Newspaper writers even described members of the jametre class as "the enemy" and "savage hordes."[70] One writer described the Carnival as "beastly" and expressed concern for the effects of the "pollution and obscenity exhibited naked before the eyes of our wives and daughters."[71] Despite their angst over the changing nature of Carnival, the elite nonetheless bore witness to the veritable impact this class of people had on the festival they once dominated.

In 1877 there were reportedly twelve bands in downtown Port of Spain, each representing a particular street or area they claimed as their own.[72] One writer strove to satisfy the curiosity of his upper-class readers by offering information on these organizations: "The 'Free-grammar' (formerly the True Blues) hail from Coburgtown; the Bois d'Inde (pronounced 'bois d'enne') or Allspice tree, from Upper Prince Street; the Bakers, from the streets behind (i.e. east of) the Market; the Danois (Danes), from the Dry river suburb (between Faure's and Samuel's Bridges); the peau de Canelle (Cinnamon bark), from the streets behind (to west of) the Gaol; the Rose barrier (Hedge-rose or rose hibiscus), from about the Toll-gate."[73] Despite their peripheral locations, these liminal spaces served as the breeding grounds for the creativity that unfolded on the streets. Still, the elite were condescending toward the jametres, reflected in the above writer's observations on the lack of social cohesion in these bands and the frequent changes in both their names and their compositions. According to this writer from the *Trinidad Chronicle*, the people who made up these bands were usually "the loose, idler, younger members of the floating portion of the populace (it would not be always correct to call them the working class)."[74] Little consideration was given to the lack of employment opportunities for the jametre class, which also included immigrants from neighboring islands and African-born men and women.[75] The prevalence of vagrancy in Port of Spain and, ultimately, in Carnival was a fiery topic of discussion in newspapers. Men, women, and children who could not afford to live in the barrack ranges would be seen roaming the streets at all hours of the day (figure 3.3). The aforesaid writer expressed much impatience about delays in the passage of a vagrancy law and the opening of reformatory schools, which he felt would eradicate this "moral leprosy."[76] The elite transferred such intolerance and condescension into their perceptions of the Jametre Carnival, as they described the various masquerades of the entire jametre collective as vagrants and vagabonds.[77]

While the elite complained, the jametre class continued its defiance, and the women were no exception. According to legend, one famous nineteenth-century chantuelle named Bodicea was a case in point. During the wake of Hannibal, a popular male chantuelle, a scuffle broke out between gangs that led to his grave being dug up and his head being carried away. A group gathered by the cemetery once news of the incident disseminated. Bodicea then accused a certain Congo Jack of the deed in an impromptu song, and when the police arrived, she tore off her dress and waved it as a banner; she was later arrested. In another incident, she viciously attacked a man after learning that he had become enamored of another chantuelle, Piti Belle Lily. Bodicea was so notorious and known to do such outrageous deeds that any young girl who exhibited rebellious traits was told: "You playing Bodicea!"[78]

The women of the jametre class often organized themselves into bands for Canboulay that had such names as "Black Ball, Dahlias, Don't-Care-

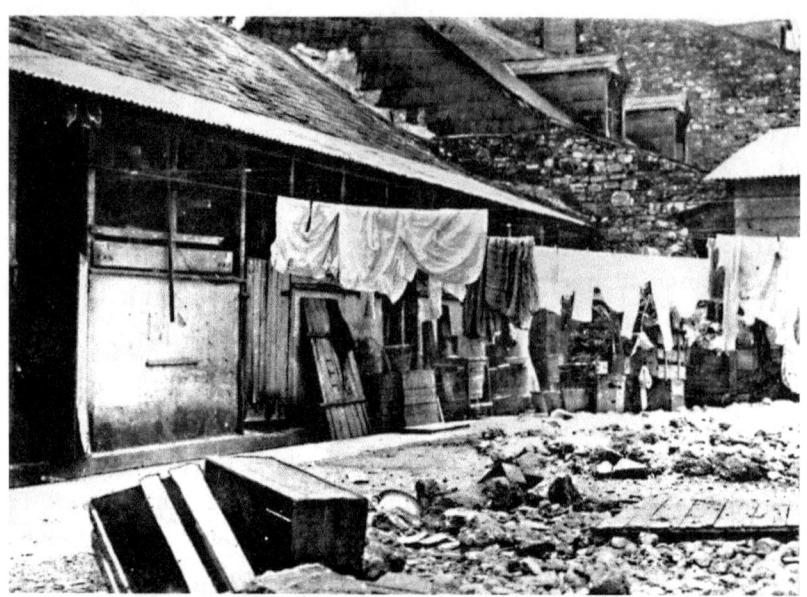

3.3 Barrack yard, East Port of Spain, Trinidad, 1930s. From Gérard Besson and Bridget Brereton, *The Book of Trinidad* (Port of Spain, Trinidad: Paria, 2010); photo from Port of Spain City Council.

A-Dams, Magentas, Maribuns (usually Maribone), Mousselines and True Blues," all of which were seen in the 1868 Carnival wearing fantastic dresses.[79] Queens accompanied by prince consorts headed these costumed bands whose members were referred to as princesses.[80] These women's participation in Carnival, however, was not pure revelry. When nineteen members of the Dahlia Band were arrested and later tried for battling against their main rivals, the Mousselines, during the Carnival of 1868, the princesses of the Mousselines admitted to concealing their batons in baskets filled with bread and cheese.[81] The Dahlias likewise carried batons in their baskets, along with stones and broken bottles.[82] The concealment of weapons seemed to be a common practice in these bands as early as 1864. In a clash between the Don't-Care-A-Dams and the Mousselines, many of these women armed themselves with horsewhips, stones, and razors, reflecting the violent culture inherent among the jametre class.[83]

A black-and-white drawing by an anonymous artist from a 1969 calendar provides us with a visual re-creation of these defiant and powerful jametre women (figure 3.4). Here, a woman stands behind a male stick

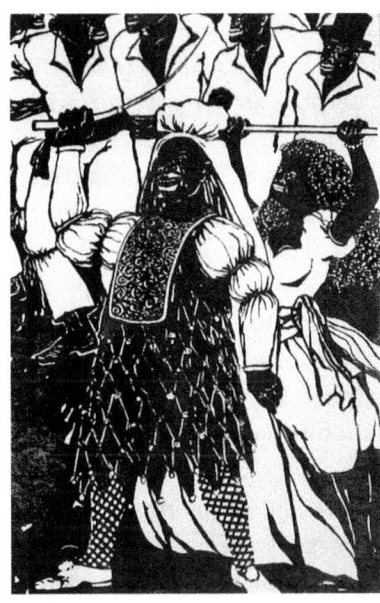

3.4 Female stick fighter. From a 1969 calendar from Trinidad and Tobago.

fighter preparing for battle. Dressed in a frock with a sash around her waist (that is probably the color for her band), she is confidently holding the stick high above her head as if ready for a fight. It is noteworthy, though, that she is the only woman in this image, which appears to capture a confrontation between two stick bands. The viciousness of slavery and its quasi continuation in the postemancipation era of colonial plantation society produced a class of both men and women who could inflict violence with as much vigor as they endured it.[84] As this image shows, women not only actively participated in riots and confrontations; they could be key instigators of them.[85] These women are emblematic of the courageous efforts working-class Black women exercised to reify the socioeconomic organizing of the land that instigated the conflict expressed in this image. Ultimately, this is an attempt at self-assertion that encapsulates the spirit of Black modernism whereby jamettes aspired to reclaim geographic spaces despite institutionalized oppression.

For the elite, the Black masses encroached on what they thought of as their parade. Members of the upper classes incessantly complained about the costumes and movements of the jametre men and women, and they saw Jametre Carnival practices as degenerate and eventually "dying a natural death."[86] At the same time, their own past actions contradicted their complaints. The French elite often replicated the attire, dances, and songs of the Africans during slavery.[87] Additionally, as Bridget Brereton has pointed out, the so-called decline in Eurocentric Carnival characters and masquerades chronicled in late nineteenth-century newspapers may not have occurred; these articles were a consequence of the editors' and, in turn, the elite's preoccupation with the jametre presence in Carnival.[88] This clear prejudice toward the formerly enslaved Africans and their activities influenced the passing of two ordinances that contributed to the repression of Canboulay: the Habitual Criminals Act of 1875 that permitted police surveillance, and an 1879 ordinance that amended the law regarding punishment for riots and such disturbances.[89] This eventually led to the prohibition of Canboulay two years later.[90]

Glissant acknowledges two important forms of resistance that have shaped Caribbean culture: "the camouflaged escape of the Carnival, which I feel constitutes a desperate way out of the confining world of the plantation, and the armed flight of marronage [settlements that fugitive slaves established in mountains and forests throughout the Caribbean], which is the most widespread act of defiance in that area of civilization that concerns us."[91] Like their counterparts in other slave societies in the Americas who settled in clandestine maroon communities, formerly enslaved Africans in the Caribbean created alternative institutions that went against European forms of civility and society formation. The transgressive endeavor that is Carnival causes inevitable tensions of geography with the geographic domination of the colonial order purposefully being contested.[92] Given this predicament, the carnivalesque realm thus calls for a suspended disbelief in established laws and the hierarchical structures of society. And the abundance generated by the countless bodies of Black people reveling on the streets as a collective entity in late nineteenth-century Trinidad must have led to an intensely spiritual embodiment of the marvelous real, a momentary yet enriched state of being that altered their experience as recently freed slaves and subjects of a British colony.[93] Indeed, "the dramas given form . . . find their place in the conflict that pits our living desires against that real world that is unable to assure their satisfaction."[94]

Carnival as an institution of resistance understandably allowed for very contested exchanges between the members of the underclass and the authorities, culminating in the Canboulay riots of 1881 when underclass masqueraders and stick fighters fought with police officers.[95] The authorities were defeated, but there was still a slow and steady repression of the Carnival masquerades. By this time, the government had become conscious

of the jametres' deep-rooted association with Carnival. In the years after 1881, the authorities took systematic steps to establish greater control
over the proceedings, especially lewd dances and songs, and by the end of
the nineteenth century had succeeded in keeping the jametres from gath-
ering during Carnival through new laws and regulations. Many felt that
migrants from the other Caribbean islands (who brought their customs
to Trinidad) should be blamed for the island's social difficulties. Among
the perceived cultural incursions from abroad were the Creole dances of
the French islands and the indecent Quelbe songs and dances of Curaçao:
controversial importations that were thought to encourage an obscene
"winin'" style in Carnival dancing.[96] To control these new tendencies,
the Summary Convictions Ordinance, No. 11, of 1883 made the owner of
any yard that had singing and dancing accompanied by the drum, chac-
chac, or any other instrument liable to a huge fine.[97] The following year
the Peace Preservation Ordinance, No. 1, of 1884 stated that the lighting
of any torch, the beating of any drum, the blowing of any horn or other instrument, and the carrying of ten or more sticks at once were strictly prohibited.[98] Nonetheless, retaliations erupted that same year in the form of
Canboulays in towns such as Couva and Princes Town.

Once it became impossible for groups of stick fighters to use drums,
other means of percussion were invented. With tamboo bamboo, drummers and even stick fighters started to beat bamboo of different heights
to create varying tones.[99] For the next decade, the police force continued
its efforts at trying to control the masses and repress selected activities
during Carnival. In 1886 the police aggressively suppressed transvestism
as well as "immorality and obscenity whether in dress, speech or song."[100]
Notices published in newspapers spelled out the practices that were seen
as inappropriate and the consequences of these actions, heeding the ideals of decorum.[101] Of course, these measures were not always effective
since the police could not keep track of the many bands masquerading
in different locations throughout Port of Spain as well as those in towns
and villages. There was even a predominance of pisse-en-lit, a masquerade consisting of mostly female participants dressed in nightgowns who
held red-stained white cloths.[102] Therefore, transvestism, pisse-en-lit costumes, and the singing of Guinea songs still pervaded Carnival proceedings despite newspapers, the mouthpiece of the elite, never hesitating to
express their disgust with these activities.[103]

All these policing measures speak to the history of the elite's sociopolitical motivation to simultaneously reject derogated lower classes while

possessing a deep-seated and suppressed desire for them; the elite's incessant and obsessive scrutiny of the working class' activities indicates a fascination that fed the dominant culture's imaginary.[104] The subalterns' physicality and verbal banter during Carnival symbolized everything grotesque and marginal, thus defining through opposition the hegemonic classical body idealized by the middle class.[105] This system of demarcation separating varying frames was mapped onto the city as a whole, dividing uptown and downtown according to class identity.[106]

With the eventual exclusion of the jametre class by the century's end, the atmosphere in Port of Spain during Carnival had changed, as can be seen in an 1888 engraving by Melton Prior. During the winter of 1887 and 1888, the *Illustrated London News* assigned Prior to visit some of the colonies in the southern Caribbean and draw interpretations of his experiences there. He visited Trinidad during Carnival on February 13 and 14, 1888. The energy captured in the image *Carnival on Frederick Street, Port of Spain* (figure 3.5) is concentrated in the foreground, where revelers mostly of African descent are dancing on the congested main thoroughfare of Port of Spain. The lively musical accompaniment most likely consisted of a fiddle, banjo, and perhaps the then illegal percussive chac-chac and bongo drum. The accompanying text for the image notes that the attire and behavior of people formerly referred to as the jametre class "on this occasion, in former years, caused a certain degree of scandal."[107] The drawing portrays people in impressive costumes celebrating in a rather elegant fashion. However, one should leave room for the artist's subjectivity in this composition, which almost mirrors a European Carnival of sorts. Although different from what was seen a decade earlier, the dissident quality of many of these characters still vexed the upper classes. The elite were eventually successful in banning many practices and costumes associated with the Jametre Carnival.[108]

One instance of a jametre-developed Carnival character that survived the repression stands in the right foreground area of Prior's painting (figure 3.6). A woman of African descent in a baby doll costume capitalizes on the opportunity Carnival offered to directly confront a man of European descent. The priest's expression mirrors the other stoic figures that stand at the edges of the composition on the streets and on banisters overlooking the crowd. Apart from being shocked at his close proximity to the reveler, he is perhaps perturbed by what her costume represents. The Baby Doll character often wore oversized baby garb, held a baby doll, and would theatrically accost any man for not supporting her children.[109] This masquer-

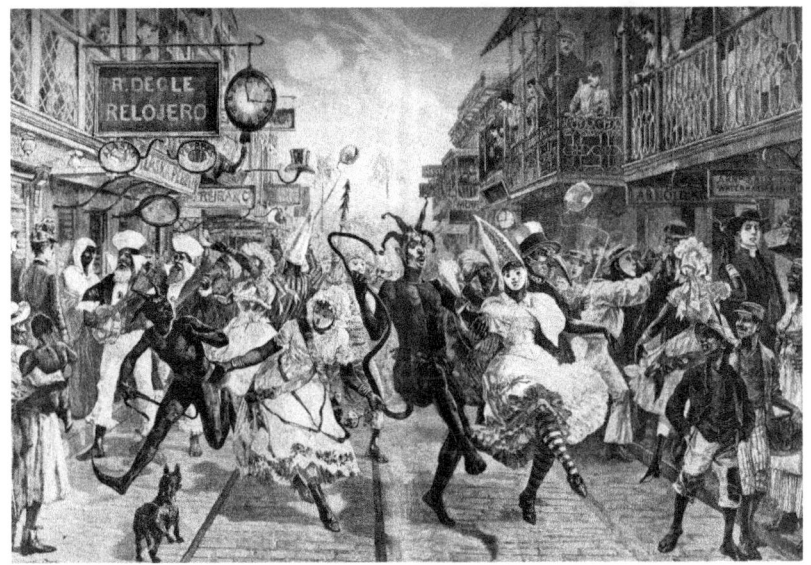

3.5 Melton Prior, *Carnival on Frederick Street, Port of Spain*, 1888. From *Illustrated London News*, May 5.

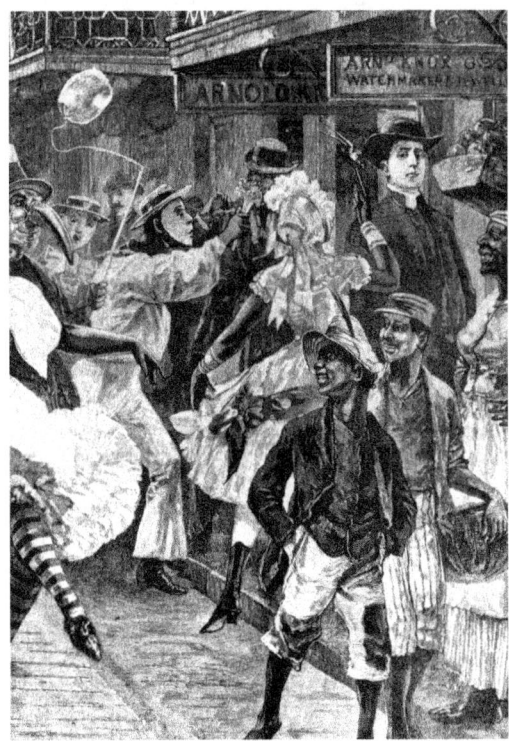

3.6 "Baby Doll" confronting a man. Detail from Melton Prior, *Carnival on Frederick Street, Port of Spain*, 1888. From *Illustrated London News*, May 5.

ade allowed these women the opportunity to say what was on their minds, confronting society about their lack of socioeconomic stability. The Baby Doll masquerade survived the repression of the Jametre Carnival, permitting women of African descent to comment on the working-class men who refused to hold themselves accountable for their children as well as the elite men who contributed to the oppression of women.[110] This bold and candid disposition signifies the fundamental nature of the jamette.

Another masquerade that characterized the brashness of the women jametres was the aforementioned pisse-en-lit. The elite were indeed keen on banning this masquerade. One *Port of Spain Gazette* contributor in 1894 writes approvingly of the long-awaited prohibition of the pisse-en-lit, expressing their pleasure in knowing that "one of the most objectionable features of the masquerade will be prohibited this year—namely, the disgusting spectacle of women appearing in the streets as '*pisse-en-lit*.'"[111] A modification of a Martinican masquerade called *chie-en-lit* (bed shitter), pisse-en-lit was named by jametre women and men who were linguistically comical with the term *pisser* to suggest menstruation in their interpretation of the masquerade.[112] The accompanying dance consisted of a quick shifting of the pelvis backward and forward and side to side while they sang obscene songs.[113] This cunning use of menses within ritual has West African precedents. Among the Yoruba, women in the midst of the menstrual cycle are believed to be so pungent that they can sometimes render a priest's powerful medicine impotent; as a result, Yoruba women sometimes use menstruation as a social weapon.[114] Far from being intended merely to stimulate repulsion, the pisse-en-lit masquerade was a manifestation of the dissent that jametre women felt strongly toward the state that consistently violated their bodies through the auspices of the police, the judicial system, and the medical profession.[115] Because of their subjugated social standing, police constantly scrutinized women of the jametre class and followed them on a regular basis and, in some cases, extorted sexual favors from them.[116] Those who did not comply might be sent to the courts to be registered as common sex workers, a marker that made them even more vulnerable to official harassment.[117]

The oppression went even further as jametre women were forced to submit themselves to monthly internal examinations at St. Ann's Hospital. If they did happen to be infected with a venereal disease such as syphilis, they were prescribed dangerous mercury treatments.[118] These women instilled a vehement fear in the state, which saw them as contaminants that threatened the well-being of the city and its inhabitants. This was in line with the general belief in Europe that Africa was the home of syphilis and that it was from there that the infectious disease spread into Europe.[119] In fact, much of the nineteenth-century medical writing in Europe recognized pathology as inherent in the Black body, often seeing dark skin and Black physiognomy as a consequence of congenital leprosy.[120]

According to the colonial, namely patriarchal and European, logic of visualization, the Black female body of the jamette is seen rather than heard and her physicality is always susceptible to scrutiny and surveillance.[121] Jametre women reacted to these condemnatory regulations using their creativity both in costume and in gesture during Carnival, protesting the outrageous bodily violations they experienced on a regular basis. This harsh reality, of course, never superseded the horrific experience of slavery, the consequences of which still impacted them. In many ways, the "space between their legs" that characterized jamettes as sexually deviant actually connected them to the terrain of the land and the movement of bodies that were mutilated, bought, sold, and trafficked.[122] The traumatic effects of both slavery and postslavery life were reflected not only in their everyday acts but also in their Carnival performances such as the pisse-en-lit (which eventually was banned in 1894).[123]

THE JAMETTE AS THE EMBODIMENT OF DEFIANCE

At the core of Victorian culture were the ideological and highly conservative tenets of respectability and reputation. Subjects of the British Empire were expected to remain within their assigned positions in the hierarchical structure of society. Jamettes did not conform their thinking or their anatomy to this hegemonic categorization. Instead, they existed in-between categories, on margins, at the thresholds. When one thinks of the term and looks at a woman who is socially demarcated as a jamette, the concept is indirectly linked to masquerade. Apart from the word's social and economic implications, it suggests that the jamette is a character, a personality that the woman assumes and thus performs, completing it with a particular attire and physical bearing. A ritual process like Carnival, in which she participated, encouraged her to escape everyday life and enter a "place for spontaneous invention and improvisation."[124] The various gestures, actions, and corporeal expressions she immersed herself in demonstrated how she established her positionality in the physical world. This embodiment of tropical aesthetics also brazenly discounts any mandate by the colonial order to render her body and sociospatial identity as being on the periphery. She is therefore emboldened by the "sayability" of the tropical landscape surrounding her.[125]

As the twentieth century progressed, African-descended and colored middle-class men (referred to as *jacket men*) sought more involvement in the development of Carnival traditions, and this impacted the freedom of jametre women. The jacket men were very much involved in the jametre subculture. Women of the jametre class were constantly present in the barrack yards, and many of them were sexually involved with jacket men.[126] However, these women's creative input through kalinda songs would be greatly hindered, since the jacket men encouraged the cultural practices of jametre men and women to adhere to traditional gender roles.[127] From the genre that jametre women innovatively developed, a new musical form called calypso, performed and recorded by working-class men, emerged.[128] The male stick fighters now transferred the energy previously used to physically challenge their opponents into musical composition, appropriating the female chantuelle's banter, gossip, and abuse.[129] Public performances of the new calypso music by women were considered taboo, as all female colonial subjects were expected to behave respectably during Carnival.[130] Newspapers published guidelines for self-presentation and deportment, and "improved" costumes and songs were introduced by the authorities that reflected the desire for Carnival to have a more "continental," European model.[131]

The agenda to silence and restrict the movements of jametre women came part and parcel with the colonial authority's intention to adamantly control female colonial subjects and enforce British standards of propriety that required women to be Christian, modest in dress, dedicated mothers, and loyal wives relegated to the home. The ideal woman in patriarchal culture is expected to be mute; she is always silent and uncomplaining, and she should avoid being a spectacle.[132] While some lower-class women recognized that rejecting jametre traits made them entitled to upward mobility, others refused to be sidelined during Carnival. There was an awareness in these more rebellious women of the body and how it could be used as a form of protest. Although these women knew that the voice was the most effective tool for expressing displeasure with social and political circumstances, they cunningly gauged the potential of the perceived anatomy as a locus of rebellious and expressive energy through which their discontent with the colonial order could be channeled. This embodied protest went against everything the female colonial subject symbolized by continuing the legacy of those such as Bodicea and Piti Belle Lilly well into the twentieth century.

Despite the attempt to eradicate working-class women from the public arena, they remained integral parts of the working-class world of Port of Spain and continued to participate in popular urban culture both within and outside the context of Carnival.[133] It is important to note that in the early twentieth century, urban working-class African Trinidadian culture tolerated, and on occasion celebrated, open female sexuality.[134] This attitude of indifference contributed to the term *jametre* becoming more associated with the women of the jametre class than the men. As the twentieth century progressed, society defined jametre behavior more and more in terms of the Black working-class woman who behaved licentiously, dressed in a provocative manner, often worked as a sex worker, and would become known as a jamette. Efforts to encourage women to garner decorum by associating Christianity and marriage with increased social status were backed up by policies in denominational and state education that emphasized the training of young girls to be wives and mothers.[135]

Still, like other working-class women, jamettes had to find a means of living. Despite the inequities the Black working class suffered, a growing Black and mixed-race middle class was a notable development of the early twentieth century.[136] Trinidad also welcomed immigrants from beyond the Caribbean region. The Lebanese and Syrian migrants who started entering the colony at the dawn of the twentieth century thrived as merchants along with the Portuguese, while European immigrants came to Trinidad in smaller numbers to work in administrative positions.[137] Meanwhile, a class of low-wage agro-proletariats of African descent worked in the fields of a thriving cocoa industry and lived in extreme poverty along with their Indian counterparts from the sugar cane plantations.[138] In the second half of the nineteenth century, Trinidad had begun to acquire the trappings of a modern capitalist state; there was remarkable growth in a diverse array of commercial ventures that included shipping agents, insurance and commission agents, oilfields and their suppliers, hardware suppliers, and food and drug importers. By 1897 petroleum had been discovered, and with the help of large-scale foreign investment, the oil industry flourished, employing thousands of workers, both men and women.[139] Most women of African descent found employment in manual labor, trade, services, and small farming in urban and rural areas; this pattern changed after 1917 when many companies in the industrial sector excluded a vast number of women from their workforce.[140] Apart from this major setback, workers did not receive adequate wages or have decent working conditions despite the flourishing of these various enterprises in the first two decades of the twentieth century. As a result, by the 1920s, members of the lower and middle classes came together to form workers' organizations and political parties that agitated against antidemocratic colonial policies.[141]

The motivation for such action may have derived from the experience some Trinidadian men had in Britain as part of the British West Indian Regiment during World War I.[142] Once in Europe, they experienced discrimination, forced to do degrading tasks such as cleaning latrines and washing linens, and given segregated and inferior canteens, hospitals, and cinemas.[143] Upon learning of the social and economic plight of other West Indian soldiers, they collectively formed a secret Caribbean league whose mission went beyond the social rights of the soldiers to consider the political future of the West Indies.[144] Upon their return home, the former soldiers mobilized to fight for social and economic rights. Uriah Buzz Butler, a Grenadian immigrant, and "Captain" A. A. Cipriani, a French Creole who fought in the regiment, became very active in leading the disenfranchised masses into activism in Trinidad.[145]

The Italo-Ethiopian War of 1935 and the Ethiopianism movement that thrived throughout the African diaspora catalyzed their efforts. Emerging in the nineteenth century, Ethiopianism was an African diaspora-wide religious and political movement that looked to a biblical prophecy in the book of Psalms in the Christian Bible and consequently interpreted biblical figures and events as being African in derivation. Black Atlantic peoples interpreted references to Ethiopia in the Bible as referring to the African continent as a whole. For some, the movement also necessitated an eventual return to the continent. Indeed, this Pan-Africanist interpretation of the Christian faith incurred a sense of unity throughout the diaspora as Black people believed it was their Africanness that united them as a collective. For Black people in Trinidad, as in other parts of the Black world, the designator "Ethiopian" was seen as synonymous with "African" or "Black." This line of thinking was further propagated by organizations such as the Universal Negro Improvement Association (UNIA), the Negro Welfare Cultural and Social Association (NWCSA), and by newspapers such as the Labour Leader and The People that became the mouthpieces of an increasingly radical, urban Black and mixed-race lower middle class.

These publications avidly reported on the buildup to the war that started with the invasion of the Italian army into Ethiopian territory in late 1934. As anthropologist Kevin A. Yelvington contends, one cannot underestimate the impact the Italo-Ethiopian War of 1935 had on the ethnic consciousness of Black Trinidadians.[146] This new political assertiveness was echoed in the Carnival, inspiring the creation of memorable calypsos and costumed bands that further reflected and commented on social and economic disparities. Glissant argues that since the transformed peoples of the Caribbean did not come to terms with their new land, they immersed themselves in "practices of diversion" as a way to deal with the impossibility of returning to their mother countries. For him, it is the individual who is able to become a nonconformist instrument of transcendence to defy the prescribed, inherently Eurocentric national ideal.[147] Attention given to the Italo-Ethiopian War and the Ethiopianism movement thus diverted Black people's attention from the sociopolitical predicament and heightened the iteration of tropical aesthetics prevalent at this historical moment. The Pan-Africanist desire for home and a sense of belonging consequently became a palpable possibility for Black Trinidadians and countless other Black people throughout the diaspora, so much so that the marvelous real most likely would have been invoked during Carnival festivities of that year as a stunning revenge against a colonial regime that they had not yet succeeded in overcoming.[148]

After World War I, the major newspapers of colonial Trinidad—*The Argos* (which had a large Black middle-class readership), the *Port of Spain Gazette* (the mouthpiece of the elite), and the *Trinidad Guardian*—felt compelled to carry the banner for an improved Carnival in Trinidad, though with conflicting agendas. The focus of the *Trinidad Guardian*, the other upper-class-aligned newspaper, was on having an "improved" and well-dressed costume aesthetic that would reflect the "Continental model."[149] Although more sympathetic to the Black working class's Carnival, *The Argos* mounted a successful campaign in favor of a more elitist Carnival, sending out committee members to lecture on how to improve Carnival behavior and recommending approved costumes that included French peasants, Italian fishermen, Cinderellas, and Daisy Queens.[150]

If the attempts of the two newspapers were not enough, further reprobations were provided in 1920 by a new ordinance, which forbade the portrayal of the diametre and pisse-en-lit, in addition to the cross-dressing of men and women.[151] Also, anyone found guilty of indecent behavior was liable to a penalty of five pounds.[152] Attempts by the authorities to prohibit an entire class of people from reveling during Carnival could not have been any more evident. The elite continued their encroachment on the festival when, in 1927, Edgar Gaston-Johnson, the mayor of Port of Spain, organized the ad hoc Carnival Improvement Committee (CIC), made up of local businessmen and professionals.[153] Its main purpose was to "clean up" the image of Carnival that was fast being recognized as a cultural product that could be indigenously emblematic of Trinidad and to appeal to foreigners.[154] The establishment of this committee was merely a tangible representation of the steady encroachment of the elite on Carnival culture. One of the CIC's first acts of improvement was the determination that the chantuelle no longer fit the new model. The committee also continued to propagate the idea that it was taboo for women to sing kalindas.

Just as men were expected to dress and perform appropriately, if women wanted to play mas, it was imperative that they adhere to the precepts of respectable femininity and portray the mandated characters permitted by Carnival's governing organization such as the French peasants and Daisy Queens. The skirt was always considered the stipulated attire for women, so costumes such as these were thus deemed appropriate for them. One costume that was prevalent among working-class women of African descent who chose to abide by the tenets of Victorianism was the Bajan Cook (figure 3.7). This masquerade was modeled after Barbadian women immigrants who began residing in Trinidad with their male counterparts in the late nineteenth century and gained employment as domestics at a higher rate than Trinidadian women (who at that time spoke more French patois than English).[155] Although working-class Trinidadians of African descent begrudged the presence of the Barbadians and the employment they gained as the years progressed, the Bajan Cook masquerade, initially performed solely by Barbadian women, became a popular masquerade for Trinidadian women by the early decades of the twentieth century. In fact, this masquerade tradition did not promote a demure womanhood, as both Trinidadian- and Barbadian-born domestics formed a pivotal part of the labor movement, creating an arm of labor organizations that dealt specifically with issues that many working women faced.[156]

The labor movement, without a doubt, imbued within the working class a strong sense of activism that manifested in the development and further expansion of trade unions, the budding Black nationalism that produced Ethiopianism and Garveyism, and in the radical journalism found in publications such as *The Beacon*, the *Negro World*, and the previ-

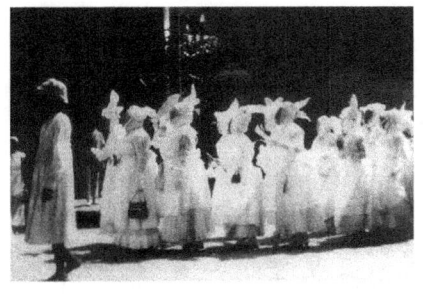

3.7 "Bajan Cooks," ca. late 1920s.
Courtesy of Adrian Camps-Campins.

ously discussed newspaper *The Argos*.[157] However, the Seditious Publication Ordinance was passed in 1920, forcing the local publications to cease operation and preventing the *Negro World* newspaper from entering the island.[158] In addition, several union leaders were arrested, imprisoned, and deported. Nonetheless, this did not deter activism, and issues of economic instability, increased prices, low wages and poor working conditions, increasing unemployment, and racial discrimination catalyzed a tumultuous period for the labor movement as working-class men and women, led by Butler and Cipriani, rallied in protests in 1937.[159] Uriah Butler and his British Empire Workers and Citizens Home Rule Party marshaled male and female workers as well as the unemployed in preparation for the disturbances. Most of the women who participated in the strikes came from a variety of fields, including sugar estate workers, domestic workers, factory workers, barmaids, food packers, and dressmakers.[160] Given the Pan-Africanist sensibility of the majority of the Black lower-middle and lower classes, it was evident that the Italo-Ethiopian War of 1935 served as a source of inspiration for these labor riots. The colonial governor of Trinidad, Sir Murchison Fletcher, declared that the labor insurrections led by Butler emerged in large part due to the political sentiments associated with the Italian invasion: "Another aspect of this racial question is the agitation which has been fostered here, and, I am afraid, is still being fostered in certain quarters, regarding the attack by Italy on Abyssinia."[161] Amid these circumstances, the anticolonialist movement was well under way, and the Black middle class, intimating a native element that justified them being rightful heirs to the state, adopted creolization as a legitimating discourse for their political power.[162] Thus, creolization became emblematic of accepted Black working-class cultural forms.

The plight of the working class, championed by the labor movement and in turn the anticolonial movement, did not prioritize the unique challenges faced by working-class women. In fact, the crusade to reduce the number of women workers that began in 1917 grew even more forceful after the labor protests of the late 1930s, when new governmental policies responded to the view that social ills existed because households did not reflect the ideal family formation.[163] The scarcity of work and the deplorable wages earned if one did find employment reflected the dire socioeconomic situation of many working-class women. This is why the women referred to as jamettes used Carnival to vent their frustrations.

It is important to consider the feminist claim that only the feminine gender is marked, thereby being defined in terms of her sex, while the masculine gender is conflated with universal personhood, thus transcending the limitations of one's physicality.[164] However, by means of a noncompliant shift, the feminine gender can attain freedom from the confines of sex by recognizing, as Simone de Beauvoir proposes, that the body can be the situation and determining factor of women's freedom rather than a defining and limiting essence.[165] This is fundamentally what jamettes did as they defied the conventions of uprightness that women of the British colonies were expected to abide by. While their distinctiveness warranted constant surveillance, they grasped the powerful impact their frames could have, both within Carnival (through the Baby Doll and pisse-en-lit masquerades) and in society at large. Furthermore, the Caribbean feminist Christine Barrow reminds us that, for economic reasons, most Caribbean women could not be restricted to the home.[166] Caribbean gender relations existed within a system of matrifocal and matrilocal families, as many Caribbean women had to be economically independent.[167]

In actuality, these women were increasingly viewed as abnormal in the context of masquerading publicly during Carnival. This abnormality specifically pertained to the lower portion of the jamette's figure, her geographical location, and her social standing.[168] Everything she represented was defined by counterdiscourses inherent in the higher end of the relevant hierarchy. Yet, as Stallybrass and White remind us, while her physicality, sexuality, and geopolitical and social positioning were all abhorred and reviled, fascination and desire simultaneously twinned the aforementioned postures.[169] As the bourgeoisie created systems of regulation governing jamettes' bodies (most notably the unmentionable lower portion), the bourgeoisie also became obsessed with the activities of the lower classes and the spaces they occupied.[170] From the elite's perspective, the jamette literally embodied the grime of the slums where she resided and thus always threatened to contaminate the purity of the bourgeois space.[171] Although she was systematically marginalized and made invisible, the jamette's physicality, imbued with negative connotation, eventually defined the parameters of the budding continental Carnival and the limits of masquerade in colonial Trinidad. Now a powerful, symbolic form, her body became the primary surface on which battles over sexual propriety and "metaphysical commitments of culture" were contested.[172] Jamettes understood how identity and space were mutually constructed, and their performances made "seeable, and sometimes fleshy, Black women's complex geographies."[173]

While hegemonic forces endorsed the image of an ideal woman and potential wife through the church and education, society used various mechanisms as tools to reaffirm these social and cultural conventions.[174] The spread of popular folkloric legends such as la diablesse in the public imaginary provided one of the most effective ways of regulating women so that they would avoid any comparison with the jamette.[175] French for "the devil woman," la diablesse is a legendary figure who seems to be a beautiful woman but really has the face of a corpse and a cloven hoof for a foot (figure 3.8).[176] She conceals her devilish appearance by wearing a wide-brimmed hat, an exquisite blouse, a long skirt, and attractive jewelry. She would appear at village social events to charm men and they would follow her, totally under her spell, deep into the woods or cane fields. Her victim tries hard to keep up with her, but la diablesse disappears, and he wanders lost and bewildered, never himself again.

The impact la diablesse had on her victims added to the mystery of the legend and the probing of whether this fearful creature really existed. Yet the real-life persona that could be referenced as the closest orientation of her was the jamette. It is plausible that this legend reflected, or even contributed to, misogynist stereotypes of jamettes as evil, demonic, and skilled in the art of deception. La diablesse's animalistic physicality, coupled with her deathlike facial features, evoked the stigma attached to the common conception of the jamette. Both la diablesse and the jamette supposedly possessed an untamed, irresistibly seductive sexuality.[177] The legend's obvious defamation of women who, like the jamette, recognized and used the power rooted in their sexualized bodies says much about the danger that such women were perceived as representing to the established order.

The now popular and socially accepted musical form of calypso also provided another avenue through which society could scrutinize and thus disparage such women. The threat that these women posed to male sexuality is captured in the calypso "Mamaguy Me" by Cobra (1937):

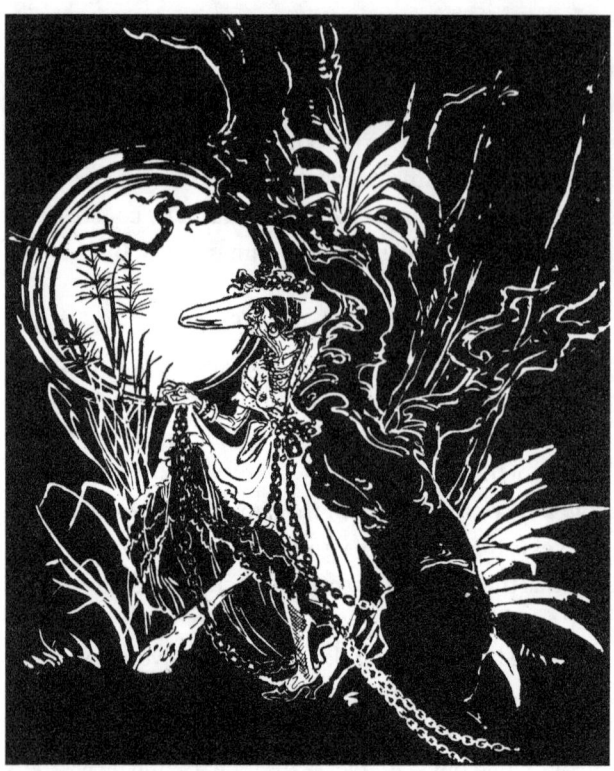

3.8 Stuart Hahn, *La Diablesse*, 2001. From Gérard Besson, *Folklore and Legends of Trinidad and Tobago* (Trinidad: Paria, 2001).

> I couldn't believe the girl was like that
> But she prove to be a vampire bat
> But when you take them down to Teteron
> You will be frightened to see the size of they craw.[178]

Here, the woman he is referring to is most likely a sex worker, and her vagina is conceptualized as a "craw." The evocation of the woman's vagina as having the ability to devour like a craw recalls the myth of *vagina dentata*, which insinuates that the woman's sexual organ is dangerous and can demolish the phallus. The view of the jamette having such an uncontrollable sexual appetite revealed men's fear of castration and emasculation, and their personal insecurities about sexual competence.[179] Despite the fact that calypsonians offered jamettes much ridicule in their compositions, many of the calypsonians still sought sex workers.

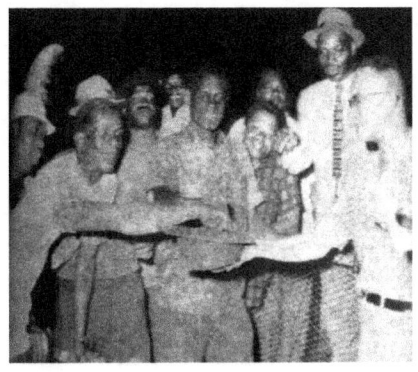

3.9 "The Draw for the Calypso King Competition," 1963. *Left to right*: Lord Blakie, Lord Cristo, Mighty Bomber, unknown woman, Lord Kitchener, Senator Ronald Williams (chair of the Carnival Development Committee). From *Evening News* (Port of Spain, Trinidad), February 22, 1963.

The calypsonian came to symbolize the celebration and reverence of Black masculinity, the epitome of the cultural ethos of the Black masses. One must be reminded of how the male figure was implicated in Trinidad Carnival. Apart from the patriarchy promoted in referring to the festival as King and to the continuous referencing of male figures in Carnival costumes, the public imaging of the calypsonian who was always a Black male contributed significantly to viewing Carnival as a masculine domain during this period (figure 3.9).[180] The Carnival of the masses was therefore beginning to be engendered as a tradition that was oriented to Black masculinity.

A young and rebellious subculture of which jamettes were a part revolved around another phenomenon, the steel pan. It was an instrument made from the base of discarded oil drums as a response to and a direct descendent of the prohibited bongo drum—which had played a crucial role in Canboulay processions—and the tamboo bamboo bands of the late nineteenth century. The musicians' incessant experimentation with different types of iron, tins, cans, and eventually oil drums resulted in the development of the steel pan.[181] It soon became a necessary part of the masquerading procession, associated with young Black men of the working class.[182] Steel bands were now the mid-twentieth-century version of the jametre class stick bands that pervaded Port of Spain in the late nineteenth century, as the *badjohns* (working-class Black men who were disorderly and sometimes above the law; they were often members of steel bands) regarded the steel pan as a metaphorical weapon of resistance. In fact, there was a violent clash between two steel bands during Carnival celebrations of 1947.[183] Just as enslaved Africans of the nineteenth century maintained underground regiments that privately observed Christmas with regalia and pageantry, steel bands served as social organizations that participated in festive occasions like Carnival.[184] As in all such organizations of this period, the roles of participants were usually gender-specific—the men often played the steel pan while the women, frequently jamettes, served as the flag bearers of the steel band.

The movements of the flag bearers on the streets during Carnival were often spectacles. Many of them were well known for being magnificent "winers"—practitioners of an undulating, gyrating, and writhing form of dance. Indeed, there are many dances from the Caribbean that incorporate such movements that originate in the hips.[185] In her research on the retention of original African dance forms and rituals in Haiti in the 1930s, Katherine Dunham noticed the isolation of the hips in the *danses grouilles* form. This dance, common during Haitian Carnival and *rara* festivals, consisted of a grinding movement of the hips and was directly associated with sexual activities.[186] These dances have always been linked to women and, in the context of Carnival in colonial Trinidad, jamettes have always performed such movements. And whenever two steel bands crossed paths on the streets, impromptu competitions broke out as flag bearers tried to outdo those of the opposing band.[187] One flag bearer of the 1940s, Mayfield Camps, who waved flag for the Trinidad All Stars Steel Orchestra, was often referred to as a "pepper sauce type of flagwoman."[188] She was known to execute dynamic routines in which she flew her flag high in the air and then low to the ground, and would finally wine bodaciously while "rolling her belly."[189] One of Trinidad's most famous jamettes, Yvonne "Bubulups" Smith, was also a flag woman for All Stars in the late 1940s.[190] She was an intimidating figure even for some of the most fearless men in steel pan such as Carlton "Zigilee" Barrow of the Bar 20 Steel Band. Barrow recalled Bubulups's defiance when she was the band's flag woman and felt compelled to lead them into battle: "When she was in front with the flag your stones was cold but it was a woman in front so you had to go."[191] Along with the constant police harassment she experienced as a sex worker, she landed in jail a number of times after violent confrontations with them or with members of steel bands.[192]

The tensions prevalent in geography that are attributable to the spatialized domination under colonialism reveal the innumerable ways racialized/gendered identities and place are reciprocally structured.[193] Nevertheless, these spirited bodily movements of the likes of Bubulups and Mayfield are exemplary of what transpires when socially produced geographies are disrupted due to the sociospatial liberation that can occur during Carnival.[194] The extent to which these legendary jamettes experienced the absolute liberty endemic in the marvelous real is clear, all of this despite the repercussions they endured living in a colony where severe prohibitions limited their everyday existence.[195]

Most of the pan men were called badjohns or saga boys, flashy dressers who lived up to their branded names as they opted to go against moral standards and reputation that were customary in the colonial Caribbean.[196] They preferred to be unemployed and many were pimps who lived off jamettes who were engaged in sex work. Their Black male counterpart, the calypsonian, presented himself as a respectable gentleman who maintained a certain reputation in the public domain and directly contrasted with these badjohns' brand of Black masculinity. As steel bands became a popular sight with costumed bands masquerading in the streets during Carnival, the authorities started seeing them as a threat to the social order. Members of the middle and upper classes perceived pan men as instigators of violence even though most were not.[197] The government responded in 1946 with a bill banning "noisy" instruments, stipulating that steel bands had to obtain a permit to play between 6:00 p.m. and 9:00 p.m.[198] When seventeen members of the Invaders steel band, two of which were women, appeared in court after a brawl with a rival band, they were all charged with malicious wounding, assault, and taking part in an unlawful assembly.[199] In the confrontations steel bands had with police, there was an underlying dynamic of rebellion that challenged] "the hierarchy of sites of discourse"; their transformative power necessitated a rethinking of what was then considered a Carnival of the elite, which the Black masses were now able to pervade.[200]

The jamettes were very involved in the endeavors of the steel bands at midcentury, serving (apart from masquerading in the sailor mas bands) as flag bearers.[201] Like the badjohns, they ignored standards of decorum by wearing the same costume as the men and sometimes even short tops and tight pants.[202] Embodying the grotesque, these women were increasingly viewed as deviant in the context of masquerading publicly during Carnival. When jamettes masqueraded in sailor mas bands or waved flags for popular steel bands, there was a rebellious quality in their movements reminiscent of the jametre class of the prior century. This deviance specifically pertained to the lower strata of society inhabited by the jamette, both her geographical location and her social standing. Everything she represented was defined by counterdiscourses inherent in the higher end of the social hierarchy. Yet while her physicality, sexuality, and geopolitical and social positioning were all abhorred and reviled by the bourgeoisie, the bourgeoisie's fascination with and desire for the jamette established an interesting dynamic between the two.[203] Since the late nineteenth century, it was known that many of the upper-class men had secret relations with the jamettes and, during the U.S. occupation of the island in the World War II years, many U.S. soldiers patronized them for their sexual services.[204]

Nevertheless, the provocative motions of their frames increasingly became an influential force in the evolution of the festival, juxtaposed against the idealized position of the classical body. The contrast between the grotesque and the classical bodies in the matrix of Carnival was discernible when costumed bands paraded on the streets. When costumed bands from the elite classes masqueraded on lorries, they avoided contact with people of other classes and races in the bands that paraded on foot.[205] As Stallybrass and White propose, when deconstructing the language of the bourgeois physique, one must reconstruct the geography of the city that always inscribes the intersection of class, race, and gender.[206] However, even when the elite removed the lorries from their processions and opted to parade on foot, they still avoided any close contact with the lower classes. By avoiding any association with and acknowledgment of the grotesque body, the collective bourgeois body clearly demonstrated the power dynamic that had to be maintained.

As part of the class of poor people of African descent in urban Trinidad, jamettes (like their male counterparts, the badjohns of the steel bands) lived a "ghetto" existence. Many of them came from extreme poverty and often were victims of sexual abuse.[207] In Tony Hall's 2001 play *Jean and Dinah* (in which two jamettes reunite after years of estrangement), one recalls how her uncle started to inappropriately touch her: "He come just so, early one Sunday morning when Aunty gone to church, and lie down on top of me on the bed. I jump up and push him off. I was always a Fighter. . . . That night he come back again. I tell him go tell Aunty and he hold me tight. He cover my mouth, he was hurting me. He say if I tell Aunty he will kill me."[208] Such traumatic home situations led these young girls to escape and venture into sex work, which ultimately made them economically independent. The existence of the Coterie of Social Workers founded by Audrey Jeffers in 1920, which sought to eradicate sex work and protect young girls who ran away from home, spoke to sex work's presence in urban centers like Port of Spain.[209] Not everyone had access to these social programs or wanted to take advantage of them. Indeed, there were cases of girls who came from respectable families and fled, or were chased away after becoming pregnant, as was the case with Bubulups.[210] It was after she moved

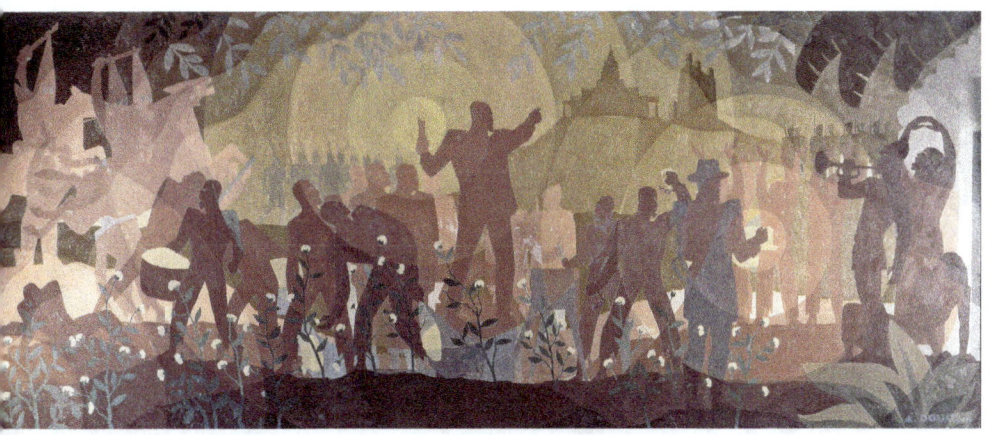

Plate 1 Aaron Douglas, *Aspects of Negro Life: From Slavery to Reconstruction*, 1934. Oil on canvas, 60 × 139 in. Schomburg Center for Research in Black Culture, New York Public Library, New York. © VAGA at Artists Rights Society (ARS), New York.

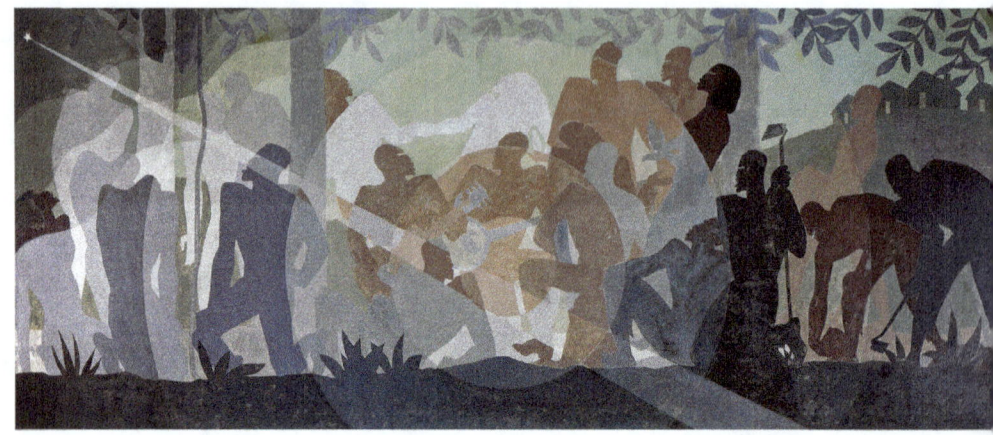

Plate 2 Aaron Douglas, *Aspects of Negro Life: An Idyll of the Deep South*, 1934. Oil on canvas, 60 × 138 in. Schomburg Center for Research in Black Culture, New York Public Library, New York. © VAGA at Artists Rights Society (ARS), New York.

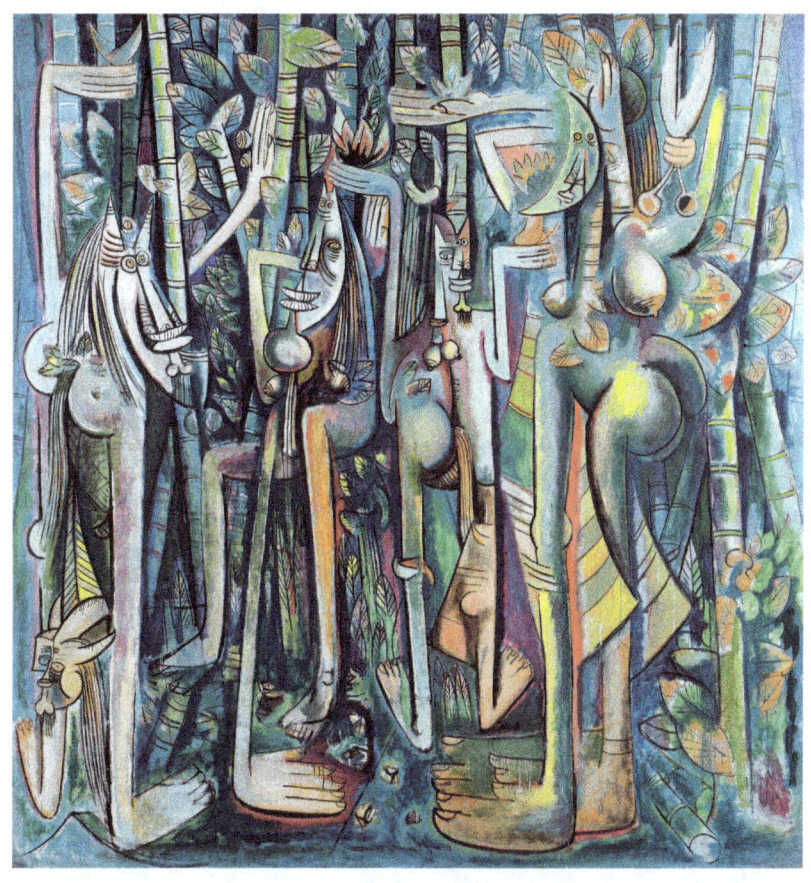

Plate 3 Wifredo Lam, *The Jungle*, 1942–44. Gouache on paper mounted on canvas, 94¼ × 90½ in. Inter-American Fund. Museum of Modern Art, New York. © Artists Rights Society (ARS), New York.

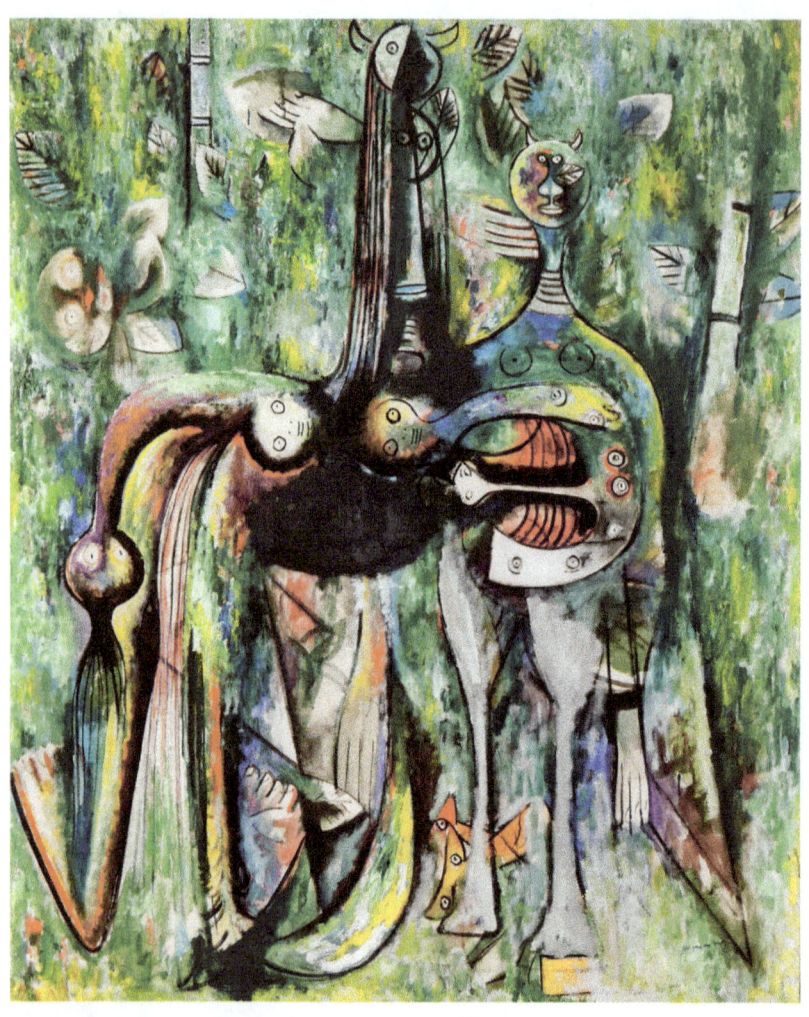

Plate 4 Wifredo Lam, *La Sombre Malembo, Dieu du Carrefour* (Malembo, God of the Crossroads), 1943. Oil on canvas, 62.2 in × 49.2 in. Collection of B. and I. Rudman, Santo Domingo. The Rudman Trust—Private Collection. © Artists Rights Society (ARS), New York / ADAGP, Paris.

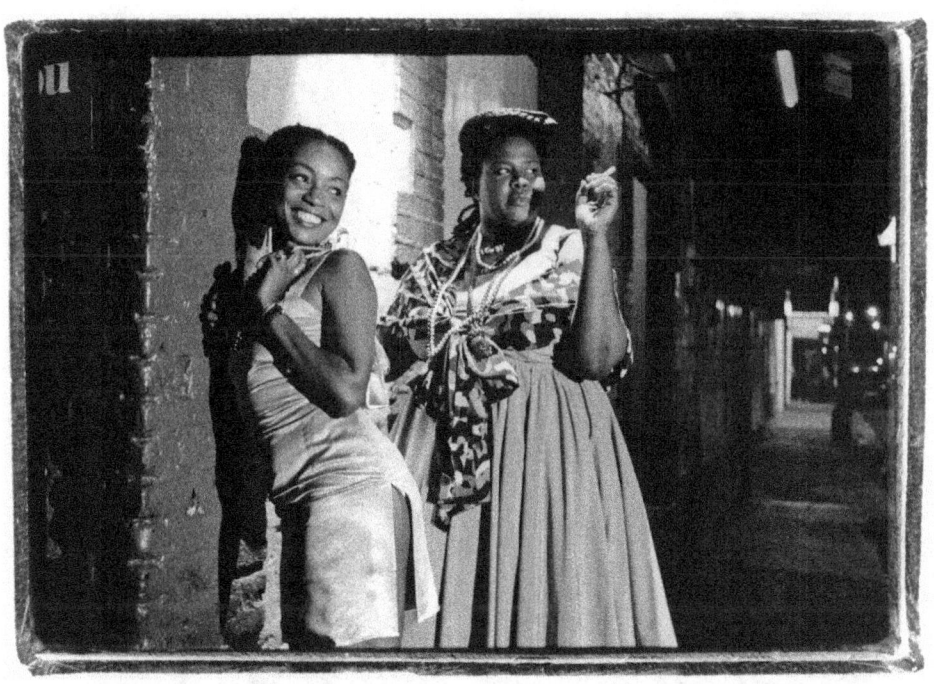

Plate 5 Penelope Spencer and Rhoma Spencer in Tony Hall, *Jean and Dinah*, 1994. Promotional photograph by Abigail Hadeed. © Abigail Hadeed. Courtesy of the artist.

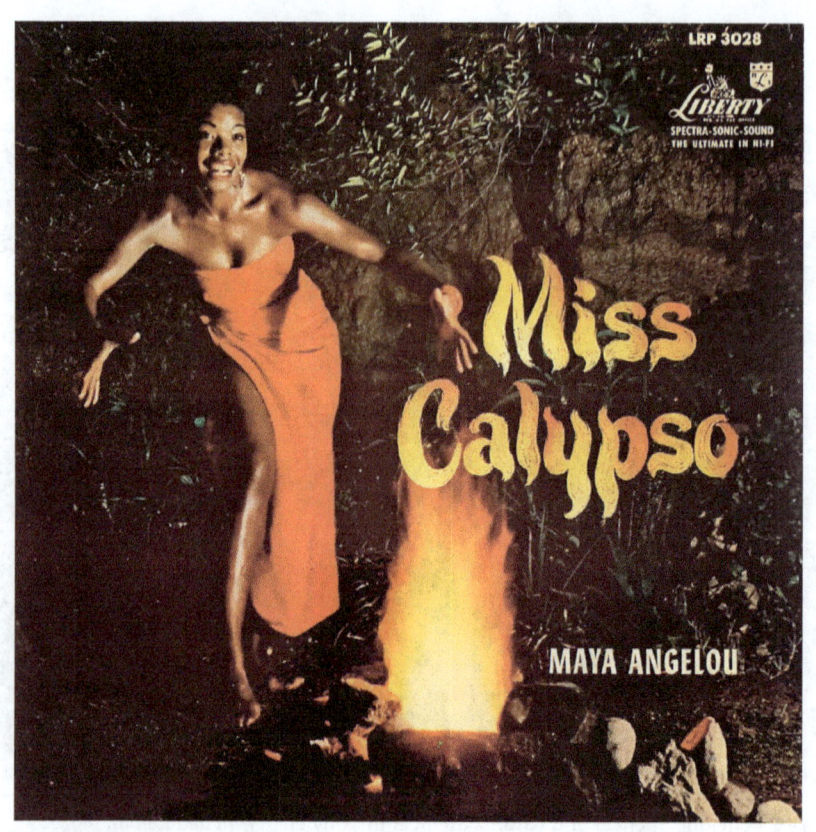

Plate 6 Maya Angelou, *Miss Calypso* album cover, 1957.
Photograph by Kenneth Wissoker.

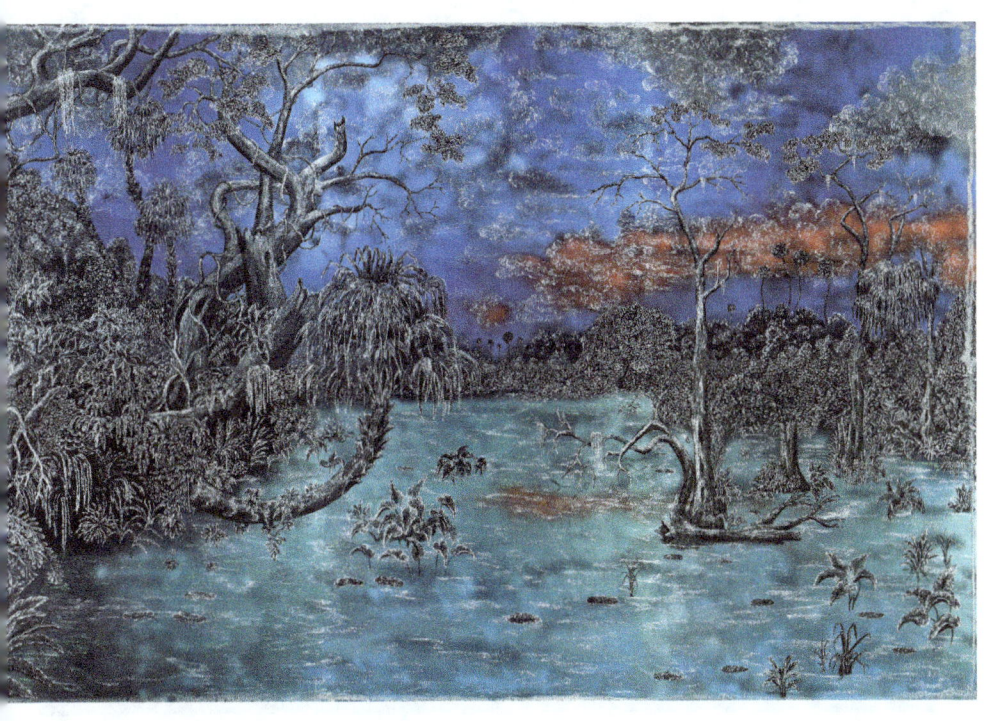

Plate 7 Edouard Duval-Carrié, *After Heade—The Great Florida Marsh*, 2013. Mixed media on aluminum, 96 × 144 in. Courtesy of the artist.

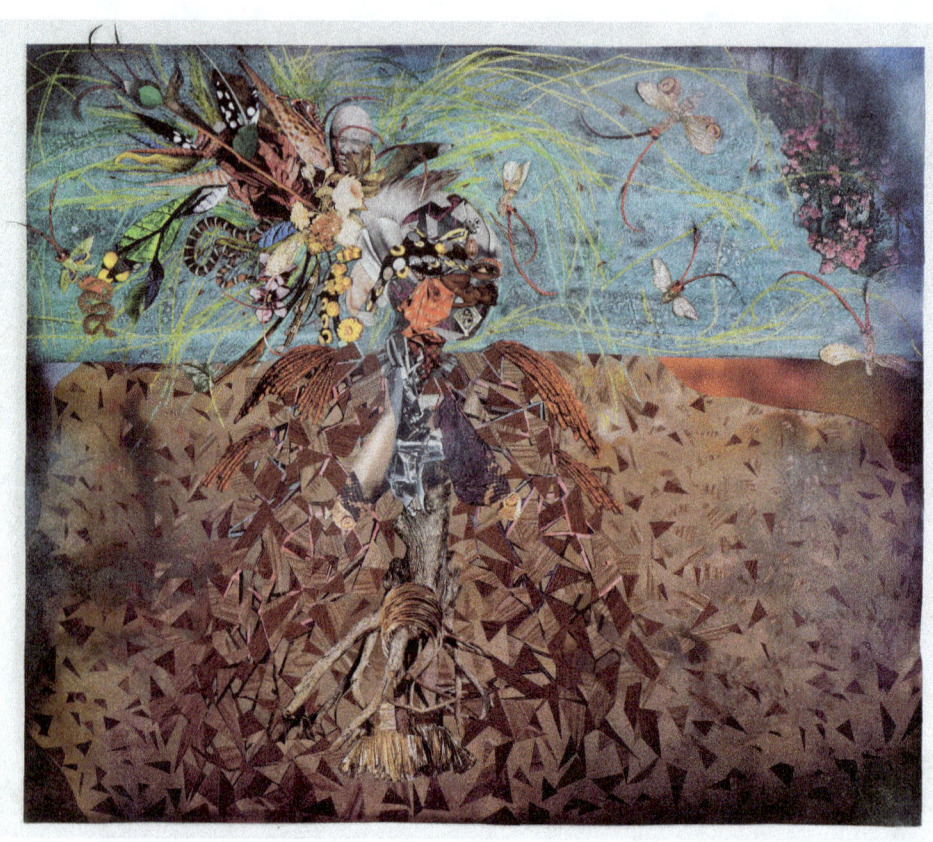

Plate 8 Wangechi Mutu, *Tropicalia*, 2015. Collage on vinyl, 35½ × 41½ in. Courtesy of the artist and Victoria Miro, London.

in with the baby's father in downtown Port of Spain that she took to the streets for company and as a means of living.[211]

Sex work became an even more viable way of making a living during the U.S. Navy's occupation of the island during World War II. In 1940 British prime minister Winston Churchill offered large plots of land in Trinidad to U.S. president Franklin Roosevelt for building naval and air bases.[212] With hundreds of American men earning decent wages (paid in "Yankee" dollars), it was more than enticing for some working-class women: not only for the sex workers but also for those whose only employment opportunity was serving the domestic needs of middle- and upper-class households.[213] The average pay for the latter was twelve dollars per month, while sex workers would often charge three, five, and sometimes as much as ten dollars for each sexual encounter.[214] American soldiers gave them more money than local men did, becoming serious competitors to their Trinidadian customers.[215]

One of the ways in which these men were able to retaliate was through the musical art form of calypso. In one song, the calypsonian Tiger ridicules a woman because of the varying complexions of her children and an absent father figure:

Some of the children brown and some little whiter
Put she to the world she can't point a father
Who it is? Me next door neighbour[216]

Calypsonians were often critical of these women, and their songs reflected what the masses felt about this cohort, relegating them to the category of jamette. In their lyrics, they often presented the moral ideals they expected women to follow, yet they seldom professed a desire to change their own behaviors.[217] However, their sense of emasculation was relieved with the end of the war and the departure of the foreigners. The sentiments of local men are best captured in the calypso "Jean and Dinah" (sung by the calypsonian the Mighty Sparrow), which warns jamettes that the "Yankees gone" and he is "taking over now." In other words, the jamettes had to accept what local men gave them and if they did not, they would suffer terribly.

The vicious nature of these consequences manifested itself physically and violently. "Jean in Town" (a character who many say was one of the jamettes about whom the Mighty Sparrow sang) ended up with a deformed arm after being attacked with a knife.[218] When Bubulups initiated a battle with her opponents, policemen arrested a naked and wounded

Bubulups.[219] Their lives became a matter of survival as they constantly had to defend themselves.[220] The difficulty of a jamette's life is best summed up in Jean's words: "Listen to me, Dinah. You could be a waiter, that is your business. The road I walk had nothing. It didn't have no money, no food. I didn't have no mother. I didn't have no father. All I ever wanted in my life was money and that is the only way I know how to do it. And that is how I going down. You hear me?"[221] This bleak reality equipped jamettes with the capacity to realize the spectacle that their bodies could inherently become. Recognizable by their posture, style of dress, and disregard for spatial and temporal precepts, jamettes threatened the controlled and repressed position that women had in society. Indeed, the mostly Black female bodies exemplified this model of the jamette but more so because society branded them vulgar.[222] As uncouth spectacles, their physiques gestured indiscretion against the repressive colonial order.[223] Vulgar now became the pejorative agent in the sociocultural framing of these Black working-class women. The anxieties of the elite and the colonial authorities centered around the vulgarity that branded the jamettes' bodies. Thus the criticism they often faced deemed them as dehumanized, degenerate, and uncontainable.

The authorities continued efforts to control the masses during Carnival with the annual publishing of a "List of Don'ts." One such list from 1946 (figure 3.10) reveals the anxieties the government still had in knowing that the potential for an insurgence could erupt during Carnival. This warning to the jamettes and badjohns evidenced the expectation that colonial subjects were to consciously and constantly practice "proper etiquette," even in the midst of revelry in Carnival. However, as the authorities were well aware, Carnival could not be possessed and controlled.

The defiant spirit of the jamette is captured in a promotional photograph from the play *Jean and Dinah* in which two women are roaming the streets alone at night (plate 5). As the image suggests, jamettes proposed a challenge to the socially acceptable idea of the colonial female subject having a sense of social responsibility by practicing self-monitoring, self-restraint, and self-containment. It is nighttime and the women are parading on the streets and stop by a building in what seems to be a designated marketplace for jamettes. While both jamettes are impeccably dressed, the one on the left wears more provocative attire and stands facing the wall, protruding her derriere as if attempting to attract attention. The other woman stands boldly and holds a cigarette to her mouth, a practice that was considered unbecoming of a lady. Standing strategically underneath the light source allows them to be noticed by potential customers as they create spectacles of themselves. Although jamettes always had the option of frequenting nightclubs to gain clientele, jamettes such as these opted to stay on the streets in the red-light districts of urban centers. Undeniably, any woman seen on the streets at night in these parts of town would immediately be considered a jamette. By doing this, they showed no concern for the social repercussions of being branded "vulgar" and for the perception they were a major hindrance to the social and economic development of the Black working class. Despite these condemnatory readings, these women were in fact able to earn incomes and thus determine their financial futures. And this corner in the grimy slum of the city served as a paradoxical space, an abhorrent location from which these two jamettes could undo traditional geographies and gain a different perspective of the urban domain, thereby solidifying their sense of place.[224]

Often jamettes were divided into two categories based on how they dressed and dealt with customers. "Low-grade" jamettes such as Yvonne "Bubulups" Smith and Gateway Elaine wore T-shirts and jeans or cheap dresses and frequented the streets at night, striking up conversations with potential customers.[225] Once the jamette gave a price, which was often low, they would go around the corner to engage in their sexual encounter. Contrastingly, "high-grade" jamettes wore stylish dresses, jewelry, and high-heeled shoes and would only do business in nightclubs.[226] Jamettes such as Delilah, Vera, and Destra would be seen in clubs like Marama and the Lucky Diamond Horseshoe Club. Here, men would invite them over to their tables and buy them a drink in an effort to seek sexual favors. Once a man agreed on the price the jamette gave, they would go to a private place to have intercourse. Although women with fair complexions and/or straighter hair textures often were immediately considered jamettes of high caliber, usually any attractive woman who dressed well would fit into this category.[227]

However, at the same time, jamettes still did not correspond with the model of the ideal woman, physically or physiognomically. Like many of the women of her class, the average jamette was Black and thus always stereotypically aligned with ugliness. At the same time, those Black women who adhered to the tenets of decency were considered socially acceptable good candidates for marriage. Despite cultural nationalist overtures to Afrocentrism in Trinidad beginning during the 1920s, the feminine ideal was, nevertheless, of European descent.[228] And no one symbolized this ideal more than the Jaycees Carnival Queen.

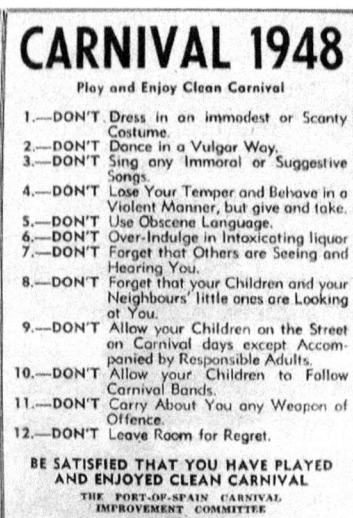

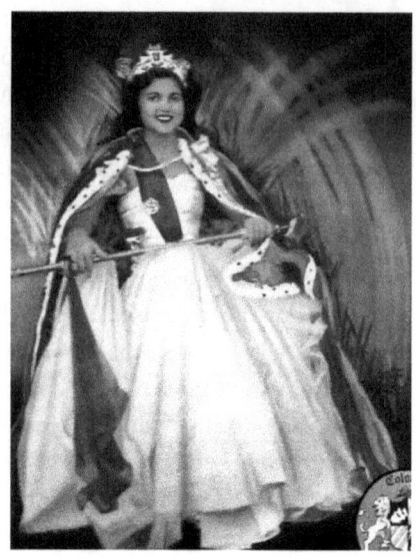

CARNIVAL 1948

Play and Enjoy Clean Carnival

1.—DON'T Dress in an immodest or Scanty Costume.
2.—DON'T Dance in a Vulgar Way.
3.—DON'T Sing any Immoral or Suggestive Songs.
4.—DON'T Lose Your Temper and Behave in a Violent Manner, but give and take.
5.—DON'T Use Obscene Language.
6.—DON'T Over-Indulge in Intoxicating liquor
7.—DON'T Forget that Others are Seeing and Hearing You.
8.—DON'T Forget that your Children and your Neighbours' little ones are Looking at You.
9.—DON'T Allow your Children on the Street on Carnival days except Accompanied by Responsible Adults.
10.—DON'T Allow your Children to Follow Carnival Bands.
11.—DON'T Carry About You any Weapon of Offence.
12.—DON'T Leave Room for Regret.

BE SATISFIED THAT YOU HAVE PLAYED AND ENJOYED CLEAN CARNIVAL

THE PORT-OF-SPAIN CARNIVAL IMPROVEMENT COMMITTEE

Per G. CABRAL, Chairman.

3.10 (*top left*) Carnival Improvement Committee, "Carnival 1948: Play and Enjoy Clean Carnival." From *Trinidad Guardian*, February 8, 1948.

3.11 (*top right*) Carnival queen Marion Halfhide, 1950. From *Carnival 1951 Souvenir Programme* (Port of Spain, Trinidad).

The Jaycees Carnival Queen represented what every woman was supposed to emulate (figure 3.11). She was almost a replica of the Queen of England, clearly standing in direct opposition to the jamette. Like the contestants of the competition, the flag woman performed in the public sphere; however, her corporeality was not exhibited in a guarded social arena like the Jaycees Carnival Queen competition. For many Black working-class men, the Carnival Queen competition served as a reminder that they could not have "the Queen." Instead, they had to settle for the "big black ugly one."[229] Although she was the least desired, a respectable and reputational Black woman always proved to be a loyal, selfless, hardworking, and chaste wife and mother. At the other end of the spectrum was the jamette. Unlike the chaste Black wife who was symbolically asexual, the jamette epitomized the sexually zealous Black woman even though she was never openly celebrated as a desired figure.

Such an association of the jamette's bodily expressions with the dark and the savage marked her as inherently primitive. As demonstrated in the regulations for Carnival behavior, her provocative gesticulations in the carnivalesque sphere received the same condemnatory reading as her perceived role in everyday society. Amid the large crowds of masqueraders in sailor mas costumed bands organized by the predominant steel bands, jamettes sustained a rebellious quality as they gyrated their pelvises that was reminiscent of the jametre class of the prior century. Their movements were akin to the steel bands, whose rhythmic and melodic sound also emitted an unruly flair as the steel pan voiced the Black masses' desire for acknowledgment of their political, social, and creative presence. The jamettes thus reveled in the music in their costumes, oscillating their hips with their arms akimbo, some waving the flags of their affiliated steel bands and others simply moving to the music while singing refrains from popular calypsos. If the jamettes were indeed primitive, it is because they were appropriating primitivity in their performances as a means of challenging the colonial order.[230]

This primitivity interrogates notions of the feminine through a type of "corporeal style," a term Judith Butler applies to gender to describe "an 'act,' as it were, which is both intentional and performative, where 'performative' suggests a dramatic and contingent construction of meaning."[231] One could argue in this context that corporeal style refers to the jamettes' disrupting the mandated corporeal style of the feminine by incorporating an aggressive and overt sexuality into their deeds. It is this idea of feminine corporeality that linked the jamette permanently to the lower strata and to the fringes of the permitted spaces for visual and physical enjoyment during Carnival.

In imagery that is rarely seen in newspapers prior to independence (because of its unconventionality), we see a woman who would be perceived as a jamette waving a flag for Tripoli Steel Band during the 1948 Carnival (figure 3.12). This woman may actually be Mable Corbin, a jamette of East Indian descent, who was a flag woman for Tripoli during this period.[232] The arm of a man standing in the foreground hides her face, but it is clear that she heads a crowd of revelers, with her hands raised and waving the band's flag. Although the steel band movement is considered a man's domain, her corporeal style constitutes a reminder of the impact of women in the development of the steel pan and the subculture surrounding it. After what may have been a quick maneuver through the crowd, she transforms into a spectacle and is immersed in an act that is both invigorating and contravening as she captures the attention of onlookers. Her monumental presence captured in the photograph also highlights her explicit command of the domain around her as she literally makes space, transforming the tropical, colonial territory as she traverses it. In that moment, Corbin

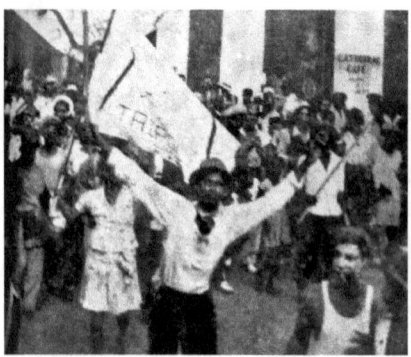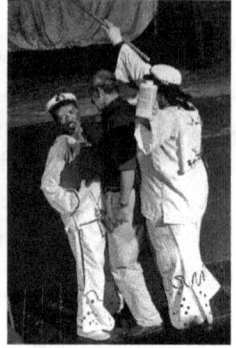

3.12 (*top left*) Flag woman from Tripoli Steel Band, 1948. From *Evening News* (Port of Spain, Trinidad), February 11, 1948.

3.13 (*top right*) Scene from the play *Jean and Dinah*, March 2006. Photograph by Jeffrey Chuck.

is immersed in absolute liberty as she actualizes the marvelous real in time and space.[233]

In another photograph from the play *Jean and Dinah*, we see the two women dressed in sailor costumes, flags in hand, and gyrating with a man positioned between them (figure 3.13). Jean and Dinah's overt sexual behavior is manifested in their direct bodily contact with the man. They may have pursued him and, like the Baby Doll character, are audacious in deciding to dance with him in such a sexual manner. In the 1940s, it was not uncommon to see women like Jean and Dinah in costumed bands organized by steel bands such as San Juan All Stars. These bands included masquerades that replicated the American sailors on the island who frequented bars and calypso tents and socialized with jamettes. More than anything, this masquerade was a parody of the American military's behavior. Yet there was a certain admiration for the Americans' rebelliousness. In fact, in 1941 the authorities prohibited the popular sailor bands from masquerading.[234] At the same time, the sailor band permitted a performance that not only explored the insertion of American culture into the colonial Trinidad context but also led the way to a new and exciting aesthetic both for costuming and for corporeal expression. Sailor bands were the most popular costumed bands to be seen parading through the streets. By 1952, of the 120 bands entered for competitions, about 40 were sailor bands.[235] The innovative aesthetic presence of the sailor band is one of the few costuming traditions of the 1940s that have survived in contemporary

Carnival, and it evokes a pivotal moment in Trinidadian history to which the jamette contributed.

An increase in the number of middle-class women masquerading in post–World War II Carnival coincided with an increase in the number of costumed bands catering to the middle class.[236] Scholar Barbara Powrie attributes the apparent "emancipation" of women as a reason for their amplified presence, identifying this revival of the women's movement as a by-product of the war.[237] Yet, along with the continued participation of jamettes and other working-class women in Trinidad Carnival, this period marks an important juncture when there was a greater presence of women in the festival. During the war years, numerous jamettes in Port of Spain continued to participate through their involvement with the steel bands and sailor mas costumed bands. The presence of the many American soldiers who resided at naval bases only accelerated the challenges to traditional moral codes already pursued by the jamettes and badjohns.[238] Furthermore, the American soldiers' validation of the calypso art form matched their attraction to the jamettes.[239] The fact that some middle-class women also had liaisons with the American soldiers may have had some impact on their wanting to participate in Carnival.[240]

The effect of the jamette and of the lower class in general was even more potent by the 1960s, since Trinidad Carnival began to embrace the cultural and corporeal practices of the working class. Part of this included a gradual co-optation by the middle and upper classes of the working class's performative tendencies. The Black masses, whose cultural contributions were "nativized" during the anticolonialist independence movement, were now seen as symbolizing the "essence" of Trinidadian culture. Since Carnival was no longer required to pay obeisance to the European discursive legacy that came with colonialism, it now became "we t'ing" and was supposed to reflect this newly constructed indigeneity.[241]

This change was also reflected in the aesthetic of the costumed bands. Bandleaders' themes began to demonstrate either a sense of nationalistic pride or ideas that were imaginative or fantasy-oriented in derivation. This less restrictive propensity flowed into the structure of the costume. For example, in 1957 Bobby Ammon produced the band La Fiesta Brava in which the costume aesthetic replicated traditional Spanish garb. The image of the band shows the revelers in costume on what seems to be the stage in Queen's Park Savannah, the main judging point for Carnival (figure 3.14). They are wearing thick long-sleeve shirts, long skirts and pants, capes, wide-brimmed hats, and black boots as they dance to music provided by wind instrumentalists, which are all in keeping with the theme of the band. Ammon's band highly contrasts with John Humphrey's 1966 presentation, Snow Kingdom. Here, masqueraders are wearing a costume with leotard and tights as its foundation, supplemented by additional pieces such as a chest piece, waistband, armbands and wristbands, a headpiece, and finally the standard. As is apparent, this new costume aesthetic and structure now provided masqueraders with more freedom of movement since there was now greater access to stretch nylons and knits, which also meant that costumes became more affordable. Carnival thus became more "democratic" and embraced revelers of different socioeconomic strata who could not afford more elaborate costumes. The deportment of masqueraders and other revelers during Carnival celebrations was less constrained and regimented, and the jamette's tremendous impact on the expressivity of the frame is obvious in this historical moment.

New designers also emerged whose costume aesthetic challenged the Eurocentric ideal that currently existed. In the mid-1950s, George Bailey, a young Black designer, arrived on the scene and embodied the desire of the Black masses for social recognition in the costumes he created. It is plausible to conclude that the Ju Ju Warrior masquerade was a significant influence on his work. The young Afro-Trinidadian designer created costumed bands such as Back to Africa, Relics of Egypt, and Somewhere in New Guinea, all of which celebrated an African heritage that had been disparaged for decades.[242] For the band Back to Africa from 1957, Bailey focused on the cultures of four precolonial African civilizations, namely the Watusi, the Masai, the Zulu, and the Zambesi.

In an image of the band Back to Africa, obvious attention is paid to the intricate detail of the leopard-printed fabric, goatskin, elaborate headpieces, ornamental jewelry, and spears as standards (figure 3.15). The vivacity of the moment is captured in the painted face of one reveler in the left foreground while others can be seen playing bongo drums. The thick horizontal lines of the textile-based costume in the center contrast the rich designs of the others, demonstrating the diversity of textile design in Africa while adding dimension to the overall presentation of the band. Bailey's penchant for intricacy and ornamentation in his costume aesthetic conveyed Africanity in a way that was dignified and elegant, harkening back to the era of Ethiopianism in 1930s Trinidad and its call for racial consciousness. Indeed, with a title like Back to Africa, one cannot escape how these words signify the Pan-Africanist call for a symbolic return to

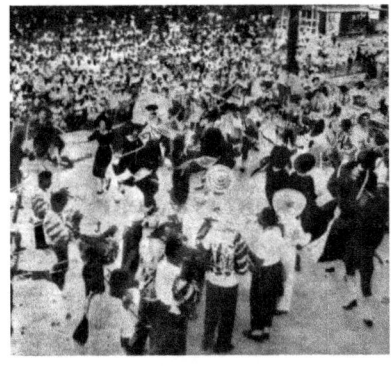
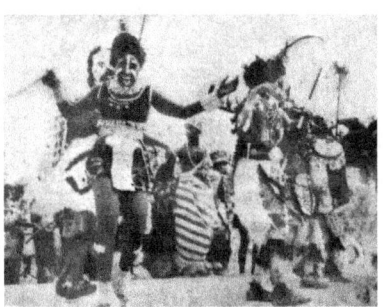

3.14 (top left) Bobby Ammon's band La Fiesta Brava, 1957. From *Trinidad Guardian*, March 6, 1957.

3.15 (top right) George Bailey's band Back to Africa, Band of the Year, 1957. From *Trinidad Guardian*, March 6, 1957.

the continent. Bailey's band won the Band of the Year competition and, with the sociocultural statement he made by representing the cultures of continental Africa, he no doubt encouraged a reevaluation of the pretty mas aesthetic.[243]

Other bands continued this sentiment. One band in 1953 looked to the Middle East for inspiration to produce Followers of Abdul Ahmed. Here, the designer went at great lengths to create costumes that simulated the grandeur of Arabian garb. The design of each costume is embellished with great ornamentation, as can be seen from the masquerader in the center of the image, who stands with legs apart and arms outstretched (figure 3.16). The full effect of the expansive sleeves, together with the headpiece, pants, shoes, and scimitar, can be experienced by any onlooker. When costumed bands such as this one used non-European themes, they countered the negative stereotypes prevalent in the public imagination and simultaneously responded to the dichotomized convention of aesthetics prevalent in Carnival.

By 1962, when Trinidad and Tobago gained independence, it became clear that the promotion of the festival as exemplary of the indigenous culture was part of the nationalist enterprise of the new government. Second, and more important, this cultural form was supposed to epitomize the Black masculinity of the masses. Nowhere are these facts more palpable than in Bailey's award-winning Band of the Year presentation Somewhere in New Guinea.[244] Bailey's continuing development as a designer is evident in the photograph of a section of his costumed band of 1962 (figure

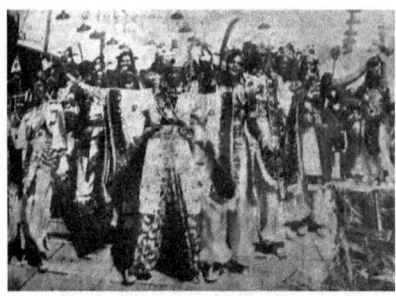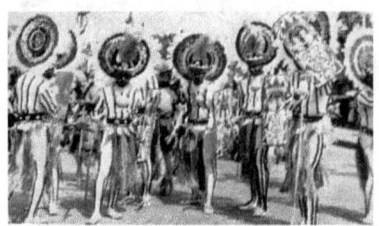

3.16 *(top left)* Followers of Abdul Ahmed. From *Trinidad Guardian*, February 18, 1953.

3.17 *(top right)* George Bailey's band Somewhere in New Guinea, Band of the Year, 1962. From *Trinidad Carnival and Calypso, 1963*, National Archives of Trinidad and Tobago.

3.17), which is a departure from his approach to the 1957 band. The male masqueraders appear majestic in their white, fitted body suits detailed with black lines that add dimension. The circular headpieces complete the presentation with their intricate and detailed designs. The bourgeoisie still managed to maintain its influence through the ever-present Eurocentrism explicit in many costumed bands and the prestigious Jaycees Carnival Queen, who seemed to replicate the Queen of England. No one could dispute the changes occurring in the festival.

History mas served a particular agenda of upholding the cultural legacy of the British Empire and the European elite while maintaining the efficacy of patriarchy. The creative yet political interjections of the likes of George Bailey in Carnival served to challenge these precepts, despite not challenging the patriarchal structure. The contributions of these innovative designers amplified the nationalist agenda of the newly independent country, for which Carnival exemplified a Creole cultural form that became "folklorized" and in turn "indigenized."

Jamettes have clearly had an unyielding presence in the history of Trinidad Carnival. In the late nineteenth century, jametre women created provocative costumes and performances. They were also pivotal in their roles as chantuelles and provided much social and political commentary via song, which led to the development of the calypso musical genre. Stigmatized with a socially imposed pejorative classification that was once the descriptor of an entire class of people, these jamettes nonetheless garnered a spirit of transgression that led to their disavowal of the "clean" Carnival mandated by the colonial elite. Their creative and cutting-edge exploits led to an eventual transformation of the performance and costume aesthetic so prevalent in Trinidad Carnival. Despite all this, jamettes have yet to be acknowledged in the festival's canon, and this speaks to how they have always been policed, silenced, and prevented from being key negotiators in the masquerading space. Jamettes serve as a testament "to the ways in which the public Black body documents where erasure and dispossession takes place; the connection with the public refuses a private, quiet, undocumented geography."[245]

Do the predominance and visibility of women who embody the spirit of the jamette during Carnival festivities today suggest that these women no longer have agency? Peggy Phelan discusses this disputed notion of assuming a connection "between representational visibility and political power."[246] She maintains that although the performativity in situations like Trinidad Carnival as masqueraded in the public sphere serves as a space for developing alternative articulations, these situations may not necessarily prove to be a useful source of catalyzing change; rather, as is the case for Carnival, they may serve the function of socially sanctioned safety valves for repressed anxieties and frustrations with one's socioeconomic predicament. However, these women are engaging in a form of "lower frequency politics," which, according to Gerard Aching, is not always intended to bring about some sort of social upheaval but instead aims at gaining and maintaining visible representation.[247] In this way, alternative sentiments that cannot otherwise be expressed are manifested. Undoubtedly the jamette, in her various incarnations, continues to be a central figure in the evolution of performance in Trinidad Carnival. Rooted in the collective embodied masquerade of a late nineteenth-century underclass that used the streets of Port of Spain as its site of protest during the pre-Lenten festival, this often-overlooked figure pioneered the full exploitation of the body in Carnival.

The body as a creative force can enact a *naming of place* while traversing the tropical environment, and Black Trinidadians employed imaginative tactics in the carnivalesque realm as effective strategies of space-making. The following chapter explores the ingenious efforts of stage performers who challenged cartographic reason with their provocative performances of the tropical other with facsimiles of the tropical terrain behind them. Their dynamic repertoires engendered new determinations of space in Western metropolitan centers that contested the hegemonic order with the formation of a Black transnation.

René Ménil maintained that there is an exoticism founded in nature that results from a human relation in a foreign land that could lead to disorientation, particularly when observing people in their environment. This is the very relation the European colonizer had with the colonial subject whom s/he rendered exotic.[1] Undeniably, the tropics have always been correlated with the bodies populating these equatorial regions, and since Western scholarship developed notions of the tropics as being full of hazardous natural disasters, terrible diseases, and venomous animals, its inhabitants were similarly aligned. These long-standing beliefs rendered non-Western peoples of tropical regions as inherently indolent due to the fecundity of the terrain and thereby likely to suffer from mental and physical laxity. Thus they were seen as incapable of creating civilizations. Many opined that the heat and humidity of the climate contributed to the attenuation of any moral compass, which heightened the sensuality and sexuality of these people.[2] It is from this perspective that the cultural forms emerging from Africa and its diaspora were scrutinized, and early twentieth-century dance forms and musical genres that became popular in the West were defined within the parameters of exoticism and primitivism. Indeed, Black primitivism determined the parameters of Western modernism. And despite the fact that Black cultural forms epitomized modernity, the question of Black people belonging in the modern world always persisted, since African-descended peoples were often linked with tropical localities.[3]

Efforts by African American performers to claim an affinity with Black people in other parts of the world were hugely informed by the precepts of Pan-Africanism. However, imperialist discourse often typified their brand of Black internationalism. American Black people possessed a sense of racial exceptionalism that revolved around their American national identity, and they subscribed to theories that associated racial development and attainment of civilization with the temperate zones of the world, most specifically the West.[4] Early twentieth-century African American performers did participate in representations of imperialism in which Black people from tropical parts of the world were rendered primitive and exotic. Nonetheless, these representations demonstrate an "outward seeking for identity and affiliation with extranational blacks," since "African Americans use primitivism . . . in an imperial manner to establish national belonging, alterity, and representational power."[5]

This chapter examines the ways in which the early twentieth-century Black Atlantic performances of Josephine Baker and Maya Angelou highlight the internationalist ethos of Pan-Africanism through their corporeal venerations of tropicality. I consider how these performers reproduced imperial identities of Black people who lived in these tropical terrains even while contesting and undermining conventional understandings of them. The movement of these African American performers within and beyond the center of power enabled a transformation of corporeal expression, particularly as it pertained to space-making and notions of belonging.[6] I argue that their performances employed tropical aesthetics in an effort to enact the *naming of place*.[7] The tropical aesthetics that these two performers used reveals how their corporeal manifestations proclaimed a different way of knowing and imagining the world through negotiations of national belonging and transnational desire. Within the sphere of performance, a performer can unearth the marvelous real and unexpectedly alter reality, and, as Alejo Carpentier declares, this comes with a particular intensity, given the exaltation of the spirit.[8] Performers such as Baker and Angelou thus prove how their bodily movements were means through which they created new ways of thinking about themselves as communities in their home countries or even in locations abroad.[9] They evoke tropicality to elicit a sense of symbolic belonging to Pan-Africa since the countries in which they live have not fully accepted them as part of the citizenry or the nation-state. One can thus envisage performance as a type of corporeal expression that is liberating, incisive, and even exceptional in its affect as a strategy of space-making. While the participants of Carnival in early twentieth-century Trinidad reveled in costume in the tropical, natural environment, these stage performers simulate tropicalia through the convergence of a variety of media such as music, dance, set design, and costuming. Their performances are also inspired by particular conceptions of Black diasporic corporeal expression that exist in cultural forms such as Carnival and are geographically linked to the tropics.

Integral to understanding the ways in which tropical aesthetics are present in exoticized performances of the early twentieth century is the consideration of how corporeal expressions of these Black performers are enduringly connected to the making of space and claiming a kind of geographic sovereignty. Much in the same way cabarets and music halls incorporated "jungle decor" into their furnishings to invoke the primitive, Black performers in turn exploited the tropical artifice to ritualistically engender a likeness to Black autonomy onstage or in song. This speaks to an association of the tropics with a homeland to which one belongs. Indeed, how one experiences race and space in the modern world is negotiated by bodies in motion; in the early twentieth century, "dance was the lexicon reflecting the dialectic process of modern transformation: the modern body continually reinventing itself, in and against its environment, at the same time as the environment made its claims upon the body."[10] Through song and dance, Black performers practiced an imperative of the modern era by transforming their predicament not only through self-reinvention but also through reorienting their relationship with the physical world. The defiant dancing and singing body worked to challenge "geographies of domination" and its eclipsing of "Black women's geographies," functioning against a world that regarded Black populations as ungeographic.[11]

These performers migrated from the United States, the Caribbean, Latin America, and Africa to the major European metropolises in order to capitalize on the negrophilia of the era. Most, like Josephine Baker, migrated to Paris, where they experienced favorable living and working conditions.[12] The Jazz Age was a period of anti-imperialism and international political movements. Given that Paris was a transnational space, foreign blacks could highlight their wider regional identities. Caribbean people, for example, voiced political ideas, criticized colonial racism in the metropolis just as they did in Caribbean cities, and "discussed issues of the Antilleans' disaporization and the Caribbean culture's globalization in [music and dance] venues."[13] Caribbean music and dance also contributed significantly to the development of musical genres that formed part of "contemporary anti-imperialistic and anti-racist political thought."[14] In the same way Black Atlantic peoples in Paris vehemently took on structures of cultural power with the narratives they performed that explored the dimensions of these structures and sought opportunities for manipulation and reshaping them, they also defied notions of cartographic reason through their reification of Black people's geography within these geographies of domination.[15] Early twentieth-century Paris evolved into a nucleus of the Black transnation, as it was a space where English-, French-, and Spanish-speaking Black people could be found, truly embodying what Martinican writer and philosopher Jane Nardal called Black *latinité* to refer to the cultural, social, and political exchanges that developed among Black people from Africa and the Americas who lived in Paris.[16]

Similarly, during the calypso craze that took America by storm in the 1950s, numerous African American calypso performers would profess to have Caribbean ancestry in an effort to advance their careers. Much of the appeal for this musical genre stemmed from a desire by white Americans to be entertained by exoticized Black West Indians similar to those who served them at popular tourist destinations. The power structure paralleled what existed during the antebellum period, and the exoticized Black other was expected to embody the childish naivete and carefree poverty of the invented caricature.[17] However, the attempts by Black Americans to mimic the Black primitive other symbolize a need to affiliate themselves with diasporic Black people. African American performers such as Angelou used primitivism as a means of engendering national belonging.[18] Angelou brazenly serenaded listeners and viewers through her music with lyrics of Black empowerment, self-definition, and resistance. By doing so, reclamation of land that can ultimately lead to a reclaiming of one's selfhood becomes feasible in an effort to proclaim Black geographic subjectivity.

In this chapter, I explore key performances by Maya Angelou and Josephine Baker that exemplify tropical aesthetics. First, I examine the imagery and musical recordings associated with the release of Angelou's first album, *Miss Calypso*, and take into consideration how they aided in a constructed representation of Angelou that epitomized the exotic Black primitive. Descriptions of lively performances of signature calypso tunes by Angelou provide a blueprint of how to interpret the lyrics of a number of songs in her album, which inevitably reflect the aspirations of Pan-Africanism at a local and global level. Angelou's musical recordings also encapsulate the cultural contributions of diasporic Black people, which ultimately give heed to the persistent resolve of Black empowerment, self-definition, and resistance.

The second portion of the chapter interrogates Josephine Baker's performances in the first major productions she starred in upon moving to Paris, namely *La Revue Nègre* and *La Folie du Jour*. In particular, I examine the tropical-inspired sensibility of the jungle-themed jazz performances that first characterized cabarets and music halls in New York and later became indicative of many productions in Paris. The application of the word *jungle* to these spectacles is interrogated, in addition to the word's connotation of primitivism as it pertained to the music, costuming, and scenic design of the productions featuring Baker. In addition, there was an affinity established between the jungle and Black bodies, bodies that were recognized as integral to modernity. This chapter also considers the provocative enterprise of imaging Baker to complement and publicize her performances. Imagery would often portray Baker as savage-like, overly sexual and deviant, situating her in the metropolis just as frequently as in tropical parts of the world. Nonetheless, Baker's performances implicitly reject the jungle construct and its accompanying devaluation of Black subjectivity and cultural expression. Her performances in *La Revue Nègre* and *La Folie du Jour* served as ritualized acts of space-making that purposely challenged geographies of domination.[19]

THE CALYPSO PERFORMANCES OF MAYA ANGELOU

While much is known of Maya Angelou's illustrious career as a poet, writer, and activist, very little is known of her short stint in dance and music. Born Marguerite Johnson, Angelou earned a scholarship to study theater and dance at the California Labor School during her teenage years. While taking modern dance classes in her native San Francisco, she met Alvin Ailey, with whom she formed a dance team, billing themselves as Al and Rita. They collaborated on the choreography and performed at various venues throughout the city. Shortly after marrying Tosh Angelous in 1951, Angelou gained another scholarship, this time to study in New York with Pearl Primus, the acclaimed dancer, choreographer, and anthropologist.[20] Primus and Angelou had something in common—the Caribbean island of Trinidad was the birthplace of Primus as well as the homeland of Angelou's maternal grandfather.[21] Angelou was enthusiastic and hopeful for the possible rewards this immense opportunity could present to her. However, recognizing that her lack of rigorous training and the high level of competition meant the unlikelihood of finding employment, Angelou moved back to San Francisco. Her efforts to sustain employment in the world of dance are indicative of what Jayna Brown contends is how "Black women reclaimed their bodies *in*, as well as *from*, the world of work." Due to the limited opportunities in purported legitimate economies, Black women had to pursue lives of service, menial and manual. "The very act of making money through the beauty, grace, and comedy of their bodies' talents reframed what could be produced by physical effort . . . a resilient striving for the body's creative autonomy."[22] Indeed, Angelou persevered and was persistent in her efforts to gain leverage in the cut-throat industry of show business.

Despite this major setback, she started performing as a calypso singer in 1953 at the Purple Onion, a famous basement cabaret in San Francisco.[23] In an effort to make her stage persona more intriguing, Angelou's friends thought it best to change her name and even created a new, more exotic biographical narrative that included a Watusi chieftain from Africa for her grandfather, who fell in love with a Spanish woman in Cuba. According to this story, they married and gave birth to Angelou's father.[24] It was in fact Angelou's voice coach who helped her coin the stage name Maya Angelou. Angelou's brother gave her the nickname Maya, and Angelou is a derivative of her former married surname, Angelous.[25] In an effort to advance their careers, numerous commercial singers of calypso would often feign legitimacy, while others were often mistaken for Trinidadians or someone from the Caribbean.[26] Perhaps Angelou and her friends opined that this fictitious biography would be a more effective marketing strategy than Angelou's factual Trinidadian ancestry.

Her revue at the Purple Onion led to other performance opportunities, most notably as a featured dancer in the opera *Porgy and Bess* during its European tour from 1954 to 1955. Once home, Angelou focused on mothering her then ten-year-old son and on finding employment. This was around the time of the second boom of America's calypso craze, with much of the fanfare revolving around Harry Belafonte (an American entertainer of Jamaican parentage), who was labeled the King of Calypso, much to the chagrin of calypsonians from Trinidad, the musical genre's country of origin. Calypso was created by the Black masses of Trinidad and Tobago and has its roots in Carnival of the late nineteenth century. It became an expressive tool for the working class of Trinidad and Tobago and later the wider Caribbean and its diaspora, offering social and political commentary with its witty banter given at someone else's expense, often thinning the line between humor and insult.[27] The first wave of calypso in America occurred from the late 1930s into the 1940s when a generation of New York–based Trinidadians developed a popular style of calypso that was distinct from its Trinidadian counterpart. Over time, the musical genre emerging in New York evolved into a form of popular entertainment targeted at North American listeners.[28] When the Andrews Sisters recorded their version of "Rum and Coca-Cola" in 1946, a calypso originally written and recorded by the notable Trinidadian calypsonian Lord Invader in the early 1940s, it became the most successful calypso crossover by non-Trinidadian singers.[29] This prefigured the immense popularity calypso would have in the next decade.

As calypso emerged as a viable commodity in the American music industry by the 1950s, the press enthusiastically generated a pseudobattle between calypso and rock and roll. Many people formed the opinion that the wholesome image that the calypso genre developed would lead to a welcoming demise of rock and roll and all the peril and debauchery it elicited from American youth. There was a consensus in the press that calypso possessed a childish naivete and "retains an underlying native innocence that the staid statesider can't quite comprehend."[30] The goal was to have the "degenerate Negro music" of the United States be replaced by a cultural form created by people who were a different sort of Black, a Blackness that was still provisionally erased. Calypso entertainers were consistently packaged as exoticized dark-skinned caricatures whose stage performances for white audiences relegated them to the servitude typical in Caribbean tourist destinations.[31] Dressed in bright-colored tattered clothing and straw hats, these performers were expected to portray the lighthearted poverty, innocence, and rusticity that Americans believed Caribbean blacks possessed.

It is within this symbolic register that one should consider Angelou's brief stint as a calypso singer. At the height of her success, Angelou made her film debut as a featured performer in *Calypso Heat Wave*, a 1957 musical film in which she sang the song "Run, Joe." That same year, she recorded her only album, titled *Miss Calypso*, which included her own songs as well as standards.[32] The imagery on the cover of *Miss Calypso* and the promotional photograph provide a visual equivalent to her lively singing as well as the melodic and rhythmic structure of the songs in the album. Both images are set in what appears to be a simulated "jungle" scene. Angelou is conveyed as an archetypal exotic woman in a revealing red dress. On the album cover (plate 6), she is portrayed cavorting around a large bonfire with one lunged leg exposed and bearing the body toward the camera. Her skin is glistening, illuminating the musculature and brown skin tone of her slender body. Her arms are bent and her fingers all point outward, invoking action, and along with her slightly open yet smiling mouth suggest she is in the midst of a performance.

The same themes prevail in the promotional photograph (figure 4.1). Here, the iridescent yellow lining of the dress is visible and echoes the

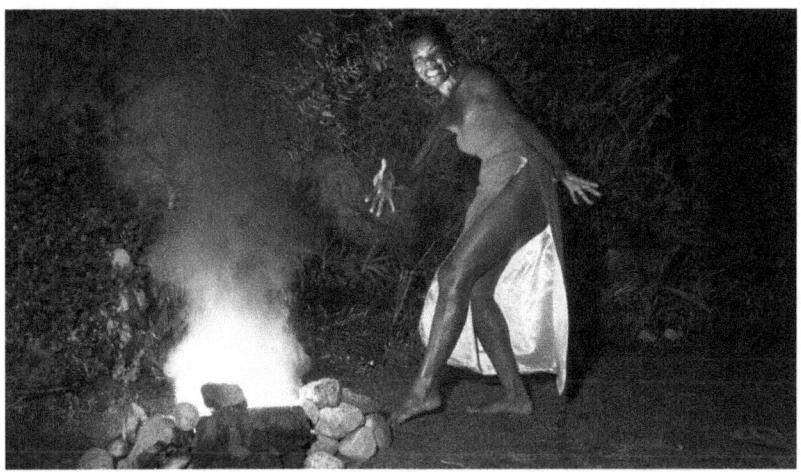

4.1 Promotional photograph for Maya Angelou's album *Miss Calypso*, 1957.

yellow hue of the fire. In both images, Angelou is rendered as a savage and sexual deviant. Her Black female body illuminated by a fire and nestled in a dark "jungle" thick with foliage epitomizes the notion of the Black hypersexualized primitive in her natural habitat. Given her artificial biographical narrative, her West Indian otherness situates her in the lower strata of imperialist relations of power. The colonialist dynamic is intensified even further if the viewer takes on a masculinist gaze, which reduces her to a feminized object who is rendered as picturesque as the environment that surrounds her.

The nature of Angelou's performances at the Purple Onion most likely informed the configuration of these photographs. Her gowns were often long and close-fitting with slits on either side reaching her hips; she also wore one-legged batik pants underneath and no shoes.[33] Collectively, this ensemble, along with the purposeful construction of her calypsonian persona— a woman from a foreign land who was half African and half Cuban—must have had an exoticizing effect meant to captivate her audience. Yet her projected image was complicated by some of the lyrics in the songs she performed, many of which were featured in her album. "Run, Joe," for example, tells the story of two men who run a candy store as well as practice fortune-telling, and are trying to avoid being captured by the police.

Loey, Loey, Loey, Loey, Loey-boy,
Joey, Joey, Joey, Joey,

Mo and Joe run the candy store,
Tellin' fortune behind a door,
The cops grabbed Mo, and as Joe ran out,
Brother Mo he began to shout,
Run Joe, hey "The Man's" at the door,
Run Joe "The Man" he won't let me go, Run Joe,
Run Joe, run as fast as you can, Run Joe de police holdin' me hand,'

Loey, Loey, Loey, Loey, Loey,
Hide the crystal ball by de fence, So dey won't find no evidence,
Get somebody to tell a lie, So I'll have me an alibi,
Hurry home and get in your bed, Call the doctor and tie your head,
Get somebody to go my bail, Don't want to stay in that rotten jail,
And, Run Joe, while the man's at the door, Run Joe,
The Man he won't let me go, Run Joe, Run Joe, as fast as you can,
Run Joe, these people is holdin' me hand.[34]

The lyrics of the calypso speak to the African continuum of divination systems of a number of sub-Saharan African religions that have been retained throughout the Americas. More important, they are a significant part of the counterideologies created by Black people for Black people that were often subjugated by the status quo throughout history. And the ongoing theme of flight is so prevalent in the song, particularly since "tellin' fortune" presented Joe and Mo opportunities to create new and redemptive meanings for their patrons out of the paradoxical spaces they occupied that were established by traditional geographies.[35] When describing her interpretation of the song, which she also performed in the film *Calypso Heat Wave*, Angelou says: "I stretched my arms and waved my hands and body in a modified hula, indicating how fast Joe made his getaway. I tugged away from an imaginary policeman showing the extent of restraint imposed on Moe. I spun in place in the small area, kneeled and bowed and swayed and swung, always in rhythm."[36]

"Mambo in Africa," a song written by Angelou, is a meditation on the cross-cultural exchanges between Africa and its diaspora elicited by mambo.

Mambo in Trinidad
Mambo in Portugal
Mambo in Mexico
Mambo in Barbados

Mambo in Bahia
Mambo in Africa
I feel like a queen and I feel like a song
I feel like the wind and I just can't go wrong
'Cause I mambo, mambo, mambo like in Africa
I feel like I'm rich and I feel like I'm tall
I feel like a bird with no worries at all
'Cause I mambo, mambo, mambo like in Africa
When I am blue, sad and sort of low
I think of the mambo and I'm rearing to go
'Cause I mambo, mambo, mambo like in Africa[37]

The short stanzas must have been among the first pieces of writing authored by the future writer and poet. The lyrics call attention to the other Caribbean musical genre, mambo, which gained its own following in New York and eventually all of the United States during the 1940s and 1950s. This Afro-Cuban musical form became another configuration in New York, blending with jazz and Afro-Cuban *danzón* and *son* rhythms. The corresponding dance also reflected the intermingling of popular dance moves of jazz as well as other Cuban and Puerto Rican musical forms.[38] The lyrics of the song tell of the popularity of mambo in different parts of the Black diaspora while also bringing to mind the disparate cultural forms that brought into being this beloved musical and dance genre. More important, Angelou establishes a link between mambo and the African continent in an effort to venerate what she deems as a significant source of this diasporic cultural derivative.

Other songs such as "Calypso Blues" contain lyrics that evoke a melancholic longing for a return to Trinidad. "Stone Cold Dead in the Market" offers social commentary, with the protagonist seeking revenge on her abusive husband by unabashedly killing him in a marketplace. A popular song during its time, "Stone Cold" was actually a Barbadian folk song first recorded by Trinidadian calypsonian Houdini in 1939 and later by African American singers Louis Jordan and Ella Fitzgerald.[39]

Given that the themes explored in many of the songs deal with the efficacy of Black cultural forms as well as liberation, to name a few, it is important to consider the pivotal historical events of the 1950s to better contextualize their character. Apart from the galvanizing developments of the civil rights movement, the landmark verdict of *Brown v. Board of Education*, the brutal killing of Emmett Till, and Rosa Parks and the Montgomery bus boycott must have provided fodder for the subversive and somewhat despondent perspective from which a number of these songs were written. However, there was also the redeeming effect of shifts in power due to decolonization and revolution in other parts of the Black world. Ghana gained independence in 1957, and that year marked the beginning of the decolonization process for other countries in Africa and the Caribbean. In 1953 Fidel Castro spearheaded the Cuban Revolution, which forced American interests out of the island. Indeed, Angelou is a calypso singer who does not have an extensive background in the musical genre. However, her performances of these songs carry out the intended purpose of the genre, with its social commentary using double entendre and innuendo. Although she is dressed in costuming intended to evoke the exotic Black other of the Caribbean, Angelou brazenly serenades listeners with lyrics of Black empowerment, self-definition, and resistance, sentiments that intimate the historical events of the period.

While female calypso singers were commonplace in the United States in the mid-twentieth century, this was not the case in Trinidad until a couple of decades later. In fact, when calypso music evolved from the musical genre of kalinda, which working-class Black women of the nineteenth century innovatively developed, into the genre it became in the early twentieth century, it became the domain of working-class Black men.[40] Black women were expected to avoid public performance of any kind, particularly the bawdy songs characteristic of kalinda.[41] Despite these constraints, a certain faction of these women went against the stipulated principles of social structure that women were supposed to practice. From the late nineteenth century until the mid-twentieth century, the poor Black woman who defied standards of propriety during Carnival and retaliated against her dehumanizing position in society was referred to as the jamette. Jamettes saw how their unruly behavior could be used for both revelry and political purposes.[42] Given the nature of Angelou's performances, she undoubtedly recalls those Trinidadian women who valued earning an individual reputation through their corporeal expressions more than being respectable. Her provocative costuming defies notions of respectability both in the Caribbean and to a certain extent in the United States, augmenting her forceful bodily movements during performances. Furthermore, the songs she covered and authored convey powerful lyrics that effectively continue the legacy of the Black female kalinda singers of nineteenth-century Trinidad.

Despite the colonial exoticism embedded in the composition of the promotional photographs and to a lesser extent the music of the album, Angelou's performances of the songs used tropical aesthetics to establish a link between the body and the land. More than anything, this embodied tropicality ritualistically manifests the social, economic, and political aspirations that Black Atlantic peoples envisioned for themselves. Through sonic and corporeal dissonance, the exoticized Black body can engage in space-making in order to incur a sense of belonging and reclamation of land that can ultimately lead to a reclaiming of one's selfhood. This was fundamental in the construction of one's identity in the mid-twentieth century. As Lowery Stokes Sims argues, "Modernism affirmed the notion that a modern individual could be an agent of change or transformation" and "represented a potential revolution in self-definition and self-image."[43] Through her animated routines, along with her ardent singing, Angelou espoused Black Atlantic peoples and was able to momentarily shift the viewer's reality so that a linking of disparate locations with the African homeland becomes possible.

Furthermore, Angelou's work can also be seen as a form of artistic cannibalism. Borrowing from Valérie Loichot's concept of literary cannibalism, artistic cannibalism requires the conscious effort of visual artists and performers to devour the visual components or tropes used to depict or embody the tropics created mostly by European and European-descended artists, representations that subjugate the "landscape, flora, fauna, humans, and texts to an imperial gaze and desire."[44] These components are exoticist and primitivist, undoubtedly created due to the colonial situation. This act of devouring is therefore an act of revenge and a call for justice. Artistic cannibalism transforms both the eater and the eaten, and it is a discursive practice with its own rules and grammaticality.[45] Through her performances of songs like "Run, Joe" and "Mambo in Africa," Angelou reproduces yet reclaims the reductive representations of Black people and in so doing entraps the Western viewers in their own trap.[46] A new vocabulary emerges to dissociate tropicalia and Black people from a Western construction, so that an avowal of Black life and sovereignty becomes more palpable.

Artistic cannibalism also permeated the early twentieth-century performances of Josephine Baker. In particular, it resonates in her performances of the famed *La Revue Nègre* at the Théâtre des Champs-Élysées and later in *La Folie du Jour* at the Folies Bergère, both in 1920s Paris. Yet the performances were meant to cater to the escapist desires of the sophisticated Parisian that were deep-rooted in colonialist and exoticist indoctrination. These productions followed the precedent of popular shows featured in the cabarets and nightclubs of early twentieth-century New York. Baker was discovered by the creator of *La Revue Nègre*, Caroline Dudley Regan, in one such venue—the Plantation Club of Midtown Manhattan. Frequented by after-theater members of the café society, like the Cotton Club in Harlem, the Plantation Club bore a name that intimated the antebellum South. The owners intended for the power structure of that era to be replicated with carefree Black employees catering to every need of the white patrons.[47] Like the featured performances, the decor incorporated furnishings that invoked the primitive, often referred to as "jungle decor." The Cotton Club, for instance, had artificial palm trees and a plantation facade, while the elegant furniture, fixtures, draperies, and tablecloths were reminiscent of the big house on a southern plantation.[48] Explicitly imbricated in these environments are "the impressions of transatlantic slavery [that] leak into the future, in essence recycling the displacement of difference." While these environments draw from "traditional geographic arrangements," one can see how the cabarets and later the music halls of Paris not only simulated the social and racial order of slavery but also implicated the geography, landscape, and spatial arrangements essential for the institution of slavery.[49]

Premiering in 1925 with twenty-five musicians and artists, *La Revue Nègre* aspired to become the first major vaudeville-style production that truly represented Black expressive cultures around the world. With a lineup that included a mélange of cultural offerings, ranging from the Dixieland music of the American South to an "authentic African" performance titled "Danse des Sauvages," the intent was to feature a bill that incorporated the many cultural manifestations attributed to Black people. The revue consisted of seven acts—"Mississippi Steam Boat Race," "New York Skyscraper," "Louisiana Camp Meeting," "Les Strutting Babies," "Darkey Impressions," "Les Pieds qui parlent," and "Charleston Cabaret"—and each act stereotypically highlighted a trait often associated with the soul of Black people: idleness, melancholy, religious fervor, and sexual ecstasy.[50]

Particularly interesting is the invocation of locality in the names of most of the seven acts. They are named after places such as Louisiana and Charleston that have long histories of slavery and colonialist oppression, and, more important, locations that are situated within the tropical and subtropical zones of the world. The set designs, costuming, musical accompaniment, and choreography of the performances all worked in concert to illuminate the supposed inherent link between Black bodies and the tropical zone. It is clear in the conceptualization of the revue that the idea of the tropics served to conjure a "hot" zone—referring to climate, character, sexuality, and even food—which would consolidate the borders of Europeanness and whiteness.[51] The costuming evoked visual markers that codify Black bodies as destitute, indolent, and even impulsive, highly sexual, and exoticized beings. Baker, for instance, is noted as wearing a tattered shirt and cutoff pants in one act as well as the famed feathered miniskirt and accessories for another (figure 4.2).[52] The set design for the "Mississippi Steam Boat Race" act featured the panoramic view of a levee accented by large trees dripping with Spanish moss and a full moon glowing behind them, all of which conveyed the subtropical terrain of the southern state. Also depicted were riverboats, women clad in mammy caps and red bandanas, and bales of cotton; these are no doubt potent signifiers of the institution of slavery and the plantation-based economies of the antebellum United States.[53]

Such a tropical-inspired sensibility characterized the jungle-themed jazz performances one would have seen at the clubs, cabarets, and music halls in 1920s Harlem. The Black mecca of New York became the site of "glamorized otherness" where white patrons went to experience "the easily exploited fantasy of tropical sensuality and savage release."[54] White-trade clubs such as the Plantation Club, the Cotton Club, and Connie's Inn were located in an area of Harlem that eventually garnered the name Jungle Alley, offering an opportunity to experience an iteration of the jungle without losing white civility.[55] Caroline Dudley, the creator of the revue, would have been well aware of this trend and would have played a key role in incorporating the concept into La Revue Nègre, thereby being instrumental in exporting this cultural phenomenon to Europe. Prior to its arrival, the chorus line format predominated music-hall dancing in Paris and consisted of scantily clad women who performed more regimented routines featuring formations and high kicks. The jazz dancing

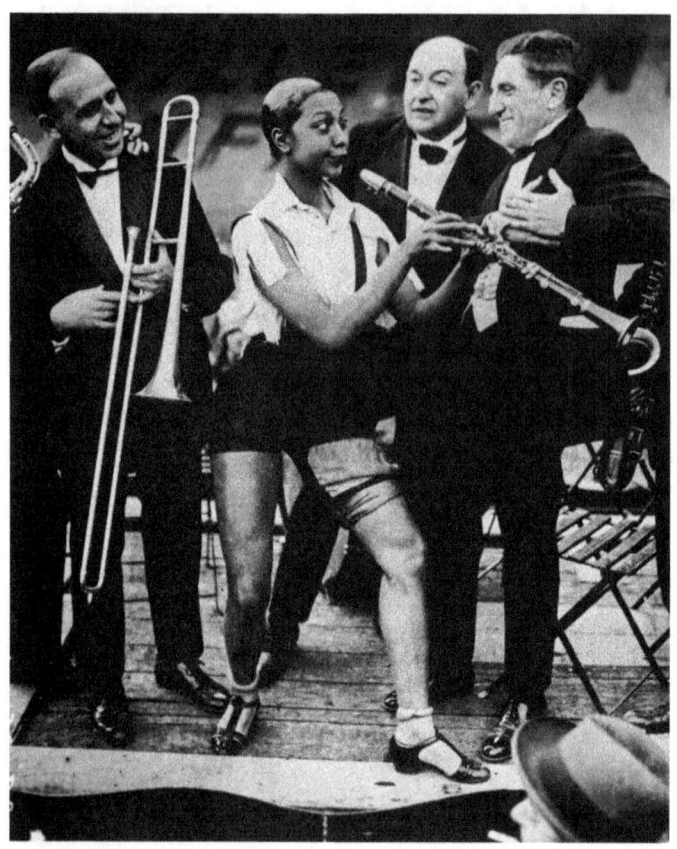

4.2 Josephine Baker in *La Revue Nègre*, Paris, 1920s. Photograph by Walery. © Bibliothèque Marguerite Durand / The Image Works.

of *La Revue Nègre* countered this structure with its free-flowing structure, since it allowed for a considerable degree of spontaneity in its lineup.[56] The dichotomy established between the two formats explicitly rendered the latter as primeval. Furthermore, although acts like the "Mississippi Steam Boat Race" are set in the United States, the costuming, the choreography, and the terrain conveyed in the set design all reflected the jungle theme. This ultimately lent to the idea of Africa since the tropical jungle was largely considered the natural habitat of Black people in the Western imaginary. The word *jungle*, after all, implied the environmental differences between Europe and tropical localities. As a social construct, jungle denoted all dense forests of the tropical world and augmented the established notion that a lack of organization and coherence in the physical environment is directly connected to a lack of organization and coherence among its inhabitants.[57]

Even the musical score of these elaborate productions included the emphatic sound of drums that was often referred to as a "jungle rhythm."[58] The Germans used the term *Urwaldmusik* (jungle music) as a descriptor for the lively musical genre. Although it was sometimes used in a pejorative sense, for most it epitomized the opposite of European intellectualism, and one could experience the rejuvenating qualities of jazz in an effort to focus not on the past but on the present, thereby embodying the so-called primitive characteristics of the Black race.[59]

For French ethnographer and surrealist writer Michel Leiris, this jungle rhythm that jazz music seemingly emitted was concomitant to the vibrancy, spontaneity, and sense of liberation that comes with modern living.

> Jazz was a sign of allegiance, an orgiastic tribute to the colors of the moment. It functioned magically, and its means of influence can be compared to a kind of possession. . . . Swept along by violent bursts of tropical energy, jazz still had enough of a "dying civilization" about it, of humanity blindly submitting to The Machine, to express quite completely the state of mind of at least some of that generation: a more or less conscious demoralization born out of war, a naïve fascination with the comfort and the latest inventions of progress . . . an abandonment to the animal joy of experiencing the influence of a modern rhythm.[60]

What is most fascinating about Leiris's choice of words is his use of the term *tropical energy*, which for him is indicative of jazz. Tropicality as Leiris conceptualizes it seems to epitomize the primitive modernism of the era. Tropical here is also synonymous with all things associated with Blackness. During this era of European colonialism in Africa, popular myths essentialized the Black body, inevitably linking all people of African descent to Africa. Whether one was a Black American or a colonial subject from Africa or the Caribbean, one was referred to as "Negro" regardless of one's racial, national, or cultural identity.[61] This practice of conflating Black subjectivities was also closely hinged to a reductive conceptualization of Africa despite the fact that members of the African diaspora were centuries removed from any direct cultural continuity with African societies and cultural forms. Moreover, what is key in the application of tropical is how it functions to characterize the sensations one experiences when listening to jazz music, a modern American musical genre, as being indicative of non-Western regions of the world. While the contextual use of the phrase "violent bursts of tropical energy" risks being pejorative, given its allusion to stereotypical mannerisms people of the tropics were believed to engender, it can still be recognized as a means through which one can attain an effervescence, a keenness, and even a stimulation necessary to thrive in modern life. While on the one hand African and African-descended peoples were historically emblematic of the primeval, timelessness, and savagery, by the 1920s, these stereotypes acquired positive connotations once American jazz became en vogue, whereby "the shock of modern rhythms, channeled by the Negro, would overtake the Western body."[62]

However, ever-present was a line of thinking that likened the popularity of jazz music to the spread of a contagious disease. One Dutch journalist exclaimed, "But this is the curse of the Nigger music. . . . They have got us all (by the balls!). . . . Is this the last symptom of the disease which began during the war and which we in the Old World still have to go through in order to emerge as being cured? Or is this the sure sign of an irreversible decline?"[63] The writer continued his rant, expressing concern that the popularity of the musical form could lead to social and cultural regression: "This is how they catch us and bring us back to a cultural level which is thousands of years closer to that of our ancestors according to the theories of Darwin."[64] Such a disposition parallels the beliefs many Europeans held with regard to living in the "torrid" zones of the tropics. The claim that Europeans should not find permanent homes in the tropics for fear that future generations would be born in a sickly and degenerate form was widely popular. Also, many believed that the tropical heat would have a negative effect on their sanity, even relaxing the mental and moral fiber and thereby leading to laxity and other excesses.[65]

Yet it was an immense curiosity about the perceived abnormality of this part of the world as well as the exoticized people often associated with these regions that attracted patrons to view *La Revue Nègre*. And the notion of the tropics as a hot and torrid zone is what the Parisian audience reacted to upon seeing Josephine Baker and Joe Alex perform their act "Danse des Sauvages." The revue's choreographer decided that this nude performance by Baker would give the production the erotic edge it needed at a climactic moment, and she conceded to this request.[66] The sexually charged performance closed the show and featured Baker and Alex in revealing costumes, with Baker wearing a feather miniskirt and feathers on her wrists and ankles (figure 4.3). The performance was in fact an interpretation of *Le Roman d'un Spahi*, a nineteenth-century work by French

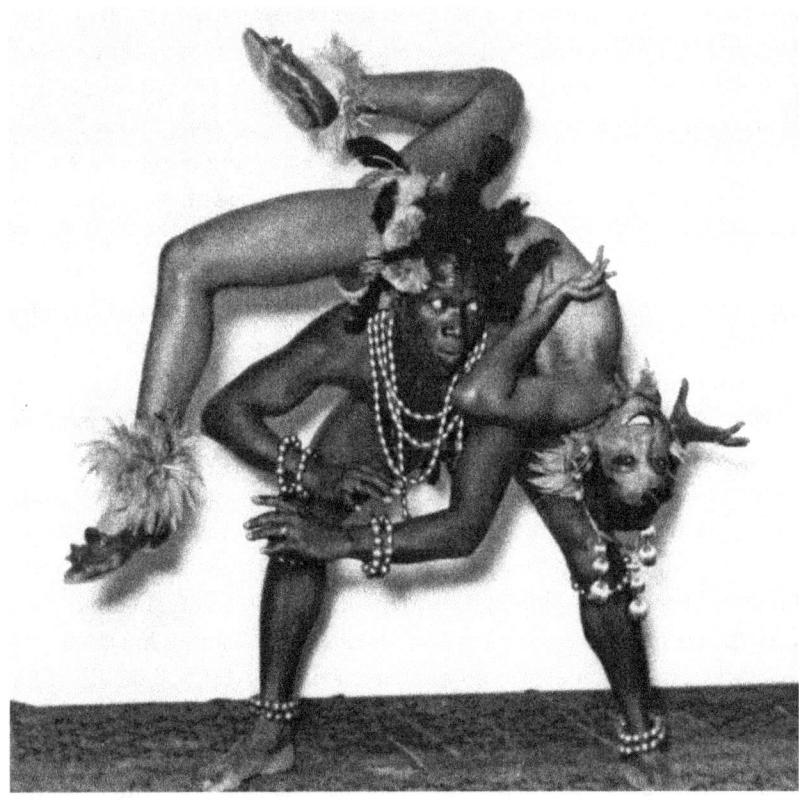

4.3 Josephine Baker and Jo Alex on opening night of *La Revue Nègre*, 1925. Photo courtesy of AKG-Images, London.

novelist Pierre Loti. Set in Senegal, it accounts the adventures of French explorer Jean Peyral. The dance reenacts the relationship Peyral had with a seductive woman, Fatou-gaye, with Baker appearing as Fatou.[67] Despite the lead protagonist in the novel being a white Frenchman, Baker's pairing with Joe Alex for this performance eclipses the focus on the European man succumbing to the beguiling African woman. Rather, the dance gave emphasis to the hypersexualization prescribed to Black people, with the conveyance of tropical Africa in the various elements of the production all serving to strengthen this representation.[68]

A polyrhythmic arrangement by the drummer served as a queue for Baker and Alex, who entered the stage with Baker positioned upside-down across Alex's back. Baker then got to her feet by doing a slow cartwheel with Alex's assistance.[69] The dance consisted of acrobatic bodily movements; there were also corporeal expressions akin to the belly dance that featured moves such as the Shake, the Shimmy, and the Mess Around, popular dances of the Jazz Age in 1920s New York. Much of these motions included quivering and sensuous gestures that were meant to convey the erotic nature of the piece.[70] Belly dancing and the shimmy were established parts of the repertoire for Salomé dancers of early twentieth-century New York. Their titillating movements were closely linked with the deviant and thus pathological sexuality of the Orient, even more so for Black female performers, whose bodies were already read as inherently primitive.[71]

Although each act in *La Revue Nègre* was carefully choreographed, Baker chose to improvise much of this dance. In many of her performances, Baker would combine elements of various American popular dances such as the Charleston, the cakewalk, and the black bottom. These dances were indeed modern, but, since she was rendered the savage Negro, Baker transformed them into "neoprimitive displays" with her ingenious improvisation of acrobatics, high kicks, and contortions.[72] One review from a French newspaper described the intricacies of these antics in which "she grimaces, crosses her eyes, puffs out her cheeks, wiggles disjointedly, does a split and finally crawls off the stage stiff-legged."[73] She even heeded to a certain level of fanaticism: "Even my teeth and eyes burned with fever. Each time I leaped I seemed to touch the sky and when I regained earth it seemed to be mine alone."[74]

On opening night, the audience was at first silent and eventually many of them erupted with cheers and clapping, some even rushing for the stage. Reviews of the show were also mixed. One critic wrote, "The plastic sense of a race of sculptors came to life and the frenzy of the African Eros swept over the audience. It was no longer a grotesque dancing girl who stood before the audience, but the black Venus that haunted Baudelaire."[75] Another critic was not so generous, characterizing her performance as "lamentable transatlantic exhibitionism, which brings us back to the monkey much quicker than we descended from the monkey."[76] These contrasting readings of Baker's performance mirror the varying reactions European critics had of jazz music. Once again, there is a conflation of Black people of America with those of Africa, with both critics conceptually shifting the location of the continent so that it is not south of Europe but rather across the Atlantic.

Nardal recognized the pitfalls that often came with the success that the likes of Baker experienced. In her clever interpretation of Baker's cultural impact in France, Nardal was steadfast to note how imperial cultural consumption played a crucial role in Baker's success. She also declared that Antillean intellectuals presented more truthful depictions of Black art that surpassed exoticism and primitivism.[77] Offering her interpretation of Baker's performances, she writes:

> Then onto the stage leaps a colored woman with lacquered hair and a sparkling smile; she is still clothed in feathers or banana leaves, but she brings the latest Broadway products (the Charleston, jazz, etc.) to the Parisians. The transition between the past and the present, the fusing of virgin forest and modernism—it is the American Negroes who are carrying it out and rendering it tangible. And the blasé artists and snobs find in them what they seek. [It is] the flavorful, spicy contrast of primitive beings in an ultra-modern frame of African frenzy, situated in the cubist décor of a night club.[78]

In these sarcastic undertones, Nardal emphasizes the continuation of primitivist fantasies that invigorate the careers of Black artists but also give life to new iterations of age-old stereotypes.[79] Nevertheless, Nardal's language still commemorates the tenacity of Black creative expression that was wholeheartedly embraced in 1920s Paris.

It is this persistence that the organizers of *La Revue Nègre* recognized in Baker, which propelled her into the limelight. They were well aware that creating imagery rendering Baker savage-like would prove to be advantageous, particularly since it aided in the sensationalizing and promotion of the revue. French poster artist Paul Colin is credited with constructing most of this visual imagery as well as those associated with the actual production. Apart from co-designing the set for the show, he also designed the poster.[80] In fact, it was his decision to highlight Baker on the poster rather than the actual star of the revue. Upon her arrival in Paris, Colin's studio was one of the first places where she was expected to reveal her nude body. She was hesitant at first, but Colin and others eventually cajoled her into abiding by the artist's wishes so that he could produce the composition (even though she is clothed in the final drawing on the poster) (figure 4.4). Baker even observed that Colin perceived her not as a woman but as an object to be painted. She admitted that it was during those sessions in his studio that her self-confidence increased and she felt beautiful for the first time. They certainly proved to be beneficial for the nude performances she was expected to perform.[81] The poster incorporates portrayals of Black people with texts in a way that exemplifies how primitivism

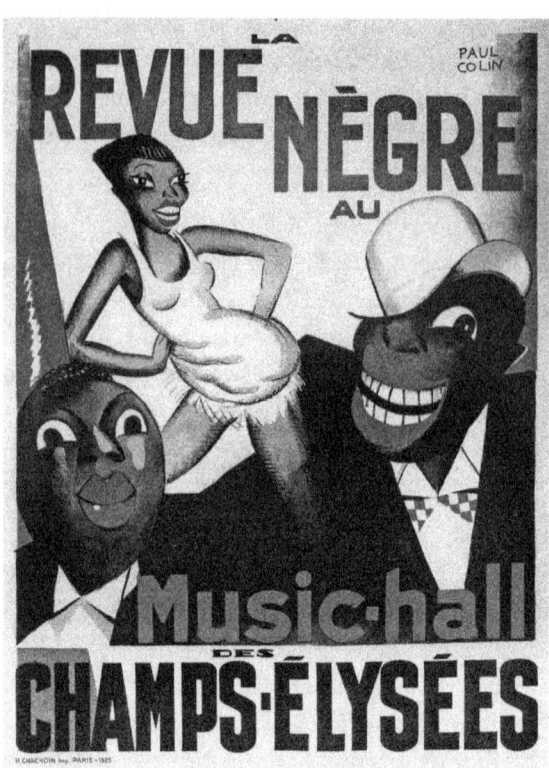

4.4 Paul Colin, poster for *La Revue Nègre*, 1925. © Artists Rights Society (ARS), New York / ADAGP, Paris.

was endemic in the representation of modernism. Most of Baker's body and the faces of two Black men are rendered in caricature-like fashion in the middle ground of the composition with the names of the show and the venue bordering them. The resemblance of the two men's faces to coon imagery is unmistakable even with their formal attire, while Baker is rendered in a sexually suggestive pose clad in a short, white shift dress.

Colin's depiction of Baker was heavily informed by a caricature that Mexican artist Miguel Covarrubias, the other set designer for the show, created for *Vanity Fair* in 1924 called "Jazz Baby."[82] Covarrubias lived in New York for many years and created illustrations depicting Black life with primitivist undertones for periodicals such as *Vanity Fair*. As a young poster artist, Colin would have picked up on the visual signifiers his contemporaries used to articulate the essence of colonial fantasies about blackness. While coon imagery is evident to a lesser extent in Colin's portrayal of Baker than in the other two figures in the *La Revue Nègre* poster, he created more disparaging imagery of Black people in his first major publication. In *Le Tumulte Noir*, a publication that included imagery celebrating the Jazz Age, Colin made direct references to minstrelsy, golliwogs, and dandies, and he also incorporated the physiognomy and other physical traits of animals such as monkeys in his representation of Black people. At this juncture, his representations of Baker transitioned from a stereotype to an actual savage persona. Many of the images fashion her in minstrel form, as in "Josephine in the City," where her minstrelized face is juxtaposed with the chic attire of the day that Baker was known for donning. In others, such as "Josephine behind Bars" (figure 4.5), Colin captures her in the midst of a dance movement but conveyed with a sense of violence and aggression. Positioned within a cage, Baker appears in white underwear with a malicious facial expression, her arms akimbo and legs splayed. A Black musician glares alarmingly at her from below, augmenting the sense of danger associated with a predatory animal.[83] "Josephine in a Palm-Tree Skirt" (figure 4.6) depicts an elongated Baker from a similar vantage point as "Josephine in a Banana Skirt" (figure 4.7). While in the latter Colin portrays her with a deportment that bespeaks Western refinement, in the former her body is more sluggish, with her arms placed in awkward positions above her head. The brown hue of her skin juxtaposed with the green-leaf skirt render her like a singular tree in a vacant terrain. Here, she is fashioned into an inanimate object, a flora that epitomizes tropicalia. Like the other pictures, this image captures the Westerners' preoccupation with Black primitivism of the early twentieth century. However, it also illuminates the indelible connection Black people were believed to possess with the tropics. Collectively, Colin's dehumanizing representations of Black people situated his work within a larger tradition of portraying blacks in advertising, not to mention Harlem music-hall posters.[84] Indeed, he was not the only one who created overtly offensive representations of Baker. The French social cartoonist Georges Goursat (known as Sem) captured the disdainful sentiments many Parisians held for Baker in one sketch. His drawing depicted her in the midst of a performance, the top half of her body lively yet elegant while her lower half included a monkey tail with a fly buzzing at its tip.[85]

Intimations to animalism were also prevalent in the words of a legend in the French cabaret world who referred to Baker as "a most beautiful panther," a phrase that undoubtedly epitomizes how Baker was framed in the French imaginary. She embodied such a disposition in a Henri Roger

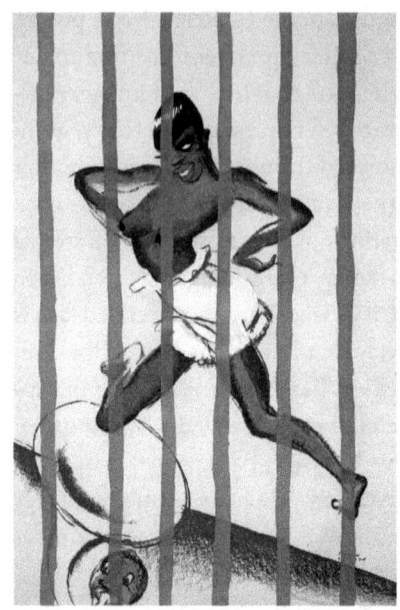

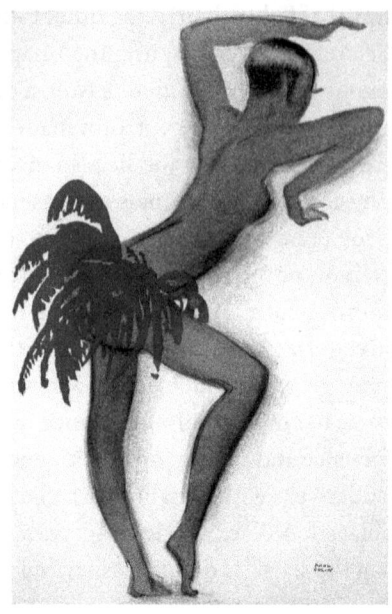

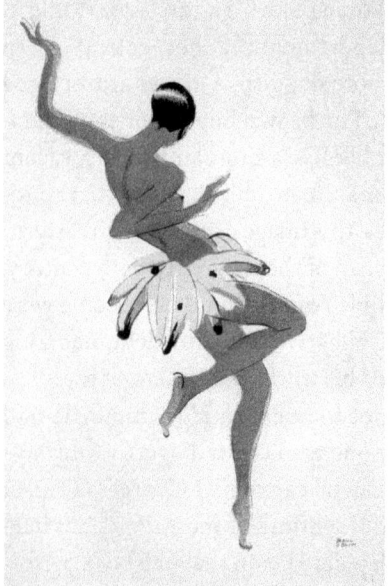

4.5 (*top left*) Paul Colin, "Josephine behind Bars," in *Le Tumulte Noir*, 1929. © Artists Rights Society (ARS), New York / ADAGP, Paris.

4.6 (*top right*) Paul Colin, "Josephine in a Palm-Tree Skirt," in *Le Tumulte Noir*, 1929. © Artists Rights Society (ARS), New York / ADAGP, Paris.

4.7 (*left*) Paul Colin, "Josephine in a Banana Skirt," in *Le Tumulte Noir*, 1929. © Artists Rights Society (ARS), New York / ADAGP, Paris.

photograph that features her lying on the floor in the nude with an intense stare on her face. Her fingers are curved and pointing downward as if to mirror the claws of a predatory animal and are strategically placed to cover her bosom. Baker is the symbol of Black savagery and sexual deviance here, participating in the construction of a persona that would benefit her career. Indeed, these evocations liken Baker to the pet leopard she owned and paraded on the streets of Paris.[86] During these outings, she successfully reified notions of the primitive that informed how she appeared in visual representations. By walking the leopard, Baker was ingeniously playing with the relative concepts of civilization and primitivism, since she displayed control over the animal realm by walking it and hence distinguished herself from association with the bestial.[87] All in all, it is impossible not to recognize the allusions to the jungle that characterized the conceptualization of blackness in the Western imaginary of the early twentieth century. This proved to be a critical aspect of Baker's public image and persona, and, when walking her pet leopard on the streets, she consciously melded her onstage and offstage identities in a way that foregrounded a tropicalist sensibility that was closely hinged to colonial conquest.

Baker's contrasting public image off the stage undoubtedly signifies an embodiment of Black modernity. She recalled the reactions people had of her at the opening-night reception for *La Revue Nègre*, for which she wore a stylish gown designed by the famous French designer Paul Poiret: "They stared at me open-mouthed. Was this the savage they had gaped at on the stage?"[88] She appears to feel empowered at this moment, commenting on the flattering reactions from men and the scornful glares from women. Baker was purposeful in creating a persona offstage that differed from the savage archetype she exemplified onstage, striving to appear what she deemed as civilized as possible in everyday life.[89] A lover of Paris fashions, Baker adored the pomp and ceremony inherent in the haute couture designs of the likes of Coco Chanel. Soon, the Baker effect was noticeable in the streets of Paris and Berlin as fashionable women covered their arms in bracelets and wore turbans, accessories the performer was famous for wearing.[90] Her impact on fashion and femininity in Europe was duly noted by Countee Cullen, who explained, "Paris is in a state of violent hysteria over her; there are Josephine Baker perfumes, costumes, bobs, statuettes; in fact, she sets the pace."[91] Baker's preoccupation with self-presentation was also cosmetic, given her obsession with keeping her skin light in complexion. She used and publicly endorsed skin lighteners

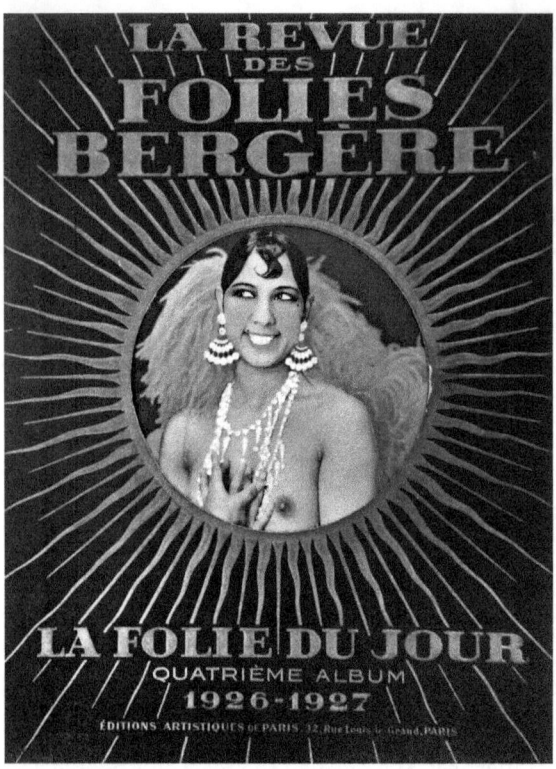

4.8 *La Folie du Jour* album cover, 1926. Courtesy
of the Wolfsonian Library, Florida International
University, University Park.

and alternative methods for doing so, although this went against the desire
of French audiences to the dark-skinned primitive onstage.[92]

In many instances, her modern offstage persona proved to be the antithesis of the primitive onstage persona in the same way the jungle was
deemed the antithesis of the metropole. Indeed, the very idea of transition-
ing from one facet of one's personality renders one ambiguous and indeci-
pherable, and it was a very modern notion for the early twentieth century.
When she incorporated these opposing sides of her image into her act,
this thwarted any possibilities of audience misconceptions.[93] Remnants
of her offstage persona are evident on the cover of the *La Folie du Jour* album from 1926 (figure 4.8). A gleaming Baker is pictured with her hair
coiffed in her signature hairstyle and decked in chandelier earrings, an
elaborate pearl necklace, and bracelets. While she is bare-chested, which
was typical of Folies Bergère female performers of the time, her costume

primarily consists of large aqua-blue feather plumes. This image captures the Black modernity inherent in her oeuvre and exhibits how adept she was in "fit[ting] the calculated incongruity between her two sides *into* her act to maximize its exposure."[94]

Since the enterprise of constructing Baker's imagery as a tropicalized other was rooted in a specific geographic location, which is entrenched in France's long-standing involvement in slavery and colonialism, costumes such as the famed banana skirt certainly emblematized tropicality. Originally conceived by Paul Colin and the French writer Jean Cocteau, the skirt was first worn by Baker early in her career, starting in the production *La Folie du Jour* in 1926 at the Folies Bergère, and it appeared in other iterations over the next ten years.[95] Folies Bergère offered its patrons escapist spectacles deeply ensconced in Orientalist forms of exotica, and the lavish extravaganzas were accented by extravagant decor of North African derivation that included luxuriant green plants and even a Turkish bath.[96] In addition, productions always included female performers who were nude from the waist up. A common practice in French music halls, nudity on the stage began in the nineteenth century with an annual contest of artists' models and eventually became a mainstream occurrence.[97]

Like all productions held at the Folies Bergère, the jungle spectacle *La Folie du Jour* was in many ways predicated on artifice and capricious frivolity. And quite a number of the shows presented at the music hall would often include the word *folie* in their titles.[98] In the French language, *folie* means madness and certainly connotes the psychological state Europeans often associated with the tropical regions of the world since the eighteenth century. Up until the early twentieth century, many held the belief that tropical heat would induce both physical and moral laxity, thereby leading to indolence and self-indulgence.[99] The name of the music hall as well as the production, *La Folie du Jour*, which translates to mean the madness of the day, undoubtedly contributes to the simulation of tropical parts of the world in the arena as well as the constructed knowledge that the exotic people who occupied these spaces embodied the antithesis of European civility.

Like other productions at the eminent music hall, *La Folie du Jour* was a large and costly one that featured more than five hundred performers with a budget of just over a half-million dollars. The set design for *La Folie du Jour* consisted of a dramatic view of thick tropical foliage with a large uprooted tree overrun with vines and moss taking up much of the middle ground as it is lying on its side (figure 4.9). A small portrayal of Baker can

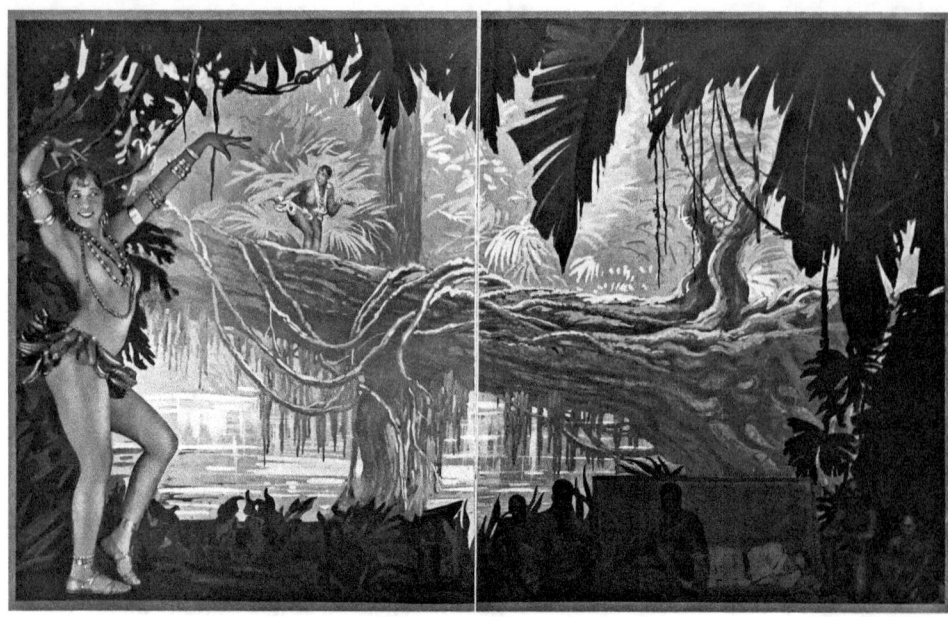

4.9 Josephine Baker in front of the set design for *La Folie du Jour*. From *La Folie du Jour* magazine, 1926. Courtesy of the Wolfsonian Library, Florida International University, University Park.

be seen playfully running along the tree's trunk but also trying to avoid falling into the body of water that flows beneath it. Just along the top foreground of the image are detailed renderings of leaves of various tropical plants, conveyed in such a way so as to extend the facsimile of tropicalia onto the stage. The tone of the colors is quite dark and it mirrors the dark colors used to render the other human figures, depicted in the lower foreground of the image. Seven figures can be seen either sitting or reclining on the ground, six of them of African descent looking straight toward the viewer while the lone white male figure, wearing a pith helmet, appears to be sleeping in a makeshift open tent. This vista not only exemplifies French colonial conquest in Africa but also characterizes the future colonial subjects as complicit in the colonialist project. Moreover, the African subjects appear indolent and docile, willing participants in this staging of fantasy-based exotica.

The jungle spectacle of *La Folie du Jour* began with two Black male drummers decked in loincloths positioned underneath a palm tree. While they beat their drums, Baker slowly reveals each limb and eventually her torso as she descends from a tree. The American poet E. E. Cummings attended the premiere and offered the following description of her performance: "She enters the show . . . through a dense electric twilight, walking backwards, on hands and feet, legs and arms stiff, down a huge jungle tree— as a creature neither infrahuman nor superhuman, but somehow both; a mysteriously unkillable Something, equally nonprimitive and uncivilized or, beyond time in the sense that emotion is beyond arithmetic."[100] She then proceeds to present her erotic repertoire of movements in a performance that actively engages with the backdrop. At one point, she moves toward the portion of the backdrop depicting the low-pitched tent where the colonialist sleeps, as if to satirically remind the audience of his vulnerable predicament of being outnumbered among cognizant African natives as well as an Africanized Baker. In the second act, a large egg-shaped ball painted in gold and decorated with flowers descended from the rafters, then slowly settled at the level of the orchestra. As the lid gradually opened, it revealed Baker, who was either crouched or standing in the mirrored interior. She wore gold bracelets, beaded necklaces, and a collection of realistic-looking bananas fastened around a waistband.[101] This particular number was very similar to the legendary "Danse des Sauvages" at the Champs-Élysées. Here, appearing as Fatou but without the partner, Baker exhibited the same level of energy and enthusiasm as she performed popular dances such as the Charleston and the black bottom, intermittently adding acrobatics and other antics.[102] The emphasis, however, lay on undulating pelvic movements, and as Baker explained, the banana skirt "slung low around my hips to accentuate my forward and backward movements."[103] Despite the fact that Baker participated in a common practice at the Folies Bergère by performing nude, she still nonetheless exemplified the unbridled sexuality and supposed primitivism that Black women and indeed Africa signified to Europe.

Baker's banana skirt ultimately became an indelible part of her performances and public image. The aesthetic structure of the skirt evolved in tandem with the evolution of Baker's career and artistic practice. While the original skirt consisted of realistic-looking bananas (figure 4.10), by the next year, they morphed into pointed spikes. In 1936 the costume changed yet again for Baker's performance at the Ziegfeld Follies, this time into a series of horizontal spikes that were donned with a pointed headpiece. In other versions of the costume, the bananas appear metallic and even bejeweled.[104] Within the framework of colonial and imperialist logic, the banana-attired Black body is often regarded as the edible, delectable other.

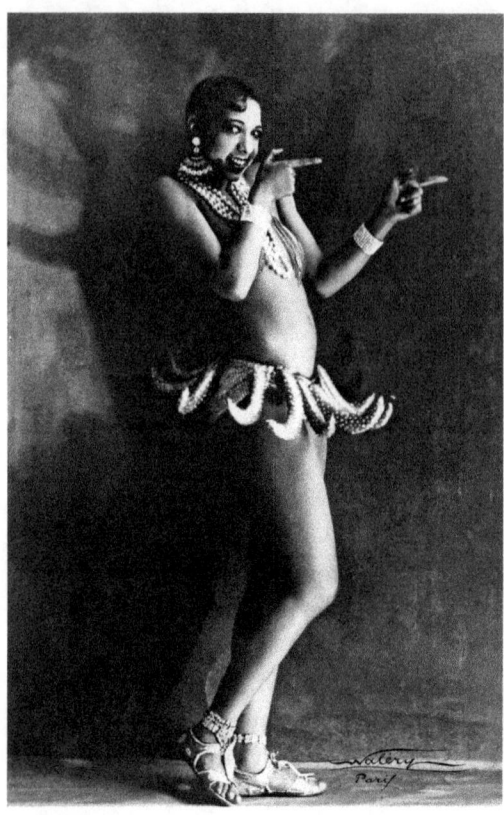

4.10 Josephine Baker wearing the banana skirt, *La Folie du Jour*, 1926. Photograph by Walery. © Bibliothèque Marguerite Durand / The Image Works.

For if the Black tropical subject is not the cannibal threat, conversely she is the consumable, tamed one; however, both relegate the tropical other to a subhuman state.[105] As Loichot reminds us, the banana skirt "both conceals the genitals and replaces them. They simultaneously strip subjects of their sex and impose upon them the fictionalized image of an unruly sexuality in a double movement of castration and grotesque exaggeration."[106] This reading can be further compounded when one considers how Baker would sometimes dress in men's suits and had female lovers.[107] Although the multiple phalli of the skirt at once signify the dichotomy of the effemization of the Black male through castration and alternatively his inherent hypermasculinization, her performance successfully emphasizes an appropriation of masculinity while also challenging heteronormativity.

In her judicious examination of Baker's oeuvre, Anne Anlin Cheng elucidates on the subject/object, viewer/viewed, colonizer/colonized paradigms around which Baker's fetishized performances orbited. Very pressing in her study is the possibility of Baker actively soliciting stereotypical expectations by wearing such ornamentation as the banana skirt. This prompts one to question the intentions of her primitivist performances, especially since, as Cheng rightly points out, it is highly probable that Baker may have gotten a different kind of pleasure from the costume. Acknowledging that racial fetishism allows for the fetishist to *have* and *be* that otherness, Cheng explains: "Instead of establishing a clear-cut dichotomy between viewer and view, subject and object, master and slave, the mise-en-scène actually enables and encapsulates a complex network of mediated desires and cross-narratives."[108]

These mediated desires and cross-narratives destabilize and even defile established dichotomies, and one can recognize the artistic cannibalism inherent in Baker's performance. In addition, Baker's Black body accentuated by the banana skirt provides an example of the tropics biting back through the disruption of the power dynamics at play. Rather than accept the pejorative value assigned to tropicality by European thought, tropical aesthetics allows us to think differently about how Baker exercised artistic cannibalism in an effort to consume reductive significations such as disparaging the tropical landscape and its association with the fetishized Black body.[109] Her performances could be viewed as fully engaged in recontextualizing these values in a way that is transformative, since it turns the colonial and imperialist logic of the fetishized Black body on its head. The pejorative connotations of the banana are at once attenuated as she dances across the stage in her costume in front of the simulated African jungle. Baker's corporeal expressions function as a ritualized devouring of significations embedded in the banana, the African tropical landscape, and, more important, the Black body. Furthermore, when considering the set design for *La Folie du Jour*, one can acknowledge how this replicated terrain conjures the idea of Africa as a homeland that connects Black people of all nationalities, such as those living in Paris, and signifies the possibility of Black sovereignty. This surreptitious ode to Africa reinstates the truth that all African-descended people in and out of the continent persistently engage in modern life.

The popular dances Baker sampled during her performances proved to be just as effective in demystifying the Black body's relation with tropical and subtropical landscapes. Most if not all of the popular dances that

Baker appropriated in her performances were rooted in the long-standing tradition during the eighteenth and nineteenth centuries of enslaved African Americans parodying the music and dancing of their white masters. An immensely popular dance in France, the cakewalk was originally a plantation harvest dance that combined the European quadrille with strutting imitations of the planters' class.[110] The Charleston lampooned the square dances of the planters' class in addition to Africanizing and reconceptualizing the quadrille.[111] What is fascinating about this early twentieth-century popular dance is that it is named after a city that was the epicenter for the American institution of slavery. The Charleston dance seems to encapsulate a ritualized yet subversive reclaiming of the land toiled by the ancestors of the people who created it. And the "unrefinement" of this dance genre reflected the supposed primitivism whites thought African Americans inherently possessed, given the perceived awkwardness of their performances. However, as literary scholar Michael Borshuk argues, in the spirit of slaves parodying the dances and actions of their masters, the Charleston does not highlight the "failure for the black performer to emulate the 'innate' grace of whites [but] the performer's movements instead exaggerate white sophistication itself as affected instead of inherent."[112] Baker continued this tradition in her performances by expanding on the parodying of white affectations that ultimately called into question the notion of white superiority.[113]

Undoubtedly, performing on stage was an immersive experience for Baker, who sometimes approached her acts as exercises of athletic endurance.[114] Her decision to improvise her performances by incorporating antics that were established parts of her repertoire not only demonstrates her innovative rigor but also is telling of how dancing allowed for transformation and self-assertion, an expression of modernity in her own terms via the body "in and against its environment."[115] She was also keenly aware of the constructions created around Black women's sexuality and steadfastly personified the "sexual beast that needed to be captured or contained."[116] There is an appropriation of stereotypes at play here whereby her repertoire of bodily movements ambiguously serves as commentary on these dehumanizing portrayals, despite the reductive ways in which the audience must have consumed her on stage. Baker's performances adeptly "diminish[ed] the negative power of governing stereotypes . . . by situating herself at the exaggerated limits of those distorted representations."[117] To this end, Jayna Brown's appeal that one should "allow these artists an interiority, to understand their agency" is valuable, including her assessment that "on the black variety stage, racial authenticity and gendered imitation, natural proclivity and skillful artifice frequently interchanged and remained ambiguous."[118] It is this ambiguity, or this liminal space that performances such as this occupied in the sphere of European popular culture, that bolstered the performers with a level of clout, however temporary this power would last. The stage thus becomes a domain that they can occupy in order to experience cultural power and freedom.[119] The stage is therefore a locus for the marvelous real, during which certain categories of reality become amplified, making this cultural power a potent force.[120]

While Baker ingeniously delegitimized pseudoscientific claims of Black female sexual deviance and Black inferiority through her bodily movements on stage, her performances should also be viewed as blaring repudiations of the jungle construct. Black performers would have been keenly aware of how their bodies signified conventional understandings of the African jungle, the locale indicative of the primeval, which supposedly justified the atavistic tendencies of Black folk.[121] Therefore, they fully immersed themselves into the creation of the jungle spectacle, and Baker incited such spectacles during her performances. As mentioned earlier, Black dance forms such as the cakewalk and the Charleston sociopolitically commented on the supposed preeminence of the Europeans. Yet they also effectively served as ritualized acts of making space, a way of giving the depreciated terrains of Africa and even the southern United States a new kind of eminence. The frenetic motions of Black performers as they commanded the stages that were transformed into jungle spectacles could be interpreted as dancing Black bodies working to challenge "geographies of domination" and their attenuation of Black people's geographies.[122] Through the dynamic gestures emitted while performing the Charleston or the cakewalk, these dancers called to mind the parodying not only of the white masters during slavery but also of the land the planters claimed as their own, which under the Eurocentric hegemonic order deemed white populations as geographic and Black populations as inherently ungeographic.[123]

Indeed, the transformation of the French music hall into the ungeographic domain of the jungle via the sound of jazz music, the jungle imagery of the set design, and the frenzied dancing of Black performers all worked in concert to bring into fruition the world of mythic Black primitivism. Every night, the Music-Hall des Champs-Élysées essentially became a simulated version of the imagined primitivist Africa and the southern United States. There is something carnivalesque and parodying about these jungle spectacles, especially since Paris was a Black transnation all its own. While performers adhered to the desired misrepresentations of blackness that the white audiences wanted to see, after curtain call, they would go to neighborhoods such as Montmartre and Montparnasse, where Black modernity was fully practiced and embodied. Once World War I ended, many Black American soldiers moved to Paris, where jazz music, minstrelsy, and vaudeville performances gained popularity at a steady pace. The majority of them earned their livelihood as musicians, singers, and entertainers in these arenas.[124]

By the 1920s, the number of Black entertainers traveling from the United States increased significantly, and there were also performers coming from the Caribbean, Latin America, and Africa. Collectively they discovered the favorable working conditions in the Paris entertainment world. Like Baker, they lived in La Butte, the nickname people used to refer to Montmartre. The area previously made famous by bohemian artists and writers of the prewar era who eventually moved across the Seine to the Latin Quarter would become home to Black Atlantic entertainers who found accommodations in cheap hotels and rooming houses.[125] The sounds and dance moves of Harlem, Havana, and Fort-de-France now became commonplace in the French capital. For many, it was not unusual to run into people one knew from one's home country. One reporter from the *Pittsburgh Courier* noted, "The Boulevard de Clichy is the 42nd and Broadway of Paris. Most of the night life of Paris centers around it, and most of the colored folks from the States, too. If you hear that some friend from the States is in Paris, just circulate around this boulevard from the Moulin Rouge down Rue Pigalle as far as the Flea Pit. . . . And it is a hundred to one shot that you'll encounter him or her, at least twice during the night."[126]

Evidently, early twentieth-century Paris evolved into a nucleus of the Black transnation, where the people of the Black Atlantic and their cultural forms began shaping the cultural milieu of the French city.[127] For Nardal, this phenomenon was the manifestation of Black *latinité*, a neologism she created that was a call for racial consciousness. The term first appeared in an essay she authored on Black internationalism in 1928 in which she astutely thanks white elitists for their fascination with Black art, music, and dance that took over the French music halls and in so doing united Black people from different parts of the Atlantic through an acknowledgment of their common origin of Africa.[128] Given the inevitability of the various exchanges that developed among Black people from Africa, the Americas, and the Caribbean who lived in Paris, Nardal believed in the possibility of Black latinité galvanizing into a "transnational circuit of Black modern culture among intellectuals whose . . . education has not necessarily driven them to deny their race."[129]

Black latinité offers a refreshing way of contextualizing Josephine Baker's performances in the context of early twentieth-century Paris. In addition, Nardal's concept of Black latinité is worthwhile for appreciating the cultural practice of Black internationalism in large Black diasporic communities such as what existed in Montmartre. It makes plausible Carpentier's pronouncement of how the marvelous real could usher in an "unexpected alteration of reality" that can occur due to the "exaltation of the spirit that leads it to a kind of extreme state."[130] This amplification of a perceived reality perhaps typifies the experience members of the Black transnation would have encountered in Montmartre, particularly when one heard the music from one's home country among the cacophony of sounds from the Black diaspora, not to mention seeing familiar faces from your respective countries. Indeed, an established link was created between Paris, Africa, and the various countries of the Americas.

Through ritualized embodiments of tropicalia, Baker and Angelou reproduced imperial identities even while contesting and undermining conventional understandings of Black people who lived in these tropical terrains. Their dynamic and provocative bodily expressions generated the symbolic sovereignty of Pan-Africa, an affinity many early twentieth-century Black people necessitated. Indeed, both Angelou and Baker performed constructions of blackness and Black otherness that they did not ultimately control. At the same time, they were among many Black performers who participated in and contributed to discourses of the primitive.[131] As Ménil insists in his hypothesis of early twentieth-century poetry from the Caribbean, "we assume the same image for ourselves and simply embellish it differently. Usually we are content with simply reversing the colors and quantities whilst maintaining the colonialists' image."[132] Through words uttered and performances generated, these individuals did in fact agree with postulations about the existence of primitive societies while also questioning the validity of such claims. Such conundrums in the experiences of early twentieth-century Black performers are constant reminders that "ideologies of power rooted in hierarchy and racism can at times coexist with agendas to assert racial equality and Black humanity even as the very terms of representations insist upon the opposite."[133] Ultimately, shifts inevitably occurred in the way Black people molded their identities, insisting that one developed a strong sense of place in this endeavor.

CONCLUSION * *The Black Body, Tropicality,*
and the Black Speculative

Black Atlantic artists and performers of the Caribbean and the United States created imaginative art that responded to colonial and hegemonic regimes using a tropicalist oeuvre. Their creative manifestations privileged the land and how a sense of place was critical in their early twentieth-century identity formations. Aaron Douglas, Wifredo Lam, Josephine Baker, Maya Angelou, and masqueraders and designers of Trinidad Carnival unquestionably contributed to the development of modernism. Tropicality encourages a new understanding of the African diasporic experience, one that connects the Black Atlantic with Africa. Tropicality therefore reorients the Pan-African world as one that is inherently modern. Early twentieth-century Black Atlantic peoples sought to engender a sense of belonging to the citizenry and a particular kind of claim to the land that they inhabit that speaks to a desire for home.

Since geography in a material and discursive sense is never fully secure, given that three-dimensional space is socially produced, the idea that belonging to a place could lead to a sociospatial liberation is seldom realized for many Black people. Due to these limitations, tropical aesthetics allows for a reification of social geographies by manifesting "alternative geographic formulations."[1] In many ways, this reconceptualization of the physical realm is demonstrative of Afro-Atlantic speculation, a series of imaginings that envision a return to Africa, given the need to perceive tropicalia as desirable and utopic, indeed a place to which one could escape.[2] The concept of tropical aesthetics offers an emboldened means to project affirmative identity politics for a people so often linked to equatorial regions of the world that were also disparaged. By eradicating reductive visual representations of Black Atlantic peoples and the land they inhabit, tropical aesthetics brings about a reclamation of humanity and dignity. This becomes plausible through the Afro-Atlantic speculative turn whereby Black people located in various regions across the Black Atlantic imagine and reconfigure in order to remember Africa.[3] The terrain and an affinity to place were crucial in the identity formation of early twentieth-century Black Atlantic peoples. Visual artists and performers of this period fortified their grounding through creative expressions that epitomized Black social, cultural, and political autonomy in societies marred by institutionalized subjugation. These artists' and performers' ingenious endeavors sought to challenge the precept that the tropical terrains of the world—otherwise disparagingly referred to as jungles—were not sites of danger, disease, and moral laxity. Rather, tropicalia should be characterized as possessing salient features that are full of beauty, promise, and grandeur.

In keeping with that idea, this conclusion considers iterations of tropicality evident in contemporary visual art. Given that misconceptions about the terrains of equatorial regions still persist, quite a number of postmodern artists create works that interrogate the production of this knowledge and in turn complicate and reconfigure its signification through the visual realm. First, I explore the significance of Brazil's Tropicalism movement, which was galvanized by artist Hélio Oiticica in the 1960s. The prolific movement aspired to cannibalize foreign modern and contemporary artistic styles, which they believed would eventually redeploy the power of the colonizers in an effort to create a new art of Brazil. Although this movement is particular to the idiosyncrasies of the Brazilian art world of the mid-twentieth century, it can be seen as an example of a larger cultural effort to challenge the reductive connotations of cultural forms imposed by the West and in turn redefine these meanings to create a new signification. I thus consider the cultural and political context from which Oiticica and the Tropicalism movement came into being by examining the efforts made as early as the 1920s in defining a Brazilian art that reflected a nationalist imperative. I then examine Oiticica's artistic and political inclination that led to the creation of his seminal work, *Tropicália*.

Another artist who aspired to demystify imposed significations of tropicality in the contemporary imaginary is the Haitian-born Edouard Duval-Carrié. A series of striking compositions he created in 2014 seeks to excavate and transform nineteenth-century renderings of landscapes of Latin America, the southern United States, and the Caribbean, renderings that have in turn contributed to how tropical landscapes are archetypically represented even today. Duval-Carrié transformed the works of Frederic Edwin Church, Martin Johnson Heade, and others into mural-size duplicates created primarily with multiple aluminum square panels and silver glitter. In doing so, the artist forces the viewer to look at the terrain and its accompanying greenery in a different way while also acknowledging the lives of the indigenous populations and enslaved Africans who endured many atrocities on these landscapes. Finally, I investigate two works of Kenyan artist Wangechi Mutu. Known for his thought-provoking imagery, Mutu created fantastic multimedia pieces that portray otherworldly environments that lend to the notion of the Black speculative. These imaginative landscapes coupled with the hybrid beings that inhabit them tackle a variety of subject matter, including the impact of colonization and the eroticization of the Black female body. While the imaginative landscapes are not geographically specific, they are most often references to the African terrain. Given that African people have always been disparaged for having a deep affinity with nature, since this countered how Europeans perceived its purpose in society, Mutu's art masterfully challenges this dichotomy while also underscoring how fundamental the natural landscape is to the progression of humanity and its civilizations.

*

Understanding the politics of Brazilian national identity and efforts in national self-making that began in the late nineteenth century is necessary to truly grasp the counterideological stance that Oiticica's oeuvre catalyzed decades later. Indeed, as is often the case in most societies, the significance of modernity largely depends on particular histories and mythologies associated with nationalism. In Brazil, stakeholders wanted desperately to rid the image of the country as a spectacle of exotic nature and instead promulgate the notion of an empire of commerce and enterprise. The country soon became invested in organizing itself through machine and technology and particularly through urban and industrial development.[4]

Despite this modernist turn, a burgeoning sentiment against the European ideal was growing among Brazil's modernist creative enclave. Members of the artistic and literary circles sought an alternative ideology to the discourses interrogating the "national problem" and wanted to create cultural forms that reflected Brazilian realities. Although artists, writers, musicians, and architects looked to Europe for artistic inspiration, they denounced the stereotypes Europeans often associated with Brazilian cultural and creative forms. This ultimately set the tone for creative innovation that was untethered from any European influence.[5] At the helm of this undertaking was Oswald de Andrade, a poet and leader of the modernist group. His "Pau-Brazil Poetry Manifesto" of 1922 championed a positionality that was liminal in orientation, that is, between the tropical and the modern. For him, poetry should be "like the country, barbaric and modern, skeptical and naïve, 'of the jungle' and 'of the school.'"[6] As discussed in chapter 2, Andrade also published his "Manifesto Antropófago" (Cannibalist Manifesto) in 1928 in which he challenged the binary opposites that have characterized Brazil's relationship with Europe since the colonial era. Andrade espoused on the benefits of anthropophagism, a cannibalism that literally and figuratively absorbs the "sacred enemy." For him, anthropophagism is revitalizing and liberates the mind in an effort to spawn creativity, and Andrade effectively situates cannibalism in the limitless bounds of sentiment that defy the rigidity of academic conformity.[7]

This ideological framework proved to be just as significant decades later to Brazilian musicians, writers, and artists of the 1960s. One artist in particular, Hélio Oiticica, cites his rediscovery of Andrade's "Cannibalist Manifesto" as being immensely profound for him, particularly because of "the critical and political consciousness that emerged with it."[8] This consciousness is indicative of a unique and constructive will, a characteristic Oiticica asserts is found in innovative movements, including the movement led by Andrade that epitomized the reduction of all external influences in Brazilian creative forms. In 1967 Oiticica used the term New Objectivity to refer to the formulation that encapsulated the efforts of the Brazilian avant-garde who aimed to foster a general creative state that would ultimately aid in developing a distinct cultural milieu.[9] For Oiticica, the avant-garde was not an issue for the elite but a broad cultural issue; he deemed that the avant-garde should seek dialogue using a broader cultural constitution. Indeed, he firmly believed that popular culture would become the means through which artists could revolutionize the contents of their practices, and in doing so, they could attract a wider audience. Given the political state of the country in the 1960s with its repressive government, Oiticica's main impetus was to reconsider the very conceptualization of Brazilian culture as well as its national identity, which is crucial for bringing about significant transformation in the arts.[10]

Such a decisive trajectory for the Brazilian avant-garde eventually led to the emergence of the Tropicalism movement. The goal of the movement was "to fashion itself as a mechanism capable of incorporating—assimilating anthropophagically and therefore selectively—the complex totality of Brazilian cultural reality, with the goal of unleashing a process of radical transformation."[11] And this endeavor would mean envisioning both culture and national identity as being in a constant state of development and evolution, not with a resolve to search for origins, so often associated with the European model, but to selectively incorporate cultural influences from the world over.[12] Indeed, this widely held claim that Europe is the custodian of originality, which is dependent on the precept that artists of the periphery are mere imitators, has been challenged by scholars of many disciplines who have evidenced European masters appropriating the works of others.[13] Nonetheless, Oiticica was steadfast in his confidence of what Tropicalism could accomplish, asserting that "it is the consciousness of not being conditioned by established structures, hence it is highly revolutionary in its entirety. Any conformity, be it intellectual, social, or existential, is contrary to its principal idea."[14] This "name-monument," as curator Carlos Basualdo refers to the movement, ought to be seen less as a musical or visual aesthetic form and more as a collective cultural project that was implemented in the last years of the 1960s.[15] It is telling that this venture, which refused to adhere to the established structures of the European and American art worlds, is in many ways aligned with the earnest undertakings of the artists and performers I have explored in this book. They employed tropical aesthetics not only to recontextualize the portrayals of equatorial territories but also to geopolitically unite disparate regions of the Black Atlantic with the African continent in order to achieve a sense of belonging that they could not achieve in the Western world, thereby fortifying their sense of identity and purpose. Similarly, Tropicalism advocated for creativity within the context of the natural landscape and the people of Brazil who contributed to the formation of the culture. This was essential to the Brazilian avant-garde earning a radical presence when juxtaposed with the more powerful international avant-garde.

This simulation of one's desired environment is ultimately what Oiticica pursued with his iconic work, *Tropicália* (1966–67) (figure C.1). His signature artwork proved to be a manifestation of his concept of New Objectivity and unabashedly buttressed the quintessential Brazilian image within the context of the Brazilian avant-garde.[16] Without question, this was a bold gesture on the part of Oiticica since he reclaimed the Brazilian landscape and the architecture of the favelas (squatter housing on the hillside of Rio de Janeiro) by incorporating them into the artwork. The piece consists primarily of two structures, which he referred to as *penetrables*, or something that can be penetrated by the spectator. They are both surrounded by an experimental image field in which he created a stereotypical tropical environment with soil, tropical plants, live macaws, and pebbles. The first *penetrable*, PN2 "Purity is a Myth," is an open-roofed square booth with the words "Purity is a Myth" stenciled on its surface

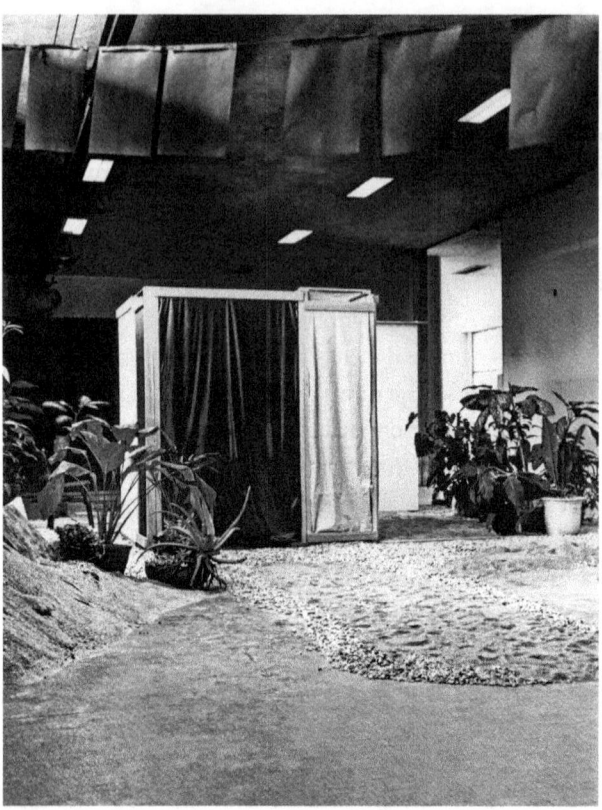

c.1 Hélio Oiticica, *Tropicália*, 1966–67. Installation view of the Exhibition Nova Objetividade Brasileira, Museo de Arte Moderna, Rio de Janeiro. Reproduced from the archives of the Projeto Hélio Oiticica.

and accessed with a swinging door. One would then continue this multisensory experience upon entering the second, much larger *penetrable*, PN3 "Imagético." This is composed of a small labyrinth and incorporates the architecture of the favelas in its construction. The spectator enters a small corridor and as one ventures further, the hall darkens. Within the walls of the labyrinth, the corridors become narrower and there is a gradual loss of light and air. Toward the end of the last corridor, the spectator sees the flickering glow and hears the low sounds of a television set.[17] Oiticica asserts that "it is the image which then devours the participant, because it is more active than his sensorial activity. Actually, this *Penetrable* gave me the powerful sensation of being devoured."[18]

It is clear that for Oiticica, this existential life experience of penetrating this work is so grandiose that not only do you devour everything you see, but the "Brazilian" image perpetuated in the visual culture of that era ultimately devours you. This notion is crucial and indelibly linked to the fact that the *Tropicália* is an experience tethered to its persuasiveness as an image.[19] Oiticica opined that *Tropicália* objectified a total "Brazilian" image, "resulting in the downfall of the universalist myth of Brazilian culture, which was a product of the European and North American mind."[20] Defiantly, this work aspired to eradicate that myth in an effort to reclaim the "Brazilian" image *for* Brazil. This is put in better context when one considers the choice of the word *penetrable* to refer to the structures that comprise the piece. This term is filled with colonialist connotation, particularly with regard to the gender-assigned power dynamics of who is penetrating and who is being penetrated. If one were to personify the spectator as the one who is penetrating in this affectation, in the end, the penetrator/colonizer/Western world is devoured by the "Brazilian" image on the T V set.

Oiticica poignantly articulated his experience of traversing through the *penetrables* as a sensation of "'treading the earth' once again."[21] This powerful declaration of an affinity to the Earth in many ways mirrors the early twentieth-century ideas of the Caribbean surrealists Aimé and Suzanne Césaire. The former wrote candidly about how Caribbean identity was rooted in the soil as it is the nucleus of the landscape, while the latter epitomized the relationship between man and the natural environment with the term *plant-man* since the plant is the means through which humanity can be redeemed and empowered.[22] Undoubtedly, Oiticica's ideological posturing is in tandem with those of the Césaires, given their celebration of the terrain and national identity as well as their shared intolerance for anti-imperialism. These ruminations are undeniably reflected in Oiticica's aspirations for Brazilian art of the 1960s: "Ever since I invented the term *Tropicália* . . . , I wanted to accentuate this new language with Brazilian elements, down to its smallest details, in an extremely ambitious attempt to create a language that would be ours, characteristic of us, that would stand up to the images of international pop and op, in which a good many of our artists were submerged."[23] These monumental possibilities the artist saw in the Tropicalism movement are in keeping with how Oiticica thought his art and, in turn, the movement should be deciphered. For him, the visual language to which he refers should not be limited to the image alone. While it is indeed important in his work, Oiticica believed that the image should always be deferential to the lived experience.[24] This is crucial, given the significance he placed on Tropicália Synthesis, a concept that acknowledges not only the "Brazilian" image but also everything that encompasses the visual richness of Brazil. So, ultimately, Tropicália is not an artistic movement but something greater that is a synthesis of cinema, theater, plastic arts, and pop music.[25]

Oiticica grew increasingly skeptical of the popularity of the movement in Brazilian culture. The media's focus on the representational attributes of Tropicalism troubled him deeply, since what often emerged was "the glorification of the bananas."[26] Yet it is this reductive tendency that critics of the movement, like Roberto Schwartz, recognized as inevitable, since the oeuvre of Tropicalism combined the archaic and the modern. While the movement was indeed radical in many ways, the effort to establish an idiosyncratically Brazilian avant-garde practice based on the "backwardness of the country" may not have been an effective way of recuperating past attempts at national modernization. Schwartz reckoned that it was typical of Tropicalism to uphold a notion of a "Brazilian poverty" that equally victimizes the rich and the poor.[27] One resounding point Schwartz seems to be highlighting is that Oiticica and other members of the Tropicalism movement are appropriating, exploiting, and to a certain extent even romanticizing the culture and aesthetics of Brazil's poor in order to revolutionize their art. Whether or not this is the case, it is clear that Oiticica's ideologies continued to shift and evolve even after the demise of the movement. He already started reassessing the problematic binary opposites of the archaic (or underdeveloped) and the modern prior to the publication of Schwartz's remarks on the Tropicalism movement. Specifically, his focus shifted from the visual qualities of the architecture of the favelas to utilizing the conceptual framework of them as a source of innovation.[28]

All in all, Oiticica was committed to carving out a space for Brazil among the international avant-garde by privileging the land, the working class, and a variety of cultural forms, ultimately going against the auspices of the art establishment. Perhaps this is why the true ethos of the movement did not gain momentum in the Brazilian cultural sphere and also why Tropicalism only lasted a few years. Nevertheless, it characterized the art of Brazil in the late 1960s.

Tropicalism is in no way Pan-Africanist in orientation. While it did venerate the natural environment of equatorial Brazil as a means to transform art-making in the country, the movement's aspirations for an international profile did not include developing a transnational agenda. At the same time, Tropicalism was unabashedly anti-imperialist and seemed to also celebrate a type of Third-Worldism that is particular to Brazil and even to Latin America at large. And the period during which Tropicalism emerged should not go unnoticed. This was a moment of military governments in Latin America, decolonization in the Caribbean and Africa, and numerous social and political movements in other parts of the globe, including the Third World. Even the Pan-Africanism movement's endeavors attenuated by the 1960s due to the energies in various countries being channeled toward attaining independence and civil rights. Yet the efforts of Tropicalism's stakeholders illuminate Brazil's affiliation with other similarly nonaligned nations that were relegated to a Third World identity. Due to the hierarchical nature of the First World and Second World categories, the explicit peripheralization of Third World nations meant that proactive steps had to be taken for them to withstand any vulnerability to the oppositional policies of countries like the United States. The Non-Aligned Movement (NAM) was one such gesture, and the nation-state members aimed to promote economic and cultural cooperation and to collectively work against colonialism, neocolonialism, and any form of hegemony.[29] In this sense, Tropicalism should be valued for its efforts to empower the social and cultural fabric of Brazil, especially with its refusal to adhere to Western aesthetic standards.

Brazil's Tropicalism movement also continues the agenda of early twentieth-century artists and performers who challenged the Western-oriented construction of the tropics, recognized the crucial linkage between land and identity, and understood the crucial role nature played in defining modernity in the Global South. Like the artistic renderings of tropical nature created by the likes of Wifredo Lam and Aaron Douglas, Oiticica's simulated garden in *Tropicália* positively manipulates tropical nature in order to propose alternative possibilities. Signified as culturally backward, the tropical landscape can at once be regarded as a space of modernity since human beings emphatically claim it as a civilization. I find Nancy Leys Stepan's idea of offering an alternative view of nature that activates different binary oppositions and dichotomies—such as the natural and the cultural, the given and the made, the temperate and the tropical—in an effort to destabilize and recombine them useful here. This effectively signifies tropical nature's complexity.[30] Just as in Stepan's readings of Brazilian landscape architect Burle Marx, it is important to examine how contemporary artists manipulate tropical nature to suggest alternative possibilities and thereby claim it as emblematic of civilization.[31] These artists are reconstituting the tropical landscape.

Haitian artist Edouard Duval-Carrié's series of paintings, which were featured in the exhibition *Edouard Duval-Carrié: Imagined Landscapes* at the Pérez Art Museum Miami in 2014, pursues this task of reconstitution through his clever excavation and transformation of certain nineteenth-century portrayals of landscapes of the Caribbean, Latin America, and the southern United States. American artists such as Frederic Edwin Church, Martin Johnson Heade, and Albert Bierstadt traveled to these regions to explore the aesthetic possibilities of the tropical terrains. Their representations of the physical arrangements were not only portrayals of the natural world but also the artist's projections of values and hopes as well as implicit fears and needs.[32] The paintings of these artists featured tropical scenery depicted with microscopic detail and a level of accuracy that reflected the dominant philosophy that privileged nature, which many believed to be synonymous with God.[33] At the same time, even though Europeans and European Americans viewed these parts of the world as tropical Edens characterized by an exotic otherness, the term *tropical* eventually connoted negativity and darkness by the eighteenth century.[34] The aesthetic breakthroughs that these paintings signify are very much connected to the political and economic interests of the colonial and imperialist nations of this era. Today, the connotations the tropics elicit are now entrenched in the collective imaginary of non-Caribbean and Caribbean peoples alike, and the legacies of colonialism and imperialism are certainly ever-present in representations of the Caribbean found in tourist advertising, films, and television.[35]

Duval-Carrié's paintings interpolate these historical renderings that have defined the Caribbean landscape for centuries, creating panoramic imagery that, although explicitly referencing compositions of nineteenth-century American painters, resolutely offers an unorthodox rumination of these geographical spaces. This body of work is not far removed from the previous artworks created by the Haitian-born artist, since the natural landscape of Haiti is a notable characteristic of his oeuvre. Given the tradition of exploring the natural terrain that came to the fore during the Haiti indigenist art and literary movements of the 1920s and 1930s, one can situate Duval-Carrié's art within a larger framework of Haitian art practice. The works of artists such as André Pierre and Philomé Obin were inspired by scenes from rural life as well as the flora and fruits that surrounded them.[36] Indeed, their art illuminated the poetic and the marvelous of Haiti, revealing the complexities of Haitian subjectivity despite the realities that constituted their everyday lives. Although the landscapes are often depicted in an idyllic, almost Eden-like manner, Duval-Carrié has stated that such depictions may be a critique of the actual state of Haiti at this historical moment.[37]

This particular political and economic conundrum that Haiti was experiencing in the early twentieth century could be tied to the country's colonial history, and Duval-Carrié's decision to focus on the era of European colonial conquest in the Caribbean is significant, since it was during this time when a particular visual vocabulary used to render the physical environment in the region was invented and soon became systemic in the history of art-making throughout the region. For Duval-Carrié, it was important to "revisit the artists that were pioneering that kind of genre."[38] However, it was important in this reexamination for him to "void these paintings of color, and the only way [he] could do it is to make them at night."[39]

The artist created the large mural-size works with multiple aluminum square panels that were painted matte black. He would then manipulate silver glitter and glue to paint the dense vegetation. For him, it was reminiscent of greenery shining after rainfall. Thin applications of aqua and royal blue would be applied to various sections of the background that required a sense of spatial depth. Once the composition was complete, Duval-Carrié would treat each panel with a thick, clear acrylic coating that created a smooth and reflective surface. The overall visual effect is striking, with the reflective glitter creating a dynamic contrast with the deep blackness of the background.[40]

This is evident in Duval-Carrié's *After Heade—Moonlit Landscape* (2013) (figure C.2). The composition directly references Martin Johnson Heade's *View from Fern-Tree Walk, Jamaica* (1887). The nineteenth-century American landscape painter created this work for his new patron, the industrialist Henry Morrison Flagler, and Heade set out to give his best effort in the work by showcasing his penchant for detail that references an earlier era of American art. The artist created a vision of the tropics that is benign and welcoming, featuring an enclave of dense tropical foliage on the left that opens up to calm seas, all of which emit a warm and hazy glow from a warm sunlight.[41] Like other artistic visions of the New World, there appears to be an absence of people in the composition, which would ultimately give the viewer the experience of "discovering" an exotic paradise for the first time.[42] In fact, Heade's romantic imagery was created with

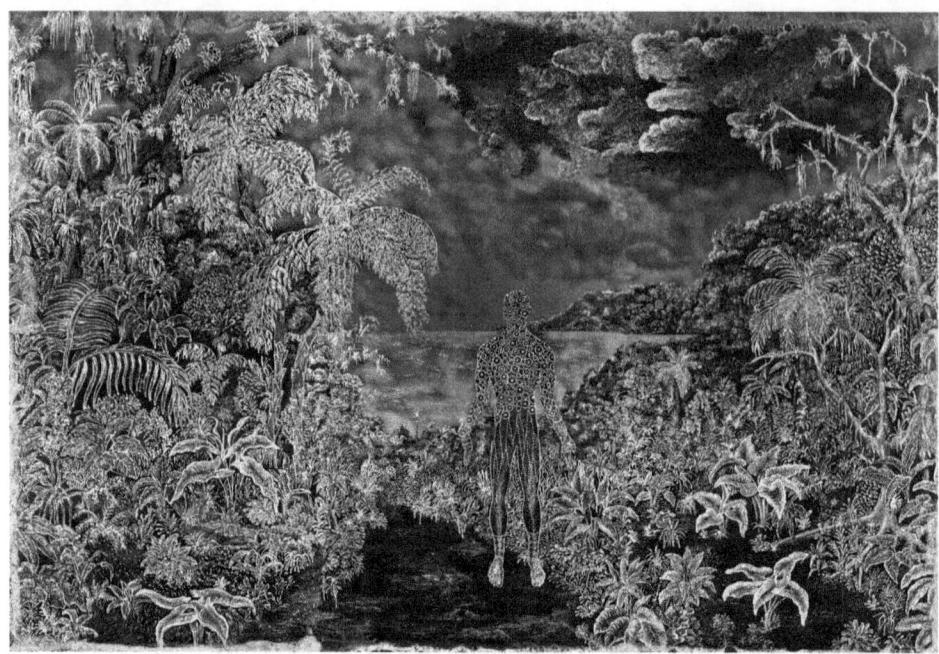

C.2 Edouard Duval-Carrié, *After Heade—Moonlit Landscape*, 2013.
Mixed media on aluminum, 96 × 144 in. Courtesy of the artist.

the intention of enticing his wealthy northern patron to someday visit the Caribbean island.[43]

The monochromatic color scheme in Duval-Carrié's *After Heade* re-orients the viewing practices often used for these panoramic paintings. The composition does use the same kind of precision and attention to detail found in the landscape painter's work. Given the limited palette, the contrast of the silver against the dark background compels the viewer to visually register the various flora being depicted in a strikingly new way. The predominant use of black recalls the monochromatic tradition in modernism as well as the reductive canvases of 1960s art movements such as hard-edge abstraction and minimalism.[44] What is interesting about Duval-Carrié's rendering of the vegetation is the heightened detailing of the configuration of each and every leaf, vine, stem, and flower, with the inclusion of shrubbery that is not even noticeable in Heade's original. On some level, Duval-Carrié's *After Heade* recalls the meticulous drawings that would accompany the texts of natural scientists of the Enlightenment period. However, here the imagery is deconstructive, revealing what is not shown in the sun-kissed vistas rendered by the likes of Heade, Church, and others. Against a deep-blue sky, the X-ray-like imaging the artist created on the picture plane is revelatory, as it allows for recognition of and a memorial for the Caribbean terrain as a signifier of a violent and painful past marred with the extermination of most of the native population, the importation of enslaved Africans within the institution of slavery, and the devastation of the natural terrain due to the exploits of the plantation-based economies.[45]

For Duval-Carrié, there is symbolism in the matte-black background and its evocation of shadow since there is "history in the shadows" and "the spirits are witness" to history. The figure standing prominently in the center of the composition is emblematic of the spirits of the members of the First Nations (the Amerindians) of the Caribbean as well as the spirits of enslaved Africans who the artist believes still occupy the natural terrain. In his native Haiti, people claim to see the spirits of the people whose land was stolen from them. The presence of these people is very much part of the lore in Haiti.[46] Duval-Carrié's series *Imagined Landscapes* is a testament to the lives of the native population and their continued reclamation of the land, even in the afterlife. Such a depiction of these people with the unique graphic markings recalls the human figures seen in the elaborate compositions of Cuban artist Belkis Ayón. Using the arduous technique of collagraphy, which combines relief and printmaking, Ayón created captivating scenes that featured subjects whose skin bore serpent-like design motifs. Although her works featured limited palettes of gradients of gray, black, and white, the scenes depicted were captivating, as they revolved around Abakuá, a Black Cuban secret religious fraternity. In works such as *La Cena* (The Dinner) (1991), Ayón's subjects are female and mouthless to represent the absence of women in the secret society.[47] Like Ayón, Duval-Carrié wants to commemorate the lives of marginalized peoples whose existence and contributions have been delegitimized by hegemonic systems of power. Such a representation of these marginalized peoples' physicality offers an iconographic means of memorializing the nameless and forgotten.

In *After Heade—The Great Florida Marsh* (2013) (plate 7), Duval-Carrié is affectively linking Florida to the Caribbean and the legacy of exploitation of both the people and the tropical terrains in this region of the world.[48] The composition borrows from Heade's *The Great Florida Marsh* (1886), which was also commissioned by his patron Flagler and was one of the largest pieces in Heade's studio.[49] Heade created this painting a few years after moving to Florida; it features moss-draped oaks, palms, palmettos, and the freshwater swamps that are so typical of the area surrounding the St. Johns River. Both Heade and Flagler were among the majority of tourists to Florida who would count a boat ride down the river as a first experience in the region. It thus makes sense why Flagler selected this view of St. Johns for the commissioned artwork, since he would eventually play an instrumental role in opening the area to development.[50] The artist used a style reminiscent of the realist paintings of the Barbizon School and the impressionists, yet he is able to present an interpretation of a quintessential Florida landscape.[51] However, unlike Heade's *View from Fern-Tree Walk, Jamaica*, *The Great Florida Marsh* conjures a sense of desolation and austerity with the darkness overpowering the lower-left section of the composition, from which emerge bulbous bottoms of trees, clumps of bushes, and winding branches that along with the remainder of the composition are collectively coated with a yellowish haze.[52]

In contrast to the somber tone of Heade's *The Great Florida Marsh*, Duval-Carrié's *After Heade—The Great Florida Marsh* incorporates colors that are more salient and offer more visual interest. The deep blue of the sky with its specks of white creates an interesting juxtaposition with the greenish-blue hues of the swamp. It typifies the true intentions that Heade and others had in creating these artworks that were part of a particular enterprise to attract people and industrial development.[53] Duval-Carrié's idiosyncratic rendering of the trees mirrors the portrayals in other works by the artist. Trees bear significant weight in his oeuvre, since they are grounding for him, given his history as a migrant, and they epitomize dignity. His use of silver glitter and glue to depict these trees seems to reflect his view that trees can be dressed. Given the lack of a human presence in the composition, the trees here emanate various persona, with Duval-Carrié "dress[ing] them with history, the best and the worst of it, with sadness and with happiness."[54]

The noticeable areas of red, mostly in the sky and in the water, seem to almost respond to the sense of desolation that is ubiquitous in Heade's original. But more important, it also serves to memorialize the violent circumstances that led to the extermination of most of the native population and the importation of enslaved Africans. This work seeks to invite us to wander through the landscape and through history.[55] Like the other paintings from the *Imagined Landscapes* exhibition, *After Heade—The Great Florida Marsh* is a memorial to these civilizations that existed before the colonial encounter and to the enslaved Africans who came from civilizations that, like the First Nations of the Caribbean and the United States, had a different relationship to nature.

Precisely this connection between people of African descent and flora occupies Kenyan artist Wangechi Mutu. Although she creates art using a variety of media, Mutu is widely known for her dynamic collages. These compositions often depict incredible and otherworldly terrains that are sometimes lush with vegetation, while others are sparse and arid. She uses a variety of materials, such as pearls, glitter, paint, feathers, and cut paper, to render these imaginative environments. Occupying these landscapes are women of African descent whose amalgamated forms are composed of human, animal, robotic, and plant parts. These wide-ranging fragments come from disparate sources such as *National Geographic*, early medical journals, and pornographic, motorcycle, and fashion magazines.[56]

Mutu's provocative artworks examine an array of topics, such as the history of colonization, consumerism, the repercussions of war, and even the eroticization of the Black female body.[57] While the captivating yet grotesque female protagonists are often the source from which these complicated subject matters are gleaned, Mutu's landscapes are just as enthralling and convoluted. She has always been drawn to the natural terrain, particularly those of her homeland. At the same time, she is fully aware of the deep dismissal of nature, given the ways in which notions of progress and intellectual advancement have been conceptualized in today's world.[58] As Mutu rightly declares, "Nature has been demonized and turned into something decorative, seen as primitive and something that ought to be controlled, something that doesn't have its own sense of self or power. Of course that is not true; nature and everything around us is every reason why we exist."[59] This recognition of the primacy of nature for humanity and the unfortunate mischaracterization of it in the Western collective imaginary is what connects Mutu's art to those of the artists explored in this book.

Of particular significance for Mutu is the connectivity that civilizations on the African continent have always had with nature. Due to the immense process of colonization in Africa, there emerged an inferiority complex among African people, since they were characterized as having a connection with nature that was drastically different from the Eurocentric conceptualization of nature, which posited that one should strive to not give it primacy since nature was not indicative of modernity.[60] Yet it is this link to nature that postcolonial Africans have inherited from previous generations that seems to be at the crux of *Tropicalia* (2015) (plate 8).

In this work, Mutu offers viewers a dissected view of her hybrid female subject, who is part human, part machine, and part plant, and in the midst of either trying to uproot herself from the ground or merely growing out of the soil. The brown earth that she inhabits appears to be imbued with activity, the artist conveying this animated milieu with numerous isometric triangles in different shades of brown that collectively give the earth a pixelated effect. We are even given glimpses of her brown shoulders and her right forearm, as well as her hand touching her face ever so slightly. A large trunk and its accompanying roots append the base of her robotic form, establishing her placement in the earth. This being looks to be reveling in her natural environment, not to mention in her complete immersion in the soil. Butterflies, snakes, and other species seem to echo her gleeful disposition.

Mutu's *Tropicalia* is imbued with Suzanne Césaire's ethos of the plant-man, who does not dominate nature but grows and lives in accord with the plant, since he is in solidarity with the rhythm of universal life.[61] Such an empowering declaration is deeply rooted in an Africa-derived worldview in which man does not dominate nature. In fact, Mutu has aptly declared that the nature she renders in these compositions knows more than she does, and she allows it to tell her what she needs to know. She firmly believes that "nature can guide us toward a place of consciousness and liberate us from these shackles of fear and human folly."[62] Perhaps this is why the scenery that Mutu creates in this work and many others comes out of her process-oriented approach to art-making. During her creative pursuits, "every decision and every mistake becomes such a marvelous part of the whole image. This way of working is similar to a life journey, an adventure or relationship, and I suppose that's why I was inspired to create landscapes. I don't believe in covering up my tracks too much."[63]

The inventive landscapes of Mutu's oeuvre also bring to mind the land of the marvelous that Alejo Carpentier and René Ménil exquisitely wrote about, which is characterized as the place where everything is possible and where one can transgress spatial boundaries and can transform into anything or anyone, since the marvelous is the image of absolute liberty.[64] In this vein, the exultation of natural topography seems to fuel Mutu's desire to create "images of an ideal world inside myself if I were to just float around in zero gravity in the universe I created."[65] In fact, for the artist, this universe would look very much like *Funkalicious Fruit Field* (2007) (figure C.3). There is a whimsical and playful quality in this work, given the unencumbered way the pink, bulbous organisms seem to float in their

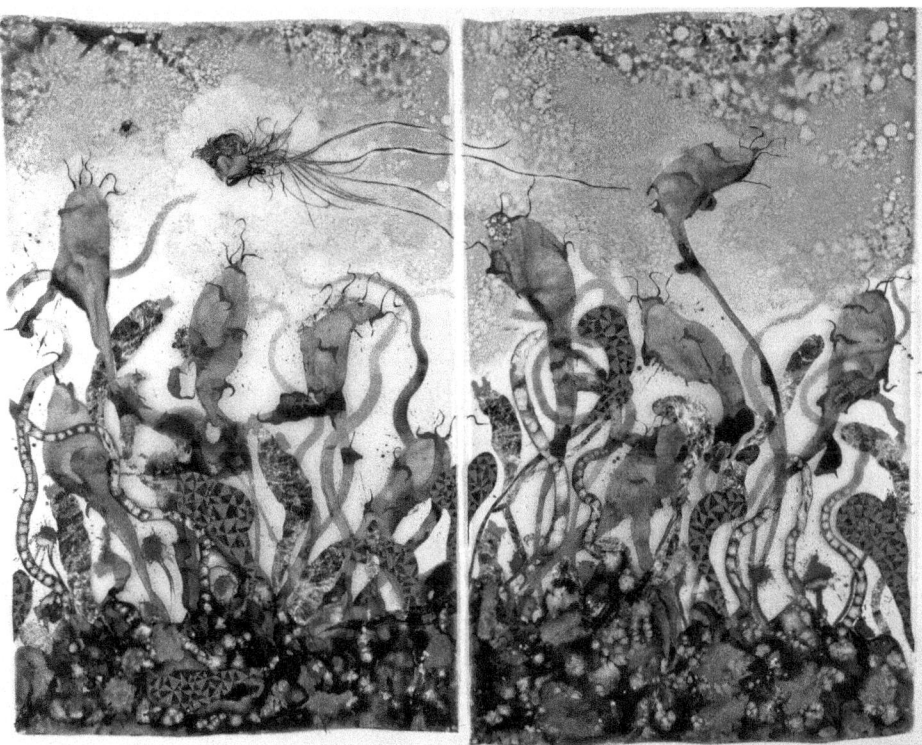

C.3 Wangechi Mutu, *Funkalicious Fruit Field*, 2007. Ink, paint, mixed media, plant materials, and plastic pearls on Mylar, 184 × 106 in. Courtesy of the artist and Victoria Miro, London.

environment. The hints of brown and specks of bright blue on their surfaces add complexity to their appearance. Juxtaposed around them are other organisms: one covered with a brown isometric design motif and the other with a deeply textured gray finish. The latter organism mirrors the color scheme in the upper portion of the picture plane, which is reminiscent of microscopic views typical in scientific imagery. Collectively, these organisms provide optical vibrancy and a great sense of movement despite being firmly rooted in place. For Mutu, there is a musical element to the movement conveyed among the creatures, and they are almost in an ocean or perhaps almost in the air.[66] The artist explains that "it is purely open space that is an interpretation of my dreams, my desire to fly and flee but in a most colorful, fantastical way."[67] The utopic vision that *Funkalicious Fruit Field* presents is ideal for an escapist urge to realize an Afrofuturist reimagining of time and space. Indeed, works such as this show how

Mutu continues the legacy of Afrofuturist pioneers who sought refuge in otherworldly realms.[68]

Without question, what binds the artistic practice of these artists with those explored in previous chapters is the notion of tropicality as it pertains to relationality. These artworks and performances collectively position the Black body in relation to the tropical landscape in a way that is transient, a relationality that is not definitive as in the concrete sense of locale. Therefore, this is a notion of belonging that is not necessarily defined by the logic of geographic location per se but hinged on translocation. This is especially true since, although manifesting as a signifier, Africa is perpetually in flux, and this buttresses the impossibility of literal returns.[69]

Pan-Africanist sensibilities certainly informed the historical relationship Black peoples in the Americas had with the land they occupied in the early twentieth century as well as the modern Black identity being molded during this time. Unquestionably, these constructions of Black identity were imbued with diasporic longing, and the renderings of subtropical and tropical landscapes in art and performance ought to be seen as providing a significant resolution to this predicament. Indeed, art allows for a creative manifestation of space, a critical imaging of space, and even a reclaiming of space that aids in the recovery of a lost sense of home. Art makes it feasible to visually render an imagined geography, an imagined Pan-Africa. And these imagined, transient tropical landscapes are integral to how tropical aesthetics functioned in Black modernism. These paintings and performances are in many instances fervent examples of Black speculative art from the early twentieth century and today, given the desire by innovative individuals to create narratives of Black histories, present, and futures from unique Black perspectives. Therefore, the materialization of these chronicles across space and time can in many ways emerge in the re-created landscapes on canvas, on stage, and even in the carnivalesque sphere.

INTRODUCTION

1 "Living Portraits: Carl Van Vechten's Color Photographs of African Americans, 1939–1964," Carl Van Vechten Papers, Yale Collection of American Literature, Beinecke Rare Book and Manuscript Library, Yale University, accessed April 13, 2020, https://beinecke.library.yale.edu/collections /highlights/living-portraits-carl-van-vechtens-color-photographs-african -americans-1939.

2 Raymond, *Beryl McBurnie*; Sörgel, *Dancing Postcolonialism*, 58–66.

3 Eldridge, "Bop Girl Goes Calypso," 11.

4 Ménil, "Concerning Colonial Exoticism," 177.

5 Ménil, "Concerning Colonial Exoticism," 177.

6 Ménil, "Concerning Colonial Exoticism," 177.

7 S. Césaire, "A Civilization's Discourse," 97; S. Césaire, *The Great Camouflage*, 112–27.

8 A number of important texts have offered substantial scholarship on the notion of tropicality as a social and cultural construct: most notably David Arnold's *Problem of Nature* (1996), J. Michael Dash's *Other America* (1998), and David C. Miller's *Dark Eden* (1989). In terms of my specific focus on how black diasporic artists challenge Western representations of tropicality in art, I am particularly in dialogue with, and indebted to, Krista Thompson's *Eye for the Tropics* (2006). However, none of these scholars offer a thorough investigation of how Caribbean and American artists of the early twentieth century responded to the colonial and hegemonic regimes through visual and performative tropicalist representation.

9 Dash, *Other America*, 29.

10 Edwards, *Practice of Diaspora*, 20–27.

11 Andrews, "Beyond Pan-Africanism."

12 See Niblett, "Arc of the 'Other America,'" for an extensive literary investigation of how the Caribbean and Latin American terrains have provided alternative visions of nature for their inhabitants.

13 Said, *Orientalism*, 202–4.

14 Rogers, *Jungle Fever*, 5–17; D. Arnold, *Problem of Nature*, 142.

15 D. Arnold, *Problem of Nature*, 141–43.

16 D. Arnold, *Problem of Nature*, 147–52; Rogers, *Jungle Fever*, 72–88.

17 Enright, *Maximum of Wilderness*, 38–50; Wilson, *Shadow and Shelter*, 4–12; D. Miller, *Dark Eden*, 1–3.

18 *Baron Alexander von Humboldt*; D. Arnold, *Problem of Nature*, 146.

19 Enright, *Maximum of Wilderness*, 7; Murray, *Islands and the Sea*, 152.

20 Humboldt, *Cosmos*, 1:13.

21 Rogers, *Jungle Fever*, 3; Pratt, *Imperial Eyes*, 119–21.

22 Rogers, *Jungle Fever*, 62–89; D. Arnold, *Problem of Nature*, 150–54.

23 Walter Raleigh, "Natural Scenery in Jamaica," *The Crayon*, May 23, 1855, 396, quoted in D. Miller, *Dark Eden*, 121.

24 Wirt, *Letters of the British Spy*, 105–6.

25 See Dash, *Other America*, 24–25, for more on the reconstruction of the Caribbean not from observation but from a psychological urge. For a discussion of the shift in creating psychological landscapes, see D. Miller, *Dark Eden*, 121.

26 Bowd and Clayton, "Tropicality," 302.

27 Enright, *Maximum of Wilderness*, 9–13; D. Miller, *Dark Eden*, 2.

28 Stepan, *Picturing Tropical Nature*, 25.

29 Humboldt, *Cosmos*, 2:93.

30 Ferber, *Hudson River School*, 9–11.

31 Novak, *Nature and Culture*, 3.

32 Kornhauser and Manthorne, *Fern Hunting*, 2–6; D. Miller, *Dark Eden*, 110–13.

33 Berger, *Sight Unseen*, 44–48, 50.

34 K. Thompson, *Eye for the Tropics*, 5.

35 K. Thompson, *Eye for the Tropics*, 5, 10–13.

36 K. Thompson, *Eye for the Tropics*, 20–21.

37 Wolf, *Art Deco*, 103–28; Hillier and Escritt, *Art Deco Style*, 21–22, 37–38.

38 Morton, *Hybrid Modernities*, 273, 290–96.

39 Glissant, *Caribbean Discourse*, 159–60.

40 Benítez-Rojo, *Repeating Island*, 5-6.

41 Dash, *Other America*, 32.

42 Gikandi, "Picasso."

43 Wilks, *Race*, 6–7.

44 Gikandi, *Writing in Limbo*, 1.

45 Alain Locke, "The New Negro," in Locke, *New Negro*, 10.

46 Powell, "Aaron Douglas Effect," 110, 122.

47 Baker, *Modernism and the Harlem Renaissance*, 31.

48 Dash, *Other America*, 42–45.

49 Poupeye, *Caribbean Art*, 49–51.

50 Glissant, *Caribbean Discourse*, 64, 100.

51 Glissant, *Caribbean Discourse*, 98.

52 Mercer, *Travel and See*, 231–34.

53 Sims, "Post-modern Modernism," 87.

54 D. Arnold, *Problem of Nature*, 128.

55 Massey, *Interior Design since 1900*, 36.

56 S. Gillespie, *Vernacular Modernism*, 3; Powell, "Re/birth of a Nation," 25.

57 Vendryes, *Barthé*, 51–58; Powell, *Black Art*, 60.
58 D. Cullen and Fuentes, *Caribbean*, 17–23; Poupeye, *Caribbean Art*, 73.
59 Hartman, "William Edouard Scott Remembered," 134–35.
60 D. Cullen and Fuentes, *Caribbean*, 22; Poupeye, *Caribbean Art*, 81.
61 Cheng, *Second Skin*, 23.
62 McKittrick, *Demonic Grounds*, xxii.
63 McKittrick, *Demonic Grounds*, xxiii.
64 McKittrick, *Demonic Grounds*, xxvi.
65 McKittrick, *Demonic Grounds*, xi, xiii, xx.
66 Franklin and Moss, *From Slavery to Freedom*, 281–84.
67 T. Martin, *Caribbean History*, 197–234.
68 Carpentier, "On the Marvelous Real in America," 86.
69 Ménil, "Introduction to the Marvellous," 91.
70 Ménil, "Introduction to the Marvellous," 93–94.
71 Batiste, *Darkening Mirrors*, 25; Kummels, "Staging the Caribbean," 142.
72 Gilroy, *Black Atlantic*, 19.
73 Batiste, *Darkening Mirrors*, 7.
74 For more on this topic, see Commander, *Afro-Atlantic Flight*.
75 Dash, *Other America*.

CHAPTER ONE. AMERICAN TROPICAL MODERNISM

1 McKittrick, *Demonic Grounds*, xxii.
2 See Adkins, "Vigilant Torch." See also, Powell, "Aaron Douglas Effect," 63.
3 Snaith, "C. L. R. James," 219.
4 Byrd and Gates, "Afterword—'Song of the Son,'" 209.
5 Nicholls, "Jean Toomer's *Cane*," 158; Snaith, "C. L. R. James."
6 Nicholls, "Jean Toomer's *Cane*," 164.
7 Toomer, *Cane*, 97.
8 Du Bois, *Souls of Black Folk*, 75.
9 Du Bois, *Souls of Black Folk*, 57, 66.
10 My thanks to Kimberly Juanita Brown for bringing this quality in Toomer's work to my attention.
11 McKittrick, *Demonic Grounds*, xxvi.
12 Ménil, "Introduction to the Marvellous," 91.
13 McKittrick, *Demonic Grounds*, xx.
14 Noël, "Envisioning New Worlds," 77.
15 J. Johnson, *Book of American Negro Poetry*, 9.
16 Alain Locke, "The Legacy of Ancestral Arts," in Locke, *New Negro*, 255.
17 Powell, "Aaron Douglas Effect," 60.
18 Powell, "Re/birth of a Nation," 16.
19 Earle, "Harlem, Modernism, and Beyond," 28.
20 Kirschke, *Aaron Douglas*, 123; Patton, *African American Art*, 139.
21 Powell, "Paint That Thing!," 109.

22 Kirschke, *Aaron Douglas*, 132.

23 Kirschke, *Aaron Douglas*, 118.

24 Aaron Douglas, untitled, undated essay, box 4, folder 12, Aaron Douglas Papers, Special Collections, Franklin Library, Fisk University, Nashville, Tennessee.

25 Earle, "Harlem, Modernism, and Beyond," 11. Earle encourages a broader reading of Douglas's landscapes that defies a certain region; however, she still limits the landscape as being situated in the United States.

26 D. Miller, *Dark Eden*, 1–3.

27 Kirschke, *Aaron Douglas*, 2–3.

28 Earle, "Harlem, Modernism, and Beyond," 8.

29 Kirschke, *Aaron Douglas*, 27–30.

30 For more on this, see Dewiel, *Jugendstil*.

31 Douglas, untitled, undated essay.

32 Powell, *Black Art*, 30.

33 Locke, "Legacy of the Ancestral Arts," 257–58.

34 Novak, *Nature and Culture*, 3–4.

35 Quoted in Novak, *Nature and Culture*, 8.

36 Novak, *Nature and Culture*, 12.

37 Delany, *Condition, Elevation, Emigration, and Destiny*, 195–97.

38 Ketner, *Emergence of the African American Artist*, 33–36, 39.

39 Farrington, *African-American Art*, 83.

40 Bearden and Henderson, *History of African-American Artists*, 26–27.

41 Quoted in P. Miller, "Nature and the National Ego," 205–6.

42 Du Bois, *Souls of Black Folk*, 118–19.

43 Franklin and Moss, *From Slavery to Freedom*, 107–12.

44 Bearden and Henderson, *History of African-American Artists*, 19–26.

45 McKittrick, *Demonic Grounds*, xix.

46 McKittrick, *Demonic Grounds*, xxii.

47 McKittrick, *Demonic Grounds*, xix.

48 Berger, *Sight Unseen*, 44–45, 50.

49 Aaron Douglas interview recording, n.d., Aaron Douglas Papers, Special Collections, Franklin Library, Fisk University, Nashville, Tennessee.

50 See Woodruff, *American Congo*, 152-3.

51 Wynter, "Novel and History."

52 Berger, *Sight Unseen*, 50, 54. Berger discusses the "continuing sway of an entrenched European-American value system" when viewing the terrain and conveying it in cartographic form. In his comparison of European and Native American mapmaking, Berger concludes that the former only convey objective spatial relationships, while the latter reveal geographic features that are established primarily by personal experiences: "Native American maps never purported to represent topography objectively but instead sought to provide a partial record of the events associated with the natural world that gave the land its meaning."

53 Franklin and Moss, *From Slavery to Freedom*, 143.
54 Douglas, untitled, undated essay.
55 Kirschke, *Aaron Douglas*, 2–3; Earle, "Harlem, Modernism, and Beyond," 8–9.
56 McKittrick, *Demonic Grounds*, xi–xiii.
57 Kirschke, *Aaron Douglas*, 123.
58 Alexandre, *Properties of Violence*, 30.
59 Ménil, "Introduction to the Marvellous," 92.
60 D. Miller, *Dark Eden*, 1–3. Miller stresses that responses to imagery of the swamp in mid-nineteenth-century America reveal the "partial autonomy of images in shaping new cultural forms and styles and thereby influence basic attitudes and values." On a more fundamental level, he recognizes how the swamp "emerged as a metaphor of newly awakened unconscious mental processes."
61 McKittrick, *Demonic Grounds*, xi, xiii.
62 Eppse, *Negro, Too, in American History*, 159.
63 Novak, *Nature and Culture*, 30–33.
64 McKittrick, *Demonic Grounds*, xv.
65 Langston Hughes, "Lonesome Place," *Opportunity Art Folio*, 1926.
66 McKittrick, *Demonic Grounds*, xvi.
67 Roberts, *Freedom as Marronage*, 5–9.
68 Ménil, "Introduction to the Marvellous," 94.
69 Kirschke, *Aaron Douglas*, 43–45.
70 Powell, "Aaron Douglas Effect," 56–57.
71 Locke, "Legacy of the Ancestral Arts," 256, 261.
72 Leighten, "White Peril," 610.
73 Quoted in Kirschke, *Aaron Douglas*, 47.
74 Locke, "Legacy of the Ancestral Arts," 266.
75 Kirschke, *Aaron Douglas*, 45–46.
76 Lemke, "Diaspora Aesthetics," 129.
77 Earle, "Harlem, Modernism, and Beyond," 37.
78 Quoted in Cassidy, "Jazz and African American Identity," 120.
79 Powell, "Paint That Thing!," 115.
80 Gikandi, "Picasso," 458.
81 Mercer, "Introduction," 7.
82 Glissant, *Caribbean Discourse*, 98.
83 Sims, "Post-modern Modernism," 87.
84 Douglas, untitled, undated essay.
85 Locke, "New Negro," 3.
86 McKittrick, *Demonic Grounds*, xxvi.
87 Niblett, "Arc of the 'Other America,'" 52. As Niblett further elucidates, Glissant recognized the importance of affirming a regionally specific identity for the Caribbean. In his book *Poetics of Relation*, Glissant characterized the Caribbean region as the "Other America" and emphasized the specificity of its space by asserting, "This has always been a place of encounter and

connivance and, at the same time, a passageway toward the American continent. Compared to the Mediterranean, which is an inner sea surrounded by lands, . . . the Caribbean is, in contrast, a sea that explodes the scattered lands into an arc." (33)

88 Kirschke, *Aaron Douglas*, 85; K. Thompson, "Preoccupied with Haiti," 79.

89 Quoted in Kirschke, *Aaron Douglas*, 85.

90 D. Arnold, *Problem of Nature*, 149–57.

91 K. Thompson, "Preoccupied with Haiti," 80.

92 Dash, *Haiti and the United States*, 51.

93 Edwards, *Practice of Diaspora*, 48.

94 Earle, "Harlem, Modernism, and Beyond," 21.

95 K. Thompson, *Eye for the Tropics*, 103–9.

96 Powell, "Re/birth of a Nation," 26.

97 Earle, "Harlem, Modernism, and Beyond," 37.

98 J. Johnson, "Truth about Haiti," 224.

99 K. Thompson, "Preoccupied with Haiti," 90-1.

100 Stewart, *Critical Temper of Alain Locke*, 188.

101 J. Johnson, "Truth about Haiti," 223.

102 K. Thompson, "Preoccupied with Haiti," 78.

103 See K. Thompson, "Preoccupied with Haiti," for a discussion of African American artists who created portraits of historical leaders of Haiti. Johnson notes that, up until 1920, the history of Haiti was written primarily by white historians. See J. Johnson, "Truth about Haiti."

104 Powell, "Re/birth of a Nation," 30–32.

105 Herzberg, "Wifredo Lam: The Development," 45.

106 Glissant, *Caribbean Discourse*, 105.

107 Stepan, *Picturing Tropical Nature*, 231–32.

108 Powell, "Aaron Douglas Effect," 62; Sims, "Post-modern Modernism," 88.

CHAPTER TWO. BRAZENLY AVANT-GARDE

1 Herzberg, "Wifredo Lam: The Development," 45.

2 Dash, *Other America*, 24

3 Mosquera, *Beyond the Fantastic*, 127.

4 Sims, *Wifredo Lam*, 36.

5 Dash, *Other America*, 24.

6 Noël, "Envisioning New Worlds," 77.

7 Mosquera, *Beyond the Fantastic*, 124; Sims, *Wifredo Lam*, 40-43.

8 Herzberg, "Wifredo Lam: The Development," 31.

9 McKittrick, *Demonic Grounds*, xi.

10 Herzberg, "Wifredo Lam: The Development," 31.

11 Ménil, "Introduction to the Marvellous," 91.

12 McKittrick, *Demonic Grounds*, xiii.

13 Timpano, "Translating Vanguardia," 54.

14 K. Thompson, *Eye for the Tropics*, 4–10.
15 K. Thompson, *Eye for the Tropics*, 5.
16 Dash, *Other America*, 22.
17 Dash, *Other America*, 24. See also Glissant, *Caribbean Discourse*, 115.
18 Ménil, "Concerning Colonial Exoticism," 176.
19 Ménil, "Concerning Colonial Exoticism," 176–77; Mosquera, *Beyond the Fantastic*, 123.
20 Sims, *Wifredo Lam*, 89.
21 Sims, *Wifredo Lam*, 6; Fouchet, *Wifredo Lam*, 6. For more on this keen interest in African art in 1920s Paris, see Krauss, "Giacometti"; Leja, *Reframing Abstract Expressionism*; Archer-Straw, *Negrophilia*.
22 Linsley, "Wifredo Lam, " 531; Mosquera, *Beyond the Fantastic*, 125.
23 A. Arnold, *Modernism and Negritude*.
24 Kelley, "Introduction," 22.
25 A. Arnold, *Modernism and Negritude*, 46.
26 Linsley, "Wifredo Lam," 532. Aimé Césaire demonstrated his and Suzanne's immense interest in flora when he wrote, "Critics have remarked upon the recurrence of certain themes in my works, in particular plant symbols. I am in fact obsessed by vegetation, by the flower, by the root. There is nothing gratuitous in that, it is linked with my situation, that of a Black man exiled from his native soil. . . . The tree, profoundly rooted in the soil, is for me the symbol of a man who is self-rooted—the nostalgia of a lost paradise" (quoted in Linsley, "Wifredo Lam," 532.)
27 Ménil, "For a Critical Reading of *Tropiques*," 73.
28 Sims, *Wifredo Lam*, 32; Linsley, "Wifredo Lam," 529.
29 Kelley, "Introduction," 14.
30 For more on this topic, see Tythacott, *Surrealism and the Exotic*, 7; Foster, "Primitive Unconscious of Modern Art," 200.
31 Tythacott, *Surrealism and the Exotic*, 188–89.
32 Richardson, "Introduction," 7.
33 S. Césaire, "1943," 126.
34 A. Césaire, "Notebook of a Return," 45.
35 S. Césaire, "A Civilization's Discourse," 97–99.
36 Linsley, "Wifredo Lam," 532.
37 Carpentier, "On the Marvelous Real in America," 86.
38 Carpentier, "On the Marvelous Real in America," 85–88.
39 Carpentier, "On the Marvelous Real in America," 85.
40 Rodriguez-Plate, *Lydia Cabrera*, 13–14; Sims, *Wifredo Lam*, 67.
41 Herzberg notes that Cabrera has even taken credit for encouraging Lam to paint aspects of his African heritage. See Herzberg, "Wifredo Lam: The Development," 50n46.
42 Herzberg, "Wifredo Lam" (1990); Herzberg, "Wifredo Lam: The Return."
43 Pappademos, *Black Political Activism*, 125–26.
44 Fouchet, *Wifredo Lam*, 188.

45 Pérez, *On Becoming Cuban*, 450–51.

46 Mosquera, *Beyond the Fantastic*, 124. See also Blanc, "Cuban Modernism."

47 Brathwaite, *Contradictory Omens*, 6.

48 Mosquera, *Beyond the Fantastic*, 127.

49 Herzberg, "Wifredo Lam: The Development," 35–36.

50 Linsley, "Wifredo Lam," 530.

51 Holliday T. Day and Hollister Sturges, "Introduction," in Day and Sturges, *Art of the Fantastic*, 38.

52 Day and Sturges, "Introduction," 38.

53 Fouchet, *Wifredo Lam*, 183.

54 Poole, "Excess of Description," 160.

55 Herzberg, "Wifredo Lam: The Development," 42, 45.

56 McKittrick, *Demonic Grounds*, xx.

57 McKittrick, *Demonic Grounds*, xxiii.

58 Fouchet, *Wifredo Lam*, 188.

59 McKittrick, *Demonic Grounds*, xxii. Lam is even quoted as saying that he "used poetry to show the reality of acceptance and protest." See Fouchet, *Wifredo Lam*, 199.

60 Sims, *Wifredo Lam*, 48.

61 Sims, *Wifredo Lam*, 43.

62 Herzberg, "Wifredo Lam: The Development," 34–35.

63 Poupeye, *Caribbean Art*, 51–54. For more on Cuban modernism, see Martínez, *Cuban Art and National Identity*.

64 Herzberg, "Wifredo Lam: The Return," 42.

65 Enriquez's *The Abduction of the Mulatas* is largely influenced by Peter Paul Ruben's *The Rape of the Daughters of Leucippus* (1617–18).

66 Herzberg, "Wifredo Lam: The Return," 35–37.

67 Poupeye, *Caribbean Art*, 62; Sims, *Wifredo Lam*, 66–67.

68 Herzberg, "Wifredo Lam: The Return," 24.

69 Cabrera, *El Monte*, 66–67.

70 Herzberg, "Wifredo Lam: The Development," 36.

71 Bettelheim, "Palo Monte Mayombe," 36.

72 Poupeye, *Caribbean Art*, 62; Cabrera, *El Monte*, 17.

73 My thanks to Tanya L. Shields for bringing this to my attention.

74 Hewitt, *Voices out of Africa*, 29–30.

75 Coronil, "Introduction," xxvii.

76 Herzberg, "Wifredo Lam," 36–37.

77 Linsley, "Wifredo Lam," 532.

78 Fouchet, *Wifredo Lam*, 199.

79 Wilkins, "Glossary," 22, quoted in D. Arnold, "India's Place in the Tropical World," 19n34.

80 D. Arnold, "India's Place in the Tropical World," 8.

81 Fouchet, *Wifredo Lam*, 198.

82 Poupeye, *Caribbean Art*, 52–53.

83 Fouchet, *Wifredo Lam*, 198. Lydia Cabrera often took the task of naming the artworks Lam painted while in Cuba. See Herzberg, "Wifredo Lam," 40.

84 Dash, *Other America*, 24.

85 Glissant, *Caribbean Discourse*, 105.

86 McKittrick, *Demonic Grounds*, xxii.

87 McKittrick, *Demonic Grounds*, 183.

88 Pérez, *On Becoming Cuban*, 323–24.

89 Daniel, "Early Works of Wifredo Lam," 37–41.

90 Fouchet, *Wifredo Lam*, 188.

91 Pérez, *On Becoming Cuban*, 193; Fouchet, *Wifredo Lam*, 183.

92 Sims, *Wifredo Lam*, 50.

93 See Rubin, *How to Read Impressionism*, 269.

94 Herzberg, "Wifredo Lam: The Development," 45.

95 Sims, *Wifredo Lam*, 50.

96 Day and Sturges, *Art of the Fantastic*, 104.

97 Herzberg, "Wifredo Lam: The Development," 38.

98 Pappademos, *Black Political Activism*, 125–26.

99 Herzberg, "Wifredo Lam: The Development," 40.

100 Sims, *Wifredo Lam*, 75; Herzberg, "Wifredo Lam: The Development," 40.

101 Vos, Eltis, and Richardson, "Dutch in the Atlantic World," 240.

102 Sims, *Wifredo Lam*, 63.

103 Day and Sturges, *Art of the Fantastic*, 104.

104 Niblett, "Arc of the 'Other America,'" 63.

105 Lucie-Smith, "Wifredo Lam and the Caribbean," 65. Lucie-Smith states that Lam looked most notably to the Sepik mask that belonged to French surrealist poet Paul Éluard.

106 Sims, *Wifredo Lam*, 11, 18.

107 Herzberg, "Wifredo Lam: The Return."

108 Linsley, "Wifredo Lam," 533.

109 R. Thompson, *Flash of the Spirit*, 5–7; Herzberg, "Wifredo Lam: The Return," 42, 46. Herzberg explains that "Lam's presentation of the altar as still life is another example of his inclination to utilize a traditional genre in untraditional ways" (46). Other altar–cum–still life works include *Autel pour Yemayá* (1944), *Grenadine Curtain* (1944), and *Table in the Garden* (1944).

110 Cabrera, *El Monte*, 66.

111 Sims, *Wifredo Lam*, 48.

112 Sims, *Wifredo Lam*, 232.

113 Herzberg, "Wifredo Lam: The Return," 46.

114 Herzberg, "Wifredo Lam: The Development," 33–35.

115 Sims, "Post-modern Modernism," 88, quoted in Mosquera, "Mi pintura es un acto de descolonización," 10.

116 Lam, "Oeuvres recentes de Wifredo Lam," 186.

117 Glissant, *Caribbean Discourse*, 137.

118 Glissant, *Caribbean Discourse*, 105.

119 Daniel, "Early Works of Wifredo Lam," 68.

120 S. Césaire, "Civilization's Discourse," 98.

121 Herzberg, "Wifredo Lam: The Development," 33.

122 A. Césaire, "Wifredo Lam," 86, quoted in Linsley, "Wifredo Lam, 534."

123 McKittrick, *Demonic Grounds*, xx.

124 Pappademos, *Black Political Activism*, 54–56.

125 Herzberg, "Wifredo Lam: The Development," 33.

126 Richardson, "Introduction," 8.

127 Maguire, "Two Returns to the Native Land."

128 Maguire, "Two Returns to the Native Land."

129 Pratt, *Imperial Eyes*, 4.

130 Loichot, *Tropics Bite Back*, xi.

131 Tythacott, *Surrealism and the Exotic*, 6–14.

132 Tythacott, *Surrealism and the Exotic*, 14.

133 Linsley, "Wifredo Lam."

134 Richardson, "Introduction," 8.

135 Ménil, "Concerning Colonial Exoticism," 177.

136 Sims, *Wifredo Lam*, 137.

137 Sartre, *Black Orpheus*, 39.

138 Dash, *Other America*, 37–38.

139 Richardson, "Introduction," 14.

140 S. Césaire, "Great Camouflage," 160

141 Loichot, *Tropics Bite Back*, 141.

142 Loichot, *Tropics Bite Back*, 142–45.

143 Stallybrass, "Against Thinking," 1581–82.

144 Loichot, *Tropics Bite Back*, v.

145 Bary, "Oswald de Andrade's 'Cannibalist Manifesto,'" 35.

146 Bary, "Oswald de Andrade's 'Cannibalist Manifesto,'" 36.

147 Andrade, "Cannibalist Manifesto," 43.

148 Loichot uses the term "artistic cannibalism" in *Tropics Bite Back*, 145.

149 Sims, "Post-modern Modernism," 88.

150 Sims, *Wifredo Lam*, 173.

151 Sims, *Wifredo Lam*, 169–70.

152 Sims, *Wifredo Lam*, 169–70.

153 MacFarlane, "Taking Stock," 17–25.

154 Malley, *Call from Algeria*, 18.

155 Bary, "Oswald de Andrade's 'Cannibalist Manifesto,'" 35.

156 Andrade, "Cannibalist Manifesto," 39.

157 Linsley, "Wifredo Lam." Jamaican poet Louise "Miss Lou" Bennett is credited with originating this concept. For more on Bennett, see Morris, *Miss Lou*.

158 Rosemont, *Surrealist Women*, 137; Kelley, "Introduction," 16–17.

159 Niblett, "Arc of the 'Other America,'" 60.

160 Ortiz, *Cuban Counterpoint*, 71; Kutzinski, *Sugar's Secrets*, 47–48.

161 Coronil, "Introduction," xxii.

162 Wynter, "Novel and History," 96–99.

163 Glissant, *Caribbean Discourse*, 100.

164 Linsley, "Wifredo Lam," 533.

165 Herzberg, "Wifredo Lam: The Development," 33.

166 Day and Sturges, "Introduction," 38–39.

167 Mosquera, *Beyond the Fantastic*, 124.

168 A. Césaire, "Notebook of a Return"; S. Césaire, "Civilization's Discourse."

169 McKittrick, *Demonic Grounds*, xx.

170 McKittrick, *Demonic Grounds*, xix.

CHAPTER THREE. EARLY TWENTIETH-CENTURY TRINIDAD CARNIVAL

1 *Sunday Express* (Port of Spain, Trinidad), February 3, 1991, 1. Soca is the dancing music that is used in Trinidad Carnival. It is a lot faster than calypso and the lyrics are usually about partying and increasing the momentum of revelers.

2 *Sunday Express* (Port of Spain, Trinidad), February 3, 1991, 1.

3 "Just One Bad Apple," *Sunday Express* (Port of Spain, Trinidad), February 24, 1991, 31; "Intention to Wave," *Sunday Express* (Port of Spain, Trinidad), March 3, 1991, 63.

4 "Sexual Stereotypes," *Sunday Express* (Port of Spain, Trinidad), February 10, 1991, 15.

5 "'Waving Teacher' under Probe," *Sunday Express* (Port of Spain, Trinidad), February 10, 1991, 3.

6 See Franco, "'Unruly Woman.'"

7 In fact, teachers were demanding through their unions that they receive better wages that year. See "Intention to Wave," 63.

8 Liverpool, *Rituals of Power and Rebellion*, 211.

9 Franco, "'Unruly Woman.'"

10 Rohlehr, *Calypso and Society*, 55; Smith, "Performing Gender," 34.

11 McKittrick, *Demonic Grounds*, 40.

12 McKittrick, *Demonic Grounds*, xxii, 41.

13 Goldberg, *Performance Art*, 138.

14 Goldberg, *Performance Art*, 44.

15 Philip, "Race, Space," 131–32.

16 Bakhtin, *Rabelais and His World*, 33–34.

17 Sims, "Post-modern Modernism," 87.

18 Glazier and Hellwig, *Modern Catholic Encyclopaedia*, 517.

19 Bakhtin, *Rabelais and His World*, 7.

20 Eco, "Frames of Comic 'Freedom,'" 1–9.

21 Eco, "Frames of Comic 'Freedom,'" 1–9.

22 Bakhtin, *Rabelais and His World*, 10.

23 Bakhtin, *Rabelais and His World*, 19.

24 Bakhtin, *Rabelais and His World*, 317.

25 Ménil, "Introduction to the Marvellous," 90–91.

26 Carpentier, "On the Marvelous Real in America," 86.

27 Eco, "Frames of Comic 'Freedom,'" 6.

28 Eco, "Frames of Comic 'Freedom,'" 7.

29 Eco, "Frames of Comic 'Freedom,'" 7.

30 Stallybrass and White, *Politics and Poetics*, 26.

31 Stallybrass and White, *Politics and Poetics*, 14.

32 Nurse, "Globalization and Trinidad Carnival," 667

33 Shohat and Stam, *Unthinking Eurocentrism*, 304.

34 Ménil, "Introduction to the Marvellous," 92.

35 Bakhtin, *Rabelais and His World*, 256.

36 Ménil, "Introduction to the Marvellous," 94.

37 Pretty mas is the aesthetic associated historically with European culture and/or the upper class. It often consisted of elaborate costumes mostly based on Greek mythology or aspects of European culture and history. Jouvay (J'Ouvert) begins around two o'clock on Carnival Monday morning when people come out into the streets to revel. There is a wide variety of costumes associated almost exclusively with Jouvay, many of which include covering oneself with paint or mud or oil. The steel band is a band of musicians who play all the various types of steel drums. The Trinidadian term for steel drum is *pan*.

38 Schechner and Riggio, "Peter Minshall," 110.

39 Philip, "Race, Space," 134–35.

40 Brereton, "Family Strategies," 79. Brereton notes that a significant number of enslaved males were deployed in nonagrarian jobs and other skilled occupations.

41 Lewis, *Culture of Gender and Sexuality*, 17.

42 Thomas, *Modern Blackness*, 39.

43 C. Hall, "Gender Politics."

44 Wood, *Trinidad in Transition*, 48–49.

45 Millette, "Wage Problem," 56–60.

46 David Dabydeen and Brinsley Samaroo, "Introduction," in Dabydeen and Samaroo, *Across the Dark Waters*, 2.

47 Wood, *Trinidad in Transition*, 160.

48 Dabydeen and Samaroo, "Introduction," 2.

49 Dabydeen and Samaroo, "Introduction," 2.

50 Dabydeen and Samaroo, "Introduction," 2.

51 Cross, "East Indian-Creole Relations," 17.

52 Warner-Lewis, *Guinea's Other Suns*, 1; Laurence, *Immigration into the West Indies*, 13–16.

53 Liverpool, *Rituals of Power and Rebellion*, 231.

54 Liverpool, *Rituals of Power and Rebellion*, 316. This is similar to what would be seen in Jamaica at that time during John Canoe festivities. See Nunley and Bettelheim, *Caribbean Festival Arts*, 46.

55 C. Day, *Five Years' Residence*, 313.

56 The Set Girls of Jamaica were female secret societies that included a leader referred to as the Queen, or "Maam." The activities of these sets mirror those of the Ekpo in eastern Nigeria and the Egungun societies in Cameroon. See Barringer, Forrester, and Martinez-Ruiz, *Art and Emancipation in Jamaica*, 105–6, 109, 115; Nunley and Bettelheim, *Caribbean Festival Arts*, 46.

57 Brereton, "Trinidad Carnival," 47; Cowley, *Carnival, Canboulay and Calypso*, 56–74.

58 Cowley, *Carnival, Canboulay and Calypso*, 56–74.

59 Scholars such as Errol Hill and Pamela Franco use the spelling *jamet* to refer to the subjugated class of Black people of the urban dwellings apart from the women of this class. John Cowley, who gives detailed accounts of Carnival proceedings in *Carnival Canboulay and Calypso*, uses *diamete, diametre, diamette*, and *jamet*. However, very little work has been done to assess the evolution of the term to its contemporary form.

60 Scher, *Carnival*, 39.

61 E. Hill, *Trinidad Carnival*, 33; Liverpool, *Rituals of Power and Rebellion*, 86.

62 Pearse, "Carnival in Nineteenth Century Trinidad," 188.

63 Quoted in Pearse, "Mitto Sampson," 257.

64 Pearse, "Mitto Sampson," 256–59.

65 Brereton, "Trinidad Carnival," 47.

66 Brereton, "Trinidad Carnival." While the jametre class was an inherent and definitive aspect of Port of Spain, Trinidad's main urban center at that time, there certainly may have been members of this class in other parts of the colony.

67 Smith, "Performing Gender," 34.

68 Brereton, "Trinidad Carnival," 48.

69 *Trinidad Chronicle*, February 17, 1874, 3.

70 *Port of Spain Gazette*, February 11, 1880, 3.

71 *Port of Spain Gazette*, February 17, 1877, 3.

72 *Trinidad Chronicle*, February 9, 1877, 3.

73 *Trinidad Chronicle*, February 9, 1877, 3.

74 *Trinidad Chronicle*, February 9, 1877, 3.

75 Warner-Lewis, *Guinea's Other Suns*, 1; Laurence, *Immigration into the West Indies*, 13–16; Liverpool, *Rituals of Power and Rebellion*, 231.

76 See, for instance, "On Vagrancy as Social Ill," *Port of Spain Gazette*, February 14, 1874, 3.

77 See Cowley, *Carnival, Canboulay and Calypso*, 71–72; Cowley, "Traditional Masques of Carnival," 215–16.

78 Pearse, "Mitto Sampson," 261.

79 *Trinidad Chronicle*, June 16, 1868, 3. Cannes Brulees (French for "canes burning"), or Canboulay, its Creole derivative, was an imitation of a task enslaved Africans had to endure whenever a fire broke out in the plantation that the elites eventually ritualized. Once slavery was abolished, its participants consisted of the free Black masses who used it as a way to commemorate slavery.

80 *Trinidad Chronicle*, June 16, 1868, 3.

81 *Trinidad Chronicle*, June 16, 1868, 3.

82 *Trinidad Chronicle*, June 16, 1868, 3.

83 *Trinidad Chronicle*, December 23, 1864, 3.

84 Trotman, *Crime in Trinidad*, 180. By the late nineteenth century, as a result of the large influx of formerly enslaved Africans into towns and cities to seek employment, many of them took extreme measures to obtain their bare necessities. As a result, the authorities implemented stringent laws to curtail the Black masses as well as harsh forms of punishment to control them.

85 Trotman, *Crime in Trinidad*, 181.

86 *Port of Spain Gazette*, February 25, 1871, 2.

87 This included the use of drums and the sexually suggestive movements necessary for the *kalinda* dance; the English, on the other hand, were involved in "rowdy merry-making and licence" during their Christmas–New Year festivities. See Correspondent X, *Port of Spain Gazette*, March 26, 1881, 3; Pearse, "Carnival in Nineteenth Century Trinidad."

88 Brereton, "Trinidad Carnival," 49–50.

89 Brereton, "Trinidad Carnival," 51.

90 Brereton, "Trinidad Carnival," 52; E. Hill, *Trinidad Carnival*, 20.

91 Glissant, *Caribbean Discourse*, 248.

92 McKittrick, *Demonic Grounds*, 43.

93 Bakhtin, *Rabelais and His World*, 10, 19; Carpentier, "On the Marvelous Real in America," 86.

94 Ménil, "Introduction to the Marvellous," 90–91.

95 E. Hill, *Trinidad Carnival*, 25.

96 *Trinidad Review*, August 9, 1883, 3.

97 Brereton, *Race Relations in Colonial Trinidad*, 161.

98 Brereton, *Race Relations in Colonial Trinidad*, 99.

99 Stuempfle, *Steelband Movement*, 23. Stuempfle notes that this practice was also prevalent in Venezuela (where it was referred to as *quitiplas*), Haiti, and Africa.

100 *Port of Spain Gazette*, March 13, 1886, 3.

101 This was a continuation of social legislation that started about a decade earlier. According to one February 2, 1871, article published in the *Trinidad Chronicle*, "Notice on Forbidden Acts during Carnival," masking, other disguises, blowing of horns, or carrying of torches were all subject to imprisonment with hard labor (1).

102 Franco, "'Unruly Woman.'" Later in this section I provide a detailed description of how women of the jametre class developed masquerade traditions like the pisse-en-lit character.

103 *Port of Spain Gazette*, January 23, 1894, 3.

104 Stallybrass and White, *Politics and Poetics*, 4–6.

105 Stallybrass and White, *Politics and Poetics*, 22–23.

106 Stallybrass and White, *Politics and Poetics*, 145.

107 *Illustrated London News*, May 5, 1888, 475.
108 Cowley, *Carnival, Canboulay and Calypso*, 128. *Guinea songs* here may be an alternative term for what was popularly referred to as kalinda songs, which chantuelles sang for the various bands' Carnival processions.
109 E. Hill, *Trinidad Carnival*, 108–9.
110 Personal communication with Rhoma Spencer, February 19, 2006.
111 *Port of Spain Gazette*, January 23, 1894, 3.
112 Much of the literature on Carnival recognizes pisse-en-lit as a predominantly male-dominated masquerade. However, Franco has provided ample evidence that women were very involved in this masquerade, even from its inception. See Franco, "'Unruly Woman.'"
113 Brereton, "Trinidad Carnival," 48.
114 Drewal, *Yoruba Ritual*, 189.
115 Drewal, *Yoruba Ritual*. See Franco, "'Unruly Woman'" for a detailed description of how women of the jametre class developed other masquerade traditions such as the pisse-en-lit character.
116 Trotman, *Crime in Trinidad*, 251, cited in Franco, "'Unruly Woman,'" 65.
117 Franco, "'Unruly Woman,'" 67.
118 Franco, "'Unruly Woman.'" Repeated treatments of large doses of mercury sometimes led to severe liver and kidney damage.
119 Pacteau, *Symptom of Beauty*, 131.
120 Gilman, "'Black Bodies, White Bodies," 9, cited in Pacteau, *Symptom of Beauty*, 13.
121 McKittrick, *Demonic Grounds*, 49.
122 McKittrick, *Demonic Grounds*, 48.
123 For a comprehensive examination of the cultural impact of trauma and how it manifests in art, see Stiles, "Shaved Heads and Marked Bodies." For more information on the banning of pisse-en-lit, see *Port of Spain Gazette*, January 23, 1894, 3.
124 Turner, *Anthropology of Performance*, 26.
125 McKittrick, *Demonic Grounds*, xx–xxiii.
126 McKittrick, *Demonic Grounds*, 137–38; Liverpool, *Rituals of Power and Rebellion*, 337–38.
127 Kalinda songs were impromptu songs involving audience participation that *chantuelles* (lead singers) would sing to the accompaniment of drums.
128 Smith, "Performing Gender," 35
129 Smith, "Performing Gender," 35.
130 Rohlehr, *Calypso and Society*, 50. Rohlehr notes that the eventual disappearance of women from the scene may have resulted from frequent complaints from journalists, the efforts of the law, in addition to both male and female censure, all of which probably pressured urban working-class women into a concern for respectability.
131 Rohlehr, *Calypso and Society*, 92.
132 Bordo, "Body," 21.

133 Mohammed, "Blueprint for Gender,"139.

134 Mohammed, "Blueprint for Gender," 139.

135 Reddock, *Women, Labour and Politics*, 53.

136 Bridget Brereton and Kevin A. Yelvington, "Introduction," in Brereton and Yelvington, *Colonial Caribbean in Transition*, 8.

137 Brereton, *Race Relations in Colonial Trinidad*, 10, 34. Brereton notes that while the Portuguese were white, they were never part of the elite in this period. The Syrian and Lebanese were seen as Arab at this time, although most of them were Christian. The European administrators who came to work in Trinidad were on the outskirts of the elite class but could certainly move their way up.

138 Millette, "Wage Problem," 64.

139 Millette, "Wage Problem," 65–68.

140 Reddock, *Women, Labour and Politics*, 55.

141 Brereton, *History of Modern Trinidad*, 158. For a thorough examination of this topic, see Bolland, *Politics of Labour*.

142 Ryan, *Race and Nationalism*, 28.

143 Brereton and Yelvington, "Introduction," 18.

144 Brereton and Yelvington, "Introduction," 18.

145 Yelvington, "War in Ethiopia and Trinidad," 189–97.

146 Yelvington, "War in Ethiopia and Trinidad," 196–98.

147 Glissant, *Caribbean Discourse*, 15–20.

148 Ménil, "Introduction to the Marvellous," 91.

149 Rohlehr, *Calypso and Society*, 92.

150 Rohlehr, *Calypso and Society*, 92; *The Argos*, February 3, 1912, 1.

151 *The Argos*, January 24, 1920, 11.

152 *The Argos*, January 24, 1920, 11.

153 Aching, *Masking and Power*, 73; Rohlehr, *Calypso and Society*, 403.

154 Particularly after World War II, during the Carnival season *Trinidad Guardian* staff writers wrote feverishly about the cruise ships anchored in Port of Spain docks as well as the airplanes landing at the Piarco Airport bringing Americans, Canadians, Europeans, and Venezuelans, who all came to experience Carnival.

155 Franco, "'Unruly Woman,'" 66.

156 Franco, "'Unruly Woman,'" 66–67.

157 Yelvington, "War in Ethiopia and Trinidad," 192.

158 "Who Fears the Sedition Bill?," *The Guardian*, March 13, 1920. See also Rohlehr, *Calypso and Society*, 104–5.

159 Yelvington, "War in Ethiopia and Trinidad," 189; Reddock, "Women Workers' Struggles," 35.

160 Reddock, "Women Workers' Struggles," 29–35.

161 Quoted in Yelvington, "War in Ethiopia," 221.

162 Brereton, *History of Modern Trinidad*, 143.

163 D. Thomas, *Modern Blackness*, 49.

164 Butler, *Gender Trouble*, 13.

165 Beauvoir, *Second Sex*, cited in Butler, *Gender Trouble*, 17.

166 Christine Barrow, "Introduction and Overview," in Barrow, *Caribbean Portraits*, xi.

167 Momsen, "Double Paradox," 45.

168 Franco, "'Unruly Woman,'" 1–3.

169 Stallybrass and White, *Politics and Poetics*, 4–5.

170 Stallybrass and White, *Politics and Poetics*, 145.

171 Stallybrass and White, *Politics and Poetics*, 133.

172 Bordo, "Body," 13.

173 McKittrick, *Demonic Grounds*, 50.

174 Anatol, "Transforming."

175 Mohammed, "Blueprint for Gender," 144.

176 Besson, *Folklore and Legends*, 40.

177 For more on la diablesse, see Besson, *Folklore and Legends*, 40–43.

178 Rohlehr, *Calypso and Society*, 231.

179 Rohlehr, *Calypso and Society*, 231. Apart from projecting personal insecurities onto jamettes, the calypso also reveals the sense of powerlessness that Black men felt as a result of the presence, during World War II, of U.S. soldiers with more disposable income than most locals.

180 Newspaper headlines like these were very common: "King Carnival Starts First War-Time Reign in 20 Years," *Trinidad Guardian*, February 15, 1940, 3; "King Carnival Ends Hectic Two-Day Reign," *Trinidad Guardian*, February 21, 1940, 3; "King Carnival Gives Up Crown after Hectic Two-Day Reign," *Trinidad Guardian*, March 6, 1946, 1, 3.

181 Stuempfle, *Steelband Movement*, 36.

182 Stuempfle, *Steelband Movement*, 48.

183 "Carnival Fun Ends; Lenten Season Begins," *Trinidad Guardian*, February 20, 1947, 1.

184 Stuempfle, *Steelband Movement*, 70.

185 It should be noted that the dancing of Indo-Trinidadian women to chutney music also includes strong pelvic movements. Despite this, winin' is always associated with popular African Trinidadian culture.

186 Dunham, "Form and Function," 502–5.

187 Personal communication with Norman Darway, May 27, 2008.

188 Personal communication with Norman Darway, May 27, 2008; K. Johnson, "Saga of a Flagwoman," 413. The attire of these flag women often captured attention too. They sometimes wore tight pants and short tops that exposed their midriffs.

189 Personal communication with Norman Darway, May 27, 2008.

190 K. Johnson, "Saga of a Flagwoman," 411.

191 Quoted in K. Johnson, "Saga of a Flagwoman," 411.

192 K. Johnson, "Saga of a Flagwoman," 411.

193 McKittrick, *Demonic Grounds*, 43, 50.

194 McKittrick, *Demonic Grounds*, xi, xiii, xx.

195 Ménil, "Introduction to the Marvellous," 91.

196 Stuempfle, *Steelband Movement*, 47. *Pan man* is the lingua franca used in Trinidad to refer to male steel-pan musicians.

197 Stuempfle, *Steelband Movement*, 62.

198 "Visitors Arriving Here for Carnival Follies," *Trinidad Guardian*, March 2, 1946, 1.

199 "Court to Take Strong View of Clashing during Celebrations," *Trinidad Guardian*, February 16, 1950, 3. It was not mentioned in the article whether any of the women were steel pan players or jamettes.

200 Stallybrass and White, *Politics and Poetics*, 201.

201 K. Johnson, "Saga of a Flagwoman."

202 Personal communication with Norman Darway, May 27, 2008.

203 Stallybrass and White, *Politics and Poetics*, 4–5.

204 With regard to the upper-class men, see E. Hill, *Trinidad Carnival*, 25, and Pearse, "Mitto Sampson," 258–62.

205 Powrie, "Changing Attitude," 230.

206 Stallybrass and White, *Politics and Poetics*, 4–5.

207 Personal communication with Rhoma Spencer, February 19, 2006.

208 T. Hall, *Jean and Dinah*, 13. "Jean and Dinah" is also the title of a famous 1956 calypso by the Mighty Sparrow; the play is the jamettes' theatrical response to the calypsonian's lyrics.

209 Mohammed, "Blueprint for Gender," 152.

210 K. Johnson, "Saga of a Flagwoman," 410.

211 K. Johnson, "Saga of a Flagwoman," 410–11.

212 Neptune, *Caliban and the Yankees*, 1.

213 Neptune, *Caliban and the Yankees*, 183.

214 Neptune, *Caliban and the Yankees*, 183–84.

215 While most of the American servicemen still held many of their racist assumptions upon arrival in Trinidad, in due course they would be seen pursuing interracial relations with nonwhite women in public. The local men left by the wayside—which included not only patrons of sex workers but also the suitors, boyfriends, and husbands of women who did not engage in commercial sexual transactions—were no doubt resentful and many of them responded harshly and sometimes violently. For more on this topic, see Neptune, *Caliban and the Yankees*, chapter 6.

216 Neptune, *Caliban and the Yankees*, 226.

217 Rohlehr, *Calypso and Society*, 231.

218 K. Johnson, "Saga of a Flagwoman," 413.

219 K. Johnson, "Saga of a Flagwoman," 412.

220 Personal communication with Rhoma Spencer, February 19, 2006.

221 T. Hall, *Jean and Dinah*, 63–64.

222 I borrow the term *vulgar* in this context from Carolyn Cooper's pioneering text, *Noises in the Blood*.

223 Belinda Edmondson employs the term *vulgar spectacle* to describe the female public performance that is transgressive and is associated with atavistic racial recidivism. See Edmondson, "Public Spectacles."

224 McKittrick, *Demonic Grounds*, 43.

225 Personal communication with Norman Darway, May 27, 2008. In an effort to feel safe at that time of night, male friends would accompany some of these jamettes.

226 Personal communication with Norman Darway, May 27, 2008.

227 Personal communication with Norman Darway, May 27, 2008. While the patrons of jamettes did follow European standards of beauty, "high-grade" jamettes most likely included dark-skinned Black women with either European or African phenotypes.

228 Rohlehr, *Calypso and Society*, 246.

229 From the calypsonian Ziegfeld's song "Calypsonian's Ambitions," quoted in Rohlehr, *Calypso and Society*, 246.

230 Schneider, *Explicit Body in Performance*, 132–34.

231 Butler, *Gender Trouble*, 177.

232 Personal communication with Norman Darway, May 27, 2008.

233 Ménil, "Introduction to the Marvellous," 92.

234 "Carnival Goes Off with Usual Swing," *Trinidad Guardian*, February 25, 1941, 1.

235 "Most Popular by Far," *Trinidad Guardian*, February 27, 1952, 5.

236 Powrie, "Changing Attitude," 230.

237 Powrie, "Changing Attitude." For more on women in World War II, see Milkman, *Gender at Work*, 84.

238 For more, see Neptune, *Caliban and the Yankees*, 158–90.

239 Neptune, *Caliban and the Yankees*. Neptune explains that these relationships in which white American soldiers pursued Black women undermined Trinidad's racial hierarchy, even when organizations were set up to ensure that they stayed on the "appropriate side of the color line" by courting local white girls (168).

240 Neptune, *Caliban and the Yankees*, 158.

241 "We t'ing" (we thing) was an expression popularized in Trinidad during the years following independence to encapsulate the patriotism encouraged by the first prime minister, Eric Williams, and his government.

242 E. Hill, *Trinidad Carnival*, 97–98.

243 *Trinidad Guardian*, March 6, 1957, 1; Anthony, *Parade of the Carnivals*, 263.

244 *Trinidad Carnival and Calypso*, 1963, National Archives of Trinidad and Tobago.

245 McKittrick, *Demonic Grounds*, 52.

246 Phelan, *Unmarked*, 5–7.

247 Aching, *Masking and Power*, 21.

1 Ménil, "Concerning Colonial Exoticism," 176.
2 D. Arnold, *Problem of Nature*, 150–54.
3 Batiste, *Darkening Mirrors*, 9–10.
4 Little, *Disciples of Liberty*, 84–85.
5 Batiste, *Darkening Mirrors*, 5.
6 Batiste, *Darkening Mirrors*, 25.
7 McKittrick, *Demonic Grounds*, xxii.
8 Carpentier, "On the Marvelous Real in America," 86.
9 Batiste, *Darkening Mirrors*, 25; Kummels, "Staging the Caribbean," 142.
10 Jayna Brown, *Babylon Girls*, 16.
11 McKittrick, *Demonic Grounds*, x–xiii.
12 Kummels, "Staging the Caribbean," 150.
13 Kummels, "Staging the Caribbean," 142.
14 Kummels, "Staging the Caribbean," 143.
15 Batiste, *Darkening Mirrors*, 7.
16 Sharpley-Whiting, "Femme Negritude," 12–16, and Sharpley-Whiting, *Negritude Women*, 105–7, cited in Kummels, "Staging the Caribbean," 150.
17 Eldridge, "Bop Girl Goes Calypso," 3.
18 Batiste, *Darkening Mirrors*, 5.
19 McKittrick, *Demonic Grounds*, x.
20 M. Gillespie, Butler, and Long, *Maya Angelou*, 36–37.
21 Angelou, *Singin' and Swingin'*, 83.
22 Jayna Brown, *Babylon Girls*, 7.
23 Angelou, *Singin' and Swingin'*, 74.
24 Angelou, *Singin' and Swingin'*, 76.
25 Angelou, *Singin' and Swingin'*, 84. See also Angelou, *I Know Why the Caged Bird Sings*, 68.
26 Eldridge, "Bop Girl Goes Calypso," 11-12.
27 Rohlehr, *Calypso and Society*, 2, 523.
28 D. Hill, "'I Am Happy,'" 74–76.
29 D. Hill, "'I Am Happy,'" 86.
30 Sasso, "They're Going Crazy for Calypso!," 80, quoted in Eldridge, "Bop Girl Goes Calypso," 7.
31 Eldridge, "Bop Girl Goes Calypso," 7.
32 Angelou, *Heart of a Woman*, 34.
33 Angelou, *Singin' and Swingin'*, 86–87.
34 Angelou, *Singin' and Swingin'*, 95–96. "Run Joe" was composed by Louis Jordan, Walter Merrick, and Joe Willoughby.
35 McKittrick, *Demonic Grounds*, 43.
36 Angelou, *Singin' and Swingin'*, 74.
37 "Mambo in Africa" was composed by Maya Angelou.
38 McMains, *Spinning Mambo into Salsa*, 31–32.
39 D. Hill, "'I Am Happy,'" 84.

40 Smith, "Performing Gender," 35.
41 Rohlehr, *Calypso and Society*, 55.
42 Noel, "De Jamette in We," 66.
43 Sims, "Post-modern Modernism," 87.
44 Loichot, *Tropics Bite Back*, 141.
45 Loichot, *Tropics Bite Back*, 141.
46 Loichot, *Tropics Bite Back*, x.
47 Haney, *Naked at the Feast*, 41–42; Haskins, *Cotton Club*, 32–33.
48 Haskins, *Cotton Club*, 33.
49 McKittrick, *Demonic Grounds*, xvi–xvii.
50 Kummels, "Staging the Caribbean," 148.
51 Loichot, *Tropics Bite Back*, xi.
52 Haney, *Naked at the Feast*, 60.
53 Haney, *Naked at the Feast*, 59.
54 Judith Brown, *Glamour in Six Dimensions*, 123.
55 Borshuk, "Intelligence of the Body," 44.
56 Archer-Straw, *Negrophilia*, 119.
57 D. Arnold, "India's Place in the Tropical World," 8.
58 Haney, *Naked at the Feast*, 60.
59 Nenno, "Femininity," 154.
60 Leiris, *L'afrique fantôme*, 42, quoted in Clifford, "Negrophilia," 905.
61 Nenno, "Femininity," 147.
62 Jayna Brown, *Babylon Girls*, 256.
63 "De Negerrevue Black People Te Berlijin—Een Bijdrage Over Het Thema 'Der Untergang des Abendlandes,'" *Het Vaderland*, July 16, 1926, evening edition, quoted in Jayna Brown, *Babylon Girls*, 245.
64 "De Negerrevue Black People Te Berlijin."
65 D. Arnold, *Problem of Nature*, 154–55.
66 Haney, *Naked at the Feast*, 56–57.
67 Jules-Rosette, *Josephine Baker*, 47.
68 According to Ingrid Kummels, per a 1930 newspaper report, Alex was from Senegal. However, this information is not reliable, particularly since other sources identify him as Antillean. See Kummels, "Staging the Caribbean," 148.
69 Haney, *Naked at the Feast*, 60.
70 Rose, *Jazz Cleopatra*, 21.
71 Ngô, *Imperial Blues*, 130–35.
72 Jules-Rosette, *Josephine Baker*, 178–79.
73 Quoted in J. Baker and Bouillon, *Josephine*, 55.
74 J. Baker and Bouillon, *Josephine*, 51–52.
75 Quoted in Haney, *Naked at the Feast*, 64.
76 Quoted in Haney, *Naked at the Feast*, 64.
77 Sharpley-Whiting, "Femme Negritude," 12–16, and Sharpley-Whiting, *Negritude Women*, 105–7, cited in Kummels, "Staging the Caribbean,"149–50.

78 Nardal, "Pantins exotiques," 2, quoted in Edwards, *Practice of Diaspora*, 169.

79 Kummels, "Staging the Caribbean," 150.

80 Jules-Rosette, *Josephine Baker*, 129.

81 Haney, *Naked at the Feast*, 54–55. See also J. Baker and Bouillon, *Josephine*, 49–50.

82 Archer-Straw, *Negrophilia*, 122.

83 Archer-Straw, *Negrophilia*, 127–29.

84 Archer-Straw, *Negrophilia*, 121–22.

85 Haney, *Naked at the Feast*, 105.

86 Haney, *Naked at the Feast*, 68.

87 W. Martin, ""Remembering the Jungle," 321–22.

88 J. Baker and Bouillon, *Josephine*, 52.

89 J. Baker and Bouillon, *Josephine*, 52–55.

90 Steele, *Paris Fashion*, 68.

91 C. Cullen, "Dark Tower," 53.

92 Jules-Rosette, *Josephine Baker*, 64; Haney, *Naked at the Feast*, 102.

93 Borshuk, "Intelligence of the Body," 52.

94 Borshuk, "Intelligence of the Body," 52.

95 Jules-Rosette, *Josephine Baker*, 49.

96 Haney, *Naked at the Feast*, 95–96; Shack, *Harlem in Montmartre*, 8; Lahs-Gonzales, "Josephine Baker," 37.

97 Rose, *Jazz Cleopatra*, 91–92.

98 Rose, *Jazz Cleopatra*, 82, gives the name of a show, *Un Soir de Folie*, Baker went to see before accepting the Folies Bergère offer.

99 D. Arnold, *Problem of Nature*, 154–55.

100 E. E. Cummings, "Vive La Folie!" in Cummings, *E. E. Cummings*, 162.

101 J. Baker and Bouillon, *Josephine*, 61; Haney, *Naked at the Feast*, 99.

102 Rose, *Jazz Cleopatra*, 28.

103 J. Baker and Bouillon, *Josephine*, 61.

104 Jules-Rosette, *Josephine Baker*, 49–50.

105 Loichot, *Tropics Bite Back*, xix.

106 Loichot, *Tropics Bite Back*, xxi.

107 Lahs-Gonzales, "Josephine Baker," 45–47.

108 Cheng, *Second Skin*, 42–47.

109 Loichot, *Tropics Bite Back*, 141.

110 Lhamon, *Raising Cain*, 140.

111 Borshuk, "Intelligence of the Body," 47–48.

112 Borshuk, "Intelligence of the Body," 50.

113 Borshuk, "Intelligence of the Body," 50.

114 Jules-Rosette, *Josephine Baker*, 179.

115 Jayna Brown, *Babylon Girls*, 16.

116 Jayna Brown, *Babylon Girls*, 47.

117 Borshuk, "Intelligence of the Body," 41.

118 Jayna Brown, *Babylon Girls*, 6.

119 Batiste, *Darkening Mirrors*, 7.
120 Carpentier, "On the Marvelous Real in America," 86.
121 For an interesting discussion of how the atavism thesis emerged during the Jazz Age, see Edwards, *Practice of Diaspora*, 163–67.
122 McKittrick, *Demonic Grounds*, x.
123 McKittrick, *Demonic Grounds*, xiii.
124 Haney, *Naked at the Feast*, 74–75.
125 Shack, *Harlem in Montmartre*, 27.
126 Joel A. Roger, "The Pepper Pot," *Pittsburgh Courier*, July 27, 1929, quoted in Shack, *Harlem in Montmartre*, 34.
127 Kummels, "Staging the Caribbean," 146–47.
128 Kummels, "Staging the Caribbean," 150.
129 Edwards, *Practice of Diaspora*, 148. Brent Hayes Edwards offers a keen exploration of the work of Jane and Paulette Nardal in their efforts to galvanize Black internationalism in early twentieth-century Paris. See Edwards, *Practice of Diaspora*, 119–86.
130 Carpentier, "On the Marvelous Real in America," 86.
131 Batiste, *Darkening Mirrors*, 9–10.
132 Ménil, "Concerning Colonial Exoticism," 180.
133 Batiste, *Darkening Mirrors*, 10.

CONCLUSION

1 McKittrick, *Demonic Grounds*, xi, xiii, xx.
2 Commander, *Afro-Atlantic Flight*, 3.
3 Commander, *Afro-Atlantic Flight*, 5.
4 Stepan, *Picturing Tropical Nature*, 213–14.
5 G. Martin, "Literature, Music and the Visual Arts," 91–92.
6 Stepan, *Picturing Tropical Nature*, 218.
7 Andrade, "Cannibalist Manifesto."
8 Oiticica, "Tropicália: The Image Problem," 309.
9 Oiticica, "General Scheme of New Objectivity," 221–22.
10 Basualdo, "Tropicália," 13–14.
11 Basualdo, "Tropicália," 15.
12 Basualdo, "Tropicália," 15.
13 Stallybrass, "Against Thinking," 1581–82.
14 Oiticica, "Tropicália," 241.
15 Basualdo, "Tropicália," 19.
16 Oiticica, "Tropicália," 239.
17 Canejo, "Resurgence of Anthropophagy," 64–65; Oiticica, "Tropicália," 239–40; Small, *Hélio Oiticica*, 98.
18 Oiticica, "Tropicália," 240.
19 Basualdo, "Tropicália," 21.
20 Oiticica, "Tropicália," 240.

21 Oiticica, "Tropicália," 240.

22 A. Césaire, "Notebook of a Return," 45; S. Césaire, "Civilization's Discourse," 97–99.

23 Oiticica, "Tropicália," 240.

24 Basualdo, "Tropicália," 20–21.

25 Oiticica, "Tropicália: The Image Problem," 309.

26 Basualdo, "Tropicália," 20.

27 Schwartz, "Culture and Politics in Brazil," 293–94.

28 Small, *Hélio Oiticica*, 104.

29 MacFarlane, "Taking Stock," 17–25.

30 Stepan, *Picturing Tropical Nature*, 224–25, 230–32.

31 Stepan, *Picturing Tropical Nature*, 230.

32 D. Miller, *Dark Eden*, 2.

33 Novak, *Nature and Culture*, 3.

34 D. Arnold, *Problem of Nature*, 147–52.

35 Ostrander, "Tropical Values," 101.

36 Bogues, "Reinventing the Caribbean," 19.

37 Bogues, "Reinventing the Caribbean," 20, 25.

38 Duval-Carrié, "Conversation."

39 Duval-Carrié, "Conversation."

40 Ostrander, "Tropical Values," 101; Duval-Carrié, "Conversation."

41 Stebbins, *Life and Work of Martin Johnson Heade*, 150.

42 Duval-Carrié, "Conversation."

43 Stebbins, *Life and Work of Martin Johnson Heade*, 150.

44 Ostrander, "Tropical Values," 103.

45 Ostrander, "Tropical Values," 103.

46 Duval-Carrié, "Conversation."

47 Powell, *Black Art*, 240–41; Sandra E. Garcia, "Overlooked No More: Belkis Ayón, a Cuban Printmaker Inspired by a Secret Male Society," *New York Times*, April 2, 2018, D10.

48 Ostrander, "Tropical Values," 106.

49 Stebbins, *Life and Work of Martin Johnson Heade*, 150.

50 Favis, *Martin Johnson Heade in Florida*, 52.

51 Stebbins, *Life and Work of Martin Johnson Heade*, 149.

52 David C. Miller mentions that this sense of desolation was a traditional category of feeling associated with the post-romantic visions created by artists that would at times bear an intensity bordering on the surreal. See D. Miller, *Dark Eden*, 172.

53 Duval-Carrié, "Conversation."

54 Bogues, "Art, History," 39–40.

55 Duval-Carrié, "Conversation."

56 Schoonmaker, "Fantastic Journey," 26.

57 Schoonmaker, "Fantastic Journey," 21.

58 Samantha Noël, conversation with Wangechi Mutu, October 11, 2018.

59 Noël, conversation with Mutu, October 11, 2018.
60 Noël, conversation with Mutu, October 11, 2018. See Iheka, *Naturalizing Africa*, for an impressive study on the contemporary ramifications of this issue.
61 S. Césaire, "Civilization's Discourse," 99.
62 Noël, conversation with Mutu, October 11, 2018.
63 Schoonmaker, "Fantastic Journey," 22.
64 Ménil, "Introduction to the Marvellous," 90–92.
65 Ménil, "Introduction to the Marvellous," 90–92.
66 Noël, conversation with Mutu, October 11, 2018.
67 Noël, conversation with Mutu, October 11, 2018.
68 Schoonmaker, "Fantastic Journey," 26.
69 Commander, *Afro-Atlantic Flight*, 5.

Aching, Gerard. *Masking and Power: Carnival and Popular Culture in the Carib-bean*. Minneapolis: University of Minnesota Press, 2002.

Adkins, Terry. "The Vigilant Torch of an Olympian Painter." *American Studies* 49, no. 1–2 (Spring/Summer 2008): 37–43.

Alexandre, Sandy. *The Properties of Violence: Claims to Ownership in Representa-tions of Lynching*. Jackson: University Press of Mississippi, 2012.

Anatol, Giselle. "Transforming the Skin-Shedding Soucouyant: Using Folklore to Reclaim Female Agency in Caribbean Literature." *Small Axe* 7 (March 2000): 44–59.

Andrade, Oswald de. "Cannibalist Manifesto." Translated by Leslie Bary. *Latin American Literary Review* 19, no. 38 (July–December 1991): 38–47.

Andrews, Kehinde. "Beyond Pan-Africanism: Garveyism, Malcolm X, and the End of the Colonial Nation State." *Third World Quarterly* 38, no. 11 (Novem-ber 2017): 2501–16.

Angelou, Maya. *The Heart of a Woman*. New York: Random House, 1981.

Angelou, Maya. *I Know Why the Caged Bird Sings*. New York: Random House, 1969.

Angelou, Maya. *Singin' and Swingin' and Gettin' Merry Like Christmas*. New York: Bantam Books, 1976.

Anthony, Michael. *Parade of the Carnivals of Trinidad, 1839–1989*. London: Circle Press, 1989.

Archer-Straw, Petrine. *Negrophilia: Avant-Garde Paris and Black Culture in the 1920s*. New York: Thames and Hudson, 2000.

Arnold, A. James. *Modernism and Negritude: The Poetry and Poetics of Aimé Cé-saire*. Cambridge, MA: Harvard University Press, 1981.

Arnold, David. "India's Place in the Tropical World, 1770–1930." *Journal of Impe-rial and Commonwealth History* 26, no. 1 (January 1998): 1–21.

Arnold, David. *The Problem of Nature: Environment, Culture and European Ex-pansion*. Oxford: Blackwell, 1996.

Baker, Houston A., Jr. *Modernism and the Harlem Renaissance*. Chicago: Univer-sity of Chicago Press, 1987.

Baker, Josephine, and Jo Bouillon. *Josephine*. Translated by Mariana Fitzpatrick. New York: Paragon House, 1977.

Bakhtin, Mikhail. *Rabelais and His World*. Translated by Helene Iswolsky. Bloomington: Indiana University Press, 1984.

Baron Alexander von Humboldt. Staten Island: Great Neck Publishing, 2007.

Barringer, Tim, Gillian Forrester, and Barbaro Martinez-Ruiz. *Art and Emancipation in Jamaica: Isaac Mendes Belisario and His Worlds*. New Haven, CT: Yale Center for British Art in association with Yale University Press, 2008.

Barrow, Christine, ed. *Caribbean Portraits: Essays on Gender Ideologies and Identities*. Kingston: Randle, 1998.

Bary, Leslie. "Oswald de Andrade's 'Cannibalist Manifesto.'" *Latin American Literary Review* 19, no. 38 (July–December 1991): 35–37.

Basualdo, Carlos. "Tropicália: Avant-Garde, Popular Culture, and the Culture Industry in Brazil." In *Tropicália: A Revolution in Brazilian Culture, 1967–1972*, edited by Carlos Basualdo. São Paulo: Cosac Naify, 2005.

Batiste, Stephanie Leigh. *Darkening Mirrors: Imperial Representation in Depression-Era African American Performance*. Durham, NC: Duke University Press, 2011.

Bearden, Romare, and Harry Henderson. *A History of African-American Artists: From 1792 to the Present*. New York: Pantheon Books, 1993.

Beauvoir, Simone de. *The Second Sex*. Translated by H. M. Parshley. New York: Vintage Books, 1989.

Benítez-Rojo, Antonio. *The Repeating Island: The Caribbean and the Postmodern Perspective*. Translated by James Maraniss. Durham, NC: Duke University Press, 1996.

Berger, Martin A. *Sight Unseen: Whiteness and American Visual Culture*. Berkeley: University of California Press, 2005.

Besson, Gérard. *Folklore and Legends of Trinidad and Tobago*. Port of Spain, Trinidad: Paria, 2001.

Bettelheim, Judith. "Palo Monte Mayombe and Its Influence on Cuban Contemporary Art." *African Arts* 34, no. 2 (Summer 2001): 36–49.

Blanc, Giulio V. "Cuban Modernism: The Search for a National Ethos." In *Wifredo Lam and His Contemporaries, 1938–1952*, edited by Maria R. Balderrama. New York: Studio Museum in Harlem, 1992.

Bogues, Anthony. "Art, History, and the Politics of Imagination: An Interview with ED-C." In *From Revolution in the Tropics to Imagined Landscapes: The Art of Edouard Duval-Carrié*, edited by Anthony Bogues. Miami: Pérez Art Museum, 2014.

Bogues, Anthony. "Reinventing the Caribbean: Edouard Duval-Carrié, History, Politics, and the Making of a Caribbean Aesthetic." In *From Revolution in the Tropics to Imagined Landscapes: The Art of Edouard Duval-Carrié*, edited by Anthony Bogues. Miami: Pérez Art Museum, 2014.

Bolland, O. Nigel. *The Politics of Labour in the British Caribbean: The Social Origins of Authoritarianism and Democracy in the Labour Movement*. Princeton, NJ: Markus Weiner, 2001.

Bordo, Susan R. "The Body and the Reproduction of Femininity: A Feminist Appropriation of Foucault." In *Gender/Body/Knowledge: Feminist Reconstructions of Being and Knowing*, edited by Allison Jaggar and Susan R. Bordo. New York: Rutgers University Press, 1989.

Borshuk, Michael. "An Intelligence of the Body: Disruptive Parody through Dance in the Early Performances of Josephine Baker." In *Embodying Liberation: The Black Body in American Dance*, edited by Dorothea Fischer-Hornung and Allison Goeller. Piscataway, NJ: Transaction, 2001.

Bowd, Gavin, and Daniel Clayton. "Tropicality, Orientalism, and French Colonialism in Indochina: The Work of Pierre Gourou, 1927–1982." *French Historical Studies* 28, no. 2 (Spring 2005): 297–327.

Brathwaite, Kamau. *Contradictory Omens: Cultural Diversity and Integration in the Caribbean*. Mona, Jamaica: Savacou, 1974.

Brereton, Bridget. "Family Strategies, Gender and the Shift to Wage Labour in the British Caribbean." In *The Colonial Caribbean in Transition: Essays on Post-emancipation Social and Cultural History*, edited by Bridget Brereton and Kevin A. Yelvington. Gainesville: University Press of Florida, 1999.

Brereton, Bridget. *A History of Modern Trinidad, 1783–1962*. Kingston, Jamaica: Heinemann, 1981.

Brereton, Bridget. *Race Relations in Colonial Trinidad 1870–1900*. Cambridge: Cambridge University Press, 2002.

Brereton, Bridget. "The Trinidad Carnival: 1870–1900." *Savacou*, nos. 11/12 (September 1975): 46–57.

Brereton, Bridget, and Kevin A. Yelvington, eds. *The Colonial Caribbean in Transition: Essays on Post-emancipation Social and Cultural History*. Gainesville: University Press of Florida, 1999.

Brown, Jayna. *Babylon Girls: Black Women Performers and the Shaping of the Modern*. Durham, NC: Duke University Press, 2008.

Brown, Judith. *Glamour in Six Dimensions: Modernism and the Radiance of Form*. Ithaca, NY: Cornell University Press, 2009.

Butler, Judith. *Gender Trouble: Feminism and the Subversion of Identity*. New York: Routledge, 1990.

Byrd, Rudolph P., and Henry Louis Gates Jr. "Afterword—'Song of the Son': The Emergence and Passing of Jean Toomer." In *Cane*, by Jean Toomer. New York: Liveright, 2011.

Cabrera, Lydia. *El Monte: Igbo, finda, ewe orisha, vititi nfinda; Notas sobre las religiones, la magia, las supersticiones y el folklore de los negros criollos y el pueblo de Cuba*. Miami: Ediciones Universal, 1975.

Canejo, Cynthia. "The Resurgence of Anthropophagy: Tropicália, Tropicalismo and Hélio Oiticica." *Third Text* 18, no. 1 (2004): 61–68.

Carpentier, Alejo. "On the Marvelous Real in America." In *Magical Realism: Theory, History, Community*, edited by Lois Parkinson Zamora and Wendy B. Faris. Durham, NC: Duke University Press, 1995.

Césaire, Aimé. "Notebook of a Return to the Native Land." In *The Collected Po-*

etry of Aimé Césaire, edited and translated by Clayton Eshleman and Annette Smith. Berkeley: University of California Press, 1983.

Césaire, Aimé. "Wifredo Lam." *Cahiers d'art*, nos. 20–21 (1947): 86.

Césaire, Suzanne. "A Civilization's Discourse." In *Refusal of the Shadow: Surrealism and the Caribbean*, edited by Michael Richardson and Krzysztof Fijalkowski. New York: Verso, 1996.

Césaire, Suzanne. "The Great Camouflage." *Tropiques*, nos. 13–14 (1945).

Césaire, Suzanne. *The Great Camouflage: Writings of Dissent, 1941–1945*. Edited by Daniel Maximin. Translated by Keith L. Walker. Middletown, CT: Wesleyan University Press, 2012.

Césaire, Suzanne. "1943: Surrealism and Us." In *Refusal of the Shadow: Surrealism and the Caribbean*, edited by Michael Richardson and Krzysztof Fijalkowski. New York: Verso, 1996.

Cheng, Anne Anlin. *Second Skin: Josephine Baker and the Modern Surface*. Oxford: Oxford University Press, 2010.

Clifford, James. "Negrophilia." In *New Histories of French Literature*, edited by Denis Hollier. Cambridge, MA: Harvard University Press, 1989.

Commander, Michelle D. *Afro-Atlantic Flight: Speculative Returns and the Black Fantastic*. Durham, NC: Duke University Press, 2017.

Cooper, Carolyn. *Noises in the Blood: Orality, Gender, and the "Vulgar" Body of Jamaican Popular Culture*. Oxford: Macmillan Caribbean, 1993.

Coronil, Fernando. "Introduction." In *Cuban Counterpoint: Tobacco and Sugar*, by Fernando Ortiz, translated by Harriet de Onis. 2nd ed. Durham, NC: Duke University Press, 1995.

Cowley, John. *Carnival, Canboulay and Calypso: Traditions in the Making*. Cambridge: Cambridge University Press, 1996.

Cross, Malcolm. "East Indian-Creole Relations in Trinidad and Guiana in the Late Nineteenth Century." In *Across the Dark Waters: Ethnicity and Indian Identity in the Caribbean*, edited by David Dabydeen and Brinsley Samaroo. London: Macmillan Caribbean, 1996.

Crowley, Daniel J. "The Traditional Masques of Carnival." *Caribbean Quarterly* 4, no. 3/4 (1956): 215–16.

Cullen, Countee. "The Dark Tower." *Opportunity* 5 (February 1927): 53.

Cullen, Deborah, and Elvis Fuentes. *Caribbean: Art at the Crossroads of the World*. New Haven, CT: Yale University Press, 2012.

Cummings, E. E. *E. E. Cummings: A Miscellany Revised*. New York: October House, 1965.

Dabydeen, David, and Brinsley Samaroo, eds. *Across the Dark Waters: Ethnicity and Indian Identity in the Caribbean*. London: Macmillan Caribbean, 1996.

Daniel, Suzanne Garrigues. "The Early Works of Wifredo Lam, 1941–1945." PhD diss., University of Maryland, 1983.

Dash, J. Michael. *Haiti and the United States: National Stereotypes and the Literary Imagination*. New York: Macmillan, 1997.

Dash, J. Michael. *The Other America: Caribbean Literature in a New World Context.* Charlottesville: University of Virginia Press, 1998.

Day, Charles. *Five Years' Residence in the West Indies.* London: Colburn, 1852.

Day, Holliday T., and Hollister Sturges, eds. *Art of the Fantastic: Latin America, 1920–1987.* Indianapolis: Indianapolis Museum of Art, 1987.

Delany, Martin Robison. *The Condition, Elevation, Emigration, and Destiny of the Colored People of the United States.* 1852. Reprint, New York: Humanity Books, 2004.

Dewiel, Lydia L. *Jugendstil.* Koln: Dumont, 2002.

Drewal, Margaret Thompson. *Yoruba Ritual: Performers, Play, Agency.* Bloomington: Indiana University Press, 1992.

Du Bois, W. E. B. *The Souls of Black Folk.* Edited by Henry Louis Gates Jr. and Terri Hume Oliver. New York: Norton, 1999.

Dunham, Katherine. "Form and Function in Primitive Dance." In *Kaiso! Writings by and about Katherine Dunham,* edited by VèVè A. Clark and Sara E. Johnson. Madison: University of Wisconsin Press, 2005.

Duval-Carrié, Edouard. "Conversation: *Imagined Landscapes* with Edouard Duval-Carrié and Tobias Ostrander." Pérez Art Museum Miami, Florida, March 13, 2014. https://www.pamm.org/blog/2014/04/conversation-imagined -landscapes-edouard-duval-carri%C3%A9-and-tobias-ostrander.

Earle, Susan. "Harlem, Modernism, and Beyond: Aaron Douglas and His Role in Art/History." In *Aaron Douglas: African American Modernist,* edited by Susan Earle. New Haven, CT: Yale University Press; Lawrence: Spencer Museum of Art, University of Kansas, 2007.

Eco, Umberto. "The Frames of Comic 'Freedom.'" In *Carnival!,* edited by Umberto Eco, V. V. Ivanov, and Monica Rector. New York: Mouton, 1983.

Edmondson, Belinda. "Public Spectacles: Caribbean Women and the Politics of Public Performance." *Small Axe 13* (March 2003): 1–16.

Edwards, Brent Hayes. *The Practice of Diaspora: Literature, Translation, and the Rise of Black Internationalism.* Cambridge, MA: Harvard University Press, 2003.

Eldridge, Michael S. "Bop Girl Goes Calypso: Containing Race and Youth Culture in Cold War America." *Anthurium: A Caribbean Studies Journal* 3, no. 2 (December 2005): 1–28.

Enright, Kelly. *The Maximum of Wilderness: The Jungle in the American Imagination.* Charlottesville: University of Virginia Press, 2012.

Eppse, Merl R. *The Negro, Too, in American History.* Nashville: National Educational Publication, 1943.

Farrington, Lisa. *African-American Art: A Visual and Cultural History.* New York: Oxford University Press, 2017.

Fauset, Arthur Huff. *For Freedom: A Biographical Story of the American Negro.* Philadelphia: Franklin, 1927.

Favis, Roberta Smith. *Martin Johnson Heade in Florida.* Gainesville: University Press of Florida, 2003.

Ferber, Linda S. *The Hudson River School: Nature and the American Vision*. New York: Skira Rizzoli, 2009.

Foster, Hal. "The Primitive Unconscious of Modern Art, or White Skin, Black Masks." In *Recodings: Art, Spectacle, Cultural Politics*. Port Townsend, WA: Bay Press, 1985.

Fouchet, Max-Pol. *Wifredo Lam*. Barcelona, Spain: Ediciones Poligrafa, 1976.

Franco, Pamela. "The 'Unruly Woman' in Nineteenth-Century Trinidad Carnival." *Small Axe* 7 (March 2000): 60–76.

Franklin, John Hope, and Alfred A. Moss Jr. *From Slavery to Freedom: A History of African Americans*. 8th ed. New York: Alfred A. Knopf, 2000.

Gikandi, Simon. "Picasso, Africa, and the Schemata of Difference." *Modernism/Modernity* 10, no. 3 (September 2003): 455–80.

Gikandi, Simon. *Writing in Limbo: Modernism and Caribbean Literature*. Ithaca, NY: Cornell University Press, 1992.

Gillespie, Marcia Ann, Rosa Johnson Butler, and Richard A. Long. *Maya Angelou: A Glorious Celebration*. New York: Doubleday, 2008.

Gillespie, Sarah Kate. *Vernacular Modernism: The Photography of Doris Ulmann*. Athens: Georgia Museum of Art, 2018.

Gilman, Sander L. "'Black Bodies, White Bodies: Toward an Iconography of Female Sexuality in Late Nineteenth-Century Art, Medicine, and Literature." In *"Race," Writing, and Difference*, edited by Henry Louis Gates Jr. Chicago: University of Chicago Press, 1985.

Gilroy, Paul. *The Black Atlantic: Modernity and Double Consciousness*. Cambridge, MA: Harvard University Press, 1993.

Glazier, Michael, and Monika K. Hellwig, eds. *The Modern Catholic Encyclopaedia*. Collegeville, MN: Liturgical Press, 2004.

Glissant, Édouard. *Caribbean Discourse: Selected Essays*. Translated by J. Michael Dash. Charlottesville: University Press of Virginia, 1989.

Glissant, Édouard. *Poetics of Relation*. Translated by Betsy Wing. Ann Arbor: University of Michigan Press, 1997.

Goldberg, RoseLee. *Performance Art: From Futurism to the Present*. 1979. Reprint, New York: Thames and Hudson, 2001.

Hall, Catherine. "Gender Politics and Imperial Politics: Rethinking the Histories of Empire." In *Engendering History: Caribbean Women in Historical Perspective*, edited by Verene Shepherd, Bridget Brereton, and Barbara Bailey. Kingston, Jamaica: Randle, 1995.

Hall, Tony. *Jean and Dinah . . . Who Have Been Locked Away in a World Famous Calypso since 1956 Speak Their Minds Publicly*. Port of Spain, Trinidad: Tony Hall and the Lordstreet Theatre Company, 2001.

Haney, Lynn. *Naked at the Feast: A Biography of Josephine Baker*. New York: Dodd, Mead, 1981.

Hartman, Della Brown. "William Edouard Scott Remembered: Lessons from a Remarkable Life." PhD diss., Kent State University, 1994.

Haskins, Jim. *The Cotton Club*. New York: Random House, 1977.

Herzberg, Julia P. "Wifredo Lam." *Latin American Art* 2, no. 3 (Summer 1990): 18–24.

Herzberg, Julia P. "Wifredo Lam: The Development of a Style and World View, the Havana Years, 1941–1952." In *Wifredo Lam and His Contemporaries, 1938–1952*, edited by Maria R. Balderrama. New York: Studio Museum in Harlem, 1992.

Herzberg, Julia P. "Wifredo Lam: The Return to Havana and the Afro-Cuban Heritage." *Review* 37 (January–June 1987): 22–30.

Hewitt, Julia Cuervo. *Voices out of Africa in Twentieth-Century Spanish Caribbean Literature*. Lewisburg, PA: Bucknell University Press, 2009.

Heyward, DuBose, and Dorothy Heyward. *The Complete Text of Porgy*. New York: Theatre Arts, 1955.

Hill, Donald. "'I Am Happy Just to Be in This Sweet Land of Liberty': The New York City Calypso Craze of the 1930s and 1940s." In *Island Sounds in the Global City: Caribbean Popular Music and Identity in New York*, by Ray Allen and Lois Wilcken. New York: New York Folklore Society and the Institute for Studies in American Music, Brooklyn College, 1998.

Hill, Errol. *The Trinidad Carnival: Mandate for a National Theatre*. Austin: University of Texas Press, 1972.

Hillier, Belvis, and Stephen Escritt. *Art Deco Style*. London: Phaidon, 1997.

Humboldt, Baron Alexander von. *Cosmos: A Sketch of a Physical Description of the Universe*. Vol. 1. New York: Harper, 1849.

Humboldt, Baron Alexander von. *Cosmos: A Sketch of a Physical Description of the Universe*. Vol. 2. New York: Harper, 1858.

Iheka, Cajetan Nwabueze. *Naturalizing Africa: Ecological Violence, Agency, and Postcolonial Resistance in African Literature*. Cambridge: Cambridge University Press, 2018.

Johnson, James Weldon, ed. *The Book of American Negro Poetry*. Rev. ed. New York: Harcourt, Brace, 1931.

Johnson, James Weldon. "The Truth about Haiti: An N.A.A.C.P. Investigation." *Crisis* 20, no. 5 (September 1920): 217–24.

Johnson, Kim Nicholas. "Saga of a Flagwoman." In *Gendered Realities: Essays in Caribbean Feminist Thought*, edited by Patricia Mohammed. Kingston, Jamaica: University of the West Indies Press; Mona, Jamaica: Centre for Gender and Development Studies, 2002.

Jules-Rosette, Bennetta. *Josephine Baker in Art and Life: The Icon and the Image*. Urbana: University of Illinois Press, 2007.

Kelley, Robin D. G. "Introduction: A Poetics of Anticolonialism." In *Discourse on Colonialism*, by Aimé Césaire, translated by Joan Pinkham. New York: Monthly Review Press, 2000.

Ketner, Joseph D. *The Emergence of the African American Artist: Robert S. Duncanson, 1821–1872*. Columbia: University of Missouri Press, 1993.

Kirschke, Amy Helene. *Aaron Douglas: Art, Race, and the Harlem Renaissance*. Jackson: University Press of Mississippi, 1995.

Kornhauser, Elizabeth Mankin, and Katherine E. Manthorne. *Fern Hunting among the Picturesque Mountains: Frederic Edwin Church in Jamaica.* Olana Collection. Ithaca, NY: Cornell University Press, 2010.

Krauss, Rosalind. "Giacometti." In *"Primitivism" in Twentieth Century Art: Affinity of the Tribal and the Modern*, edited by William Rubin. New York: Museum of Modern Art, 1984.

Kummels, Ingrid. "Staging the Caribbean: Dialogues on Diasporic Antillean Music and Dance in Paris during the Jazz Age." In *Transatlantic Caribbean: Dialogues of People, Practice, Ideas*, edited by Ingrid Kummels. Bielefeld, Germany: Transcript, 2014.

Kutzinski, Vera. *Sugar's Secrets: Race and the Erotics of Cuban Nationalism.* Charlottesville: University Press of Virginia, 1993.

Lahs-Gonzales, Olivia. "Josephine Baker: Modern Woman." In *Josephine Baker: Image and Icon*, edited by Olivia Lahs-Gonzales. St. Louis, MO: Sheldon Art Galleries, 2006.

Lam, Wifredo. "Oeuvres recentes de Wifredo Lam." *Cahiers d'Art* 26 (1951): 181–89.

Laurence, K. O. *Immigration into the West Indies in the Nineteenth Century.* Barbados: Caribbean Universities Press, 1971.

Leighten, Patricia. "The White Peril and L'Arte negre: Picasso, Primitivism, and Anticolonialism." *Art Bulletin* 72, no. 4 (December 1990): 609–30.

Leiris, Michel. *L'afrique fantôme.* Paris: Gallimard, 1951.

Leja, Michael. *Reframing Abstract Expressionism: Subjectivity and Painting in the 1940s.* New Haven, CT: Yale University Press, 1993.

Lemke, Sieglinde. "Diaspora Aesthetics: Exploring the African Diaspora in the Works of Aaron Douglas, Jacob Lawrence, and Jean-Michel Basquiat." In *Exiles, Diasporas and Strangers*, edited by Kobena Mercer. London: Institute of International Visual Arts; Cambridge, MA: MIT Press, 2008.

Lewis, Linden, ed. *The Culture of Gender and Sexuality in the Caribbean.* Gainesville: University Press of Florida, 2003.

Lhamon, W. T. *Raising Cain: Blackface Performance from Jim Crow to Hip Hop.* Cambridge, MA: Harvard University Press, 1998.

Linsley, Robert. "Wifredo Lam: Painter of Negritude." *Art History* 11, no. 4 (December 1988): 527–44.

Little, Lawrence. *Disciples of Liberty: The African Methodist Episcopal Church in the Age of Imperialism, 1884–1916.* Knoxville: University of Tennessee Press, 2000.

Liverpool, Hollis. *Rituals of Power and Rebellion: The Carnival Tradition in Trinidad and Tobago, 1763–1962.* Chicago: Research Associates School Times, 2001.

Locke, Alain, ed. *The New Negro: Voices of the Harlem Renaissance.* New York: Boni, 1925.

Loichot, Valérie. *The Tropics Bite Back: Culinary Coups in Caribbean Literature.* Minneapolis: University of Minnesota Press, 2013.

Lucie-Smith, Edward. "Wifredo Lam and the Caribbean." In *Wifredo Lam in*

North America, edited by Curtis L. Carter. Milwaukee, WI: Patrick and Beatrice Haggerty Museum of Art, Marquette University, 2007.

MacFarlane, S. Neill. "Taking Stock: The Third World and the End of the Cold War." In *Third World beyond the Cold War: Continuity and Change*, edited by Louise Fawcett and Yezid Sayigh. New York: Oxford University Press, 1999.

Maguire, Emily A. "Two Returns to the Native Land: Lydia Cabrera Translates Aimé Césaire." *Small Axe* 17, no. 3 (November 2013): 125–37.

Malley, Robert. *The Call from Algeria: Third Worldism, Revolution, and the Turn to Islam*. Berkeley: University of California Press, 1996.

Martin, Gerald. "Literature, Music and the Visual Arts, 1870–1930." In *A Cultural History of Latin America: Literature, Music and the Visual Arts in the 19th and 20th Centuries*, edited by L. Bethell. Cambridge: Cambridge University Press, 1998.

Martin, Tony. *Caribbean History: From Pre-Colonial Origins to the Present*. Boston: Pearson, 2012.

Martin, Wendy. "'Remembering the Jungle': Josephine Baker and Modernist Parody." In *Prehistories of the Future: The Primitivist Project and the Culture of Modernism*, edited by Elazar Barkan and Ronald Bush. Stanford, CA: Stanford University Press, 1995.

Martínez, Juan A. *Cuban Art and National Identity: The Vanguardia Painters, 1927–1950*. Gainesville: University Press of Florida, 1994.

Massey, Anne. *Interior Design since 1900*. 3rd ed. London: Thames and Hudson, 2008.

McKay, Claude, *Banana Bottom*. New York: Harper, 1933.

McKittrick, Katherine. *Demonic Grounds: Black Women and the Cartographies of Struggle*. Minneapolis: University of Minnesota Press, 2006.

McMains, Juliet. *Spinning Mambo into Salsa: Caribbean Dance in Global Commerce*. Oxford: Oxford University Press, 2015.

Ménil, René. "Concerning Colonial Exoticism." In *Refusal of the Shadow: Surrealism and the Caribbean*, edited by Michael Richardson and Krzysztof Fijalkowski. London: Verso, 1996.

Ménil, René. "For a Critical Reading of *Tropiques*." In *Refusal of the Shadow: Surrealism and the Caribbean*, edited by Michael Richardson and Krzysztof Fijalkowski. New York: Verso, 1996.

Ménil, René. "Introduction to the Marvellous." In *Refusal of the Shadow: Surrealism and the Caribbean*, edited by Michael Richardson and Krzysztof Fijalkowski. New York: Verso, 1996.

Mercer, Kobena. "Introduction." In *Cosmopolitan Modernisms*, edited by Kobena Mercer. London: Institute of International Visual Arts; Cambridge, MA: MIT Press, 2005.

Mercer, Kobena. *Travel and See: Black Diaspora Art Practices since the 1980s*. Durham, NC: Duke University Press, 2016.

Milkman, Ruth. *Gender at Work: The Dynamics of Job Segregation by Sex during World War II*. Urbana: University of Illinois Press, 1987.

Miller, David C. *Dark Eden: The Swamp in Nineteenth-Century American Culture.* Cambridge: Cambridge University Press, 1989.

Miller, Perry. "Nature and the National Ego." In *Errand into the Wilderness.* New York: Harper and Row, 1964.

Millette, James. "The Wage Problem in Trinidad and Tobago, 1838–1938." In *The Colonial Caribbean in Transition: Essays on Post-emancipation Social and Cultural History,* edited by Bridget Brereton and Kevin A. Yelvington. Gainesville: University Press of Florida, 1999.

Mohammed, Patricia. "A Blueprint for Gender in Creole Trinidad: Exploring Gender Mythology through Calypsoes of the 1920s and 1930s." In *The Culture of Gender and Sexuality in the Caribbean,* edited by Linden Lewis. Gainesville: University Press of Florida, 2003.

Momsen, Janet. "The Double Paradox." In *Gendered Realities: Essays in Caribbean Feminist Thought,* edited by Patricia Mohammed. Kingston, Jamaica: University of the West Indies Press; Mona, Jamaica: Centre for Gender and Development Studies, 2002.

Morris, Mervyn. *Miss Lou: Louise Bennett and Jamaican Culture.* Oxford: Signal Books, 2014.

Morton, Patricia A. *Hybrid Modernities: Architecture and Representation at the 1931 Colonial Exposition, Paris.* Cambridge, MA: MIT Press, 2000.

Mosquera, Gerardo. *Beyond the Fantastic: Contemporary Art Criticism from Latin America.* Cambridge, MA: MIT Press, 1996.

Mosquera, Gerardo., "Mi pintura es un acto de descolonización: Entrevista con Wifredo Lam." *Bohemia* 92, no. 25 (1980): 10–13.

Murray, John A. *The Islands and the Sea: Five Centuries of Nature Writing from the Caribbean.* New York: Oxford University Press, 1991.

Nardal, Jane. "Pantins exotiques" [Exotic Puppets]. *La Dépêche Africaine* 8 (October 1928): 2.

Nenno, Nancy. "Femininity, the Primitive, and Modern Urban Space: Josephine Baker in Berlin." In *Women in the Metropolis: Gender and Modernity in Weimar Culture,* edited by Katharina von Ankum. Berkeley: University of California Press, 1997.

Neptune, Harvey R. *Caliban and the Yankees: Trinidad and the United States Occupation.* Chapel Hill: University of North Carolina Press, 2007.

Ngô, Fiona I. B. *Imperial Blues: Geographies of Race and Sex in Jazz Age New York.* Durham, NC: Duke University Press, 2014.

Niblett, Michael. "The Arc of the 'Other America': Landscape, Nature, and Region in Eric Walrond's *Tropic Death.*" In *Perspectives on the "Other America": Comparative Approaches to Caribbean and Latin American Culture,* edited by Kerstin Oloff and Michael Niblett. Amsterdam: Rodopi, 2009.

Nicholls, David G. "Jean Toomer's *Cane,* Modernization, and the Spectral Folk." In *Modernism, Inc.: Body, Memory, Capital,* edited by Jani Scandura and Michael Thurston. New York: New York University Press, 2001.

Noel, Samantha A. "De Jamette in We: Redefining Performance in Contemporary Trinidad Carnival." *Small Axe,* no. 31 (March 2010): 60–78.

Noel, Samantha A. "Envisioning New Worlds: The 'Tropical Aesthetics' in the Art of Wifredo Lam and Aaron Douglas." *Art Journal* 77, no. 3 (2018): 76–91.

Novak, Barbara. *Nature and Culture: American Landscape and Painting, 1825–1875.* 3rd ed. Oxford: Oxford University Press, 2007.

Nunley, John W., and Judith Bettelheim, eds. *Caribbean Festival Arts: Each and Every Bit of Difference.* Seattle: University of Washington Press, 1988.

Nurse, Keith. "Globalization and Trinidad Carnival: Diaspora, Hybridity and Identity in Global Culture." *Cultural Studies* 13, no. 4 (1999): 661–90.

Oiticica, Hélio. "General Scheme of New Objectivity." In *Tropicália: A Revolution in Brazilian Culture, 1967–1972,* edited by Carlos Basualdo. São Paulo: Cosac Naify, 2005.

Oiticica, Hélio. "Tropicália." In *Tropicália: A Revolution in Brazilian Culture, 1967–1972,* edited by Carlos Basualdo. São Paulo: Cosac Naify, 2005.

Oiticica, Hélio. "Tropicália: The Image Problem Surpassed by That of a Synthesis." In *Tropicália: A Revolution in Brazilian Culture, 1967–1972,* edited by Carlos Basualdo. São Paulo: Cosac Naify, 2005.

Ortiz, Fernando. *Cuban Counterpoint: Tobacco and Sugar.* 2nd ed. Translated by Harriet de Onís. Durham, NC: Duke University Press, 1995.

Ostrander, Tobias. "Tropical Values: The Imagined Landscapes of Edouard Duval-Carrié." In *From Revolution in the Tropics to Imagined Landscapes: The Art of Edouard Duval-Carrié,* edited by Anthony Bogues. Miami: Pérez Art Museum, 2014.

Pacteau, Francette. *The Symptom of Beauty.* Cambridge, MA: Harvard University Press, 1994.

Pappademos, Melina. *Black Political Activism and the Cuban Republic.* Chapel Hill: University of North Carolina Press, 2011.

Patton, Sharon. *African American Art.* Oxford: Oxford University Press, 1998.

Pearse, Andrew. "Carnival in Nineteenth Century Trinidad." *Caribbean Quarterly* 4, no. 3/4 (March–June 1956): 175–93.

Pearse, Andrew. "Mitto Sampson on Calypso Legends of the Nineteenth Century." *Caribbean Quarterly* 4, no. 3/4 (March–June 1956): 250–62.

Pérez, Louis A., Jr. *On Becoming Cuban: Identity, Nationality, and Culture.* Chapel Hill: University of North Carolina Press, 1999.

Phelan, Peggy. *Unmarked: The Politics of Performance.* New York: Routledge, 1993.

Philip, M. NourbeSe. "Race, Space, and the Poetics of Moving." In *Caribbean Creolization: Reflections on the Cultural Dynamics of Language, Literature, and Identity,* edited by Kathleen M. Balutansky and Marie-Agnes Sourieau. Gainesville: University Press of Florida, 1998.

Poole, Deborah. "An Excess of Description: Ethnography, Race, and Visual Technologies." *Annual Review of Anthropology* 34 (2005): 159–79.

Poupeye, Veerle. *Caribbean Art.* New York: Thames and Hudson, 1998.

Powell, Richard J. "The Aaron Douglas Effect." In *Aaron Douglas: African American Modernist,* edited by Susan Earle. New Haven, CT: Yale University Press; Lawrence: Spencer Museum of Art, University of Kansas, 2007.

Powell, Richard J. *Black Art: A Cultural History*. London: Thames and Hudson, 2002.

Powell, Richard J. "Paint That Thing! Aaron Douglas's Call to Modernism." *American Studies* 49, no. 1/2 (Spring/Summer 2008): 107–19.

Powell, Richard J. "Re/birth of a Nation." In *Rhapsodies in Black: Art of the Harlem Renaissance*, edited by Richard J. Powell and David A. Bailey. London: Hayward Gallery and Institute of International Visual Arts; Berkeley: University of California Press, 1997.

Powrie, Barbara E. "The Changing Attitude of the Coloured Middle Class Towards Carnival." *Carnival Quarterly* 14, no. 3/4 (1956): 224–32.

Pratt, Mary Louise. *Imperial Eyes: Travel Writing and Transculturation*. London: Routledge, 1992.

Raymond, Judy. *Beryl McBurnie*. Kingston, Jamaica: University of the West Indies Press, 2018.

Reddock, Rhoda. *Women, Labour and Politics in Trinidad and Tobago: A History*. Atlantic Highlands, NJ: Zed Books, 1994.

Reddock, Rhoda. "Women Workers' Struggles in the British Colonial Caribbean: the 1930s." In *Revisiting Caribbean Labour: Essays in Honour of O. Nigel Bolland*, edited by Constance R. Sutton. New York: Research Institute for the Study of Man, 2005.

Richardson, Michael. "Introduction." In *Refusal of the Shadow: Surrealism and the Caribbean*, edited by Michael Richardson and Krzysztof Fijalkowski. New York: Verso, 1996.

Roberts, Neil. *Freedom as Marronage*. Chicago: University of Chicago Press, 2015.

Rodriguez-Plate, Edna M. *Lydia Cabrera and the Construction of an Afro-Cuban Cultural Identity*. Chapel Hill: University of North Carolina Press, 2004.

Rogers, Charlotte. *Jungle Fever: Exploring Madness and Medicine in Twentieth-Century Tropical Narratives*. Nashville, TN: Vanderbilt University Press, 2012.

Rohlehr, Gordon. *Calypso and Society in Pre-independence Trinidad*. Port of Spain, Trinidad: G. Rohlehr, 1990.

Rose, Phyllis. *Jazz Cleopatra: Josephine Baker in Her Time*. New York: Doubleday, 1989.

Rosemont, Penelope, ed. *Surrealist Women: An International Anthology*. Austin: University of Texas Press, 1998.

Rubin, James Henry. *How to Read Impressionism: Ways of Looking*. New York: Abrams, 2013.

Ryan, Selwyn. *Race and Nationalism in Trinidad and Tobago: A Study of Decolonization in a Multicultural Society*. Toronto: University of Toronto Press, 1972.

Said, Edward. *Orientalism*. London: Penguin, 2003.

Sartre, Jean-Paul. *Black Orpheus*. Translated by S. W. Allen. Paris, 1951.

Sasso, Arthur J. "They're Going Crazy for Calypso!" *Real: The Exciting Magazine for Men* 10, no. 2 (June 1957): 76–89.

Schechner, Richard, and Milla Cozart Riggio. "Peter Minshall: A Voice to Add to the Song of the Universe." In *Carnival: Culture in Action; The Trinidad Experience*, edited by Milla Cozart Riggio. New York: Routledge, 2004.

Scher, Philip. *Carnival and the Formation of a Caribbean Transnation*. Gainesville: University Press of Florida, 2003.

Schneider, Rebecca. *The Explicit Body in Performance*. London: Routledge, 1997.

Schoonmaker, Trevor. "A Fantastic Journey." In *Wangechi Mutu: A Fantastic Journey*, edited by Trevor Schoonmaker. Durham, NC: Nasher Museum of Art, Duke University, 2013.

Schwartz, Roberto. "Culture and Politics in Brazil, 1964–1969." In *Tropicália: A Revolution in Brazilian Culture, 1967–1972*, edited by Carlos Basualdo. São Paulo: Cosac Naify, 2005.

Shack, William A. *Harlem in Montmartre: A Paris Jazz Story between the Great Wars*. Berkeley: University of California Press, 2001.

Sharpley-Whiting, T. Denean. *"Femme Negritude*: Jane Nardal, *Le Dépêche Africaine*, and the Francophone New Negros." *Souls: A Critical Journal of Black Politics, Culture, and Society* 2, no. 4 (2000): 8–17.

Sharpley-Whiting, T. Denean. *Negritude Women*. Minneapolis: University of Minnesota Press, 2002.

Shohat, Ella, and Robert Stam. *Unthinking Eurocentrism: Multiculturalism and the Media*. London: Routledge, 1994.

Sims, Lowery Stokes. "The Post-modern Modernism of Wifredo Lam." In *Cosmopolitan Modernisms*, edited by Kobena Mercer. Cambridge, MA: MIT Press, 2005.

Sims, Lowery Stokes. *Wifredo Lam and the International Avant-Garde, 1923–1982*. Austin: University of Texas Press, 2002.

Small, Irene V. *Hélio Oiticica: Folding the Frame*. Chicago: University of Chicago Press, 2016.

Smith, Hope Munro. "Performing Gender in the Trinidad Calypso." *Latin American Music Review* 25, no. 1 (Spring/Summer 2004): 32–56.

Snaith, Anna. "C. L. R. James, Claude McKay, Nella Larsen, Jean Toomer: The 'Black Atlantic' and the Modernist Novel." In *The Cambridge Companion to the Modernist Novel*, edited by Morag Shiach. Cambridge: Cambridge University Press, 2007.

Sörgel, Sabine. *Dancing Postcolonialism: The National Dance Theatre Company of Jamaica*. Bielefeld, Germany: Transcript, 2007.

Stallybrass, Peter. "Against Thinking." PMLA 122, no. 5 (2007): 1580–87.

Stallybrass, Peter, and Allon White. *The Politics and Poetics of Transgression*. Ithaca, NY: Cornell University Press, 1986.

Stebbins, Theodore E. *The Life and Work of Martin Johnson Heade: A Critical Analysis and Catalogue Raisonné*. New Haven, CT: Yale University Press, 1975.

Steele, Valerie. *Paris Fashion: A Cultural History*. Oxford: Oxford University Press, 1988.

Stepan, Nancy Leys. *Picturing Tropical Nature*. Ithaca, NY: Cornell University Press, 2001.

Stewart, Jeffrey, ed. *The Critical Temper of Alain Locke: A Selection of His Essays on Art and Culture*. New York: Garland, 1983.

Stiles, Kristine. "Shaved Heads and Marked Bodies: Representations from Cultures of Trauma." *Strategie II: Peuples Mediterraneens*, nos. 64–65 (July–December 1993): 95–117.

Stuempfle, Stephen. *The Steelband Movement: The Forging of a National Art in Trinidad and Tobago*. Philadelphia: University of Pennsylvania Press, 1995.

Thomas, Deborah. *Modern Blackness: Nationalism, Globalization, and the Politics of Culture in Jamaica*. Durham, NC: Duke University Press, 2005.

Thompson, Krista. *An Eye for the Tropics: Tourism, Photography, and Framing the Caribbean Picturesque*. Durham, NC: Duke University Press, 2006.

Thompson, Krista. "Preoccupied with Haiti: The Dream of Diaspora in African American Art, 1915–1942." *American Art* 21, no. 3 (Fall 2007): 74–97.

Thompson, Robert Farris. *Flash of the Spirit: African and Afro-American Art and Philosophy*. New York: Vintage Books, 1984.

Timpano, Nathan. "Translating Vanguardia: Wifredo Lam, Transculturation, and the Crux of Avant-Gardism." *Rutgers Art Review* 23 (2007): 48–67.

Toomer, Jean. *Cane*. New York: Liveright, 2011.

Trotman, David. *Crime in Trinidad: Conflict and Control in a Plantation Society, 1838–1900*. Knoxville: University of Tennessee Press, 1986.

Turner, Victor. *The Anthropology of Performance*. New York: PAJ, 1986.

Tythacott, Louise. *Surrealism and the Exotic*. London: Routledge, 2003.

Vendryes, Margaret Rose. *Barthé: A Life in Sculpture*. Jackson: University Press of Mississippi, 2008.

Vos, Jelmer, David Eltis, and David Richardson. "The Dutch in the Atlantic World: New Perspectives from the Slave Trade with Particular Reference to the African Origins of the Traffic." In *Extending the Frontiers: Essays on the New Transatlantic Slave Trade Database*, edited by David Eltis and David Richardson. New Haven, CT: Yale University Press, 2008.

Walrond, Eric. *Tropic Death*. New York: Liveright, 1926.

Warner-Lewis, Maureen. *Guinea's Other Suns: The African Dynamic in Trinidad Culture*. Dover, MA: Majority Press, 1991.

Wilkins, Charles. "Glossary." In *The Fifth Report from the Select Committee of the House of Commons on the Affairs of the East India Company*, vol. 3, edited by Walter Kelly Firminger. Calcutta, 1918.

Wilks, Jennifer M. *Race, Gender, and Comparative Black Modernism: Suzanne Lacascade, Marita Bonner, Suzanne Césaire, Dorothy West*. Baton Rouge: Louisiana State University Press, 2008.

Wilson, Anthony. *Shadow and Shelter: The Swamp in Southern Culture*. Jackson: University Press of Mississippi, 2006.

Wirt, William. *The Letters of the British Spy*. 10th ed. New York: Harper, 1832.

Wolf, Norbert. *Art Deco*. Translated by Cynthia Hall. New York: Preston, 2016.

Wood, Donald. *Trinidad in Transition*. London: Oxford University Press, 1968.

Woodruff, Nan Elizabeth. *American Congo: The African American Freedom Struggle in the Delta*. Cambridge, MA: Harvard University Press, 2003.

Wynter, Sylvia. "Novel and History, Plot and Plantation." *Savacou* 5 (1971): 95–102.

Yelvington, Kevin A. "The War in Ethiopia and Trinidad, 1935–1936." In *The Colonial Caribbean in Transition: Essays on Postemancipation Social and Cultural History*, edited by Bridget Brereton and Kevin A. Yelvington. Gainesville: University Press of Florida, 1999.

Page locators in italics refer to figures and plates

Haitian Revolution (1804), 13, 57
Halfhide, Marion (Trinidad Carnival Queen), *134*
Hall, Tony, 130, 132–33, *136*, *pl. 5*
Hannibal (male chantuelle), 109
Harlem (NY), 58, 155
Harlem Renaissance, 1, 5, 11, 26, 27, 49
Harpe Astrale (Lam), 63, 85–87, *86*
Heade, Martin Johnson, 178, 186; *The Great Florida Marsh*, 189–91; *View from Fern-Tree Walk, Jamaica*, 187–88, 190
Herzberg, Julia P., 61, 73, 82, 84, 203n109
Heyward, DuBose, 14, 27
Holzer, Helena, 65, 68
home: understandings of, 13–14
homeland: Africa as, 153, 171, 191; Lam and, 63, 69, 71–72; tropics as, 144, 146, 153
Houdini (Trinidadian calypsonian), 151
Hudson River School, 9–10, 28, 32–35
Hughes, Langston, 44–45
humanity and dignity, 17–18, 62, 153, 177–78
humanization, 16, 23, 36
Humboldt, Alexander von, 8, 9
Humphrey, John, 138
Hyppolite, Hector, 15

identity: Antillean, 62, 66, 85, 87; Brazilian, 179–81, 183; Cuban, 69, 80–81; cultural, 58, 157; formation of, 4, 13, 38–39, 177–78; Third World, 92–93, 185
Idyll of the Deep South, An (Douglas), 26, 40–41, 45, *pl. 2*
Illustrated London News, 114
Illustration (Reiss), 30–31
imperialism: African American performers and, 142–43; Art Deco style and, 10–11; cultural, 19, 59, 84, 88–89, 144; resistance to, 54–55
Independence Wars, 74
indigenous groups, 189–91
industrialization, 11–12, 14, 34–35, 179, 190

innovation: in Black art, 26, 32, 49, 88, 98, 179, 184
internationalism, Black, 5–6, 20, 142–44, 174–75, 217n129
Interpretation of Harlem Jazz I (Reiss), 26, 30, *30*
Italo-Ethiopian War (1935), 120–21, 123
Ivory Coast, 65

Jamaica, 7, 8, 105, 106, 207n56
jametre class, 98, 107–11, *111*, 119, 135
Jamette/Jametre Carnival (Trinidad), 20, 98, 107–9
jamettes, 20, 98, 107, 117–41, 152, 207n59; Baby Doll character, 114–16, *115*, 124, 136; categories of, 133–34, *134*; *chantuelles* (lead singers of costumed bands), 98, 108, 118, 122, 140; and employment, 119–20, 123–24, 128–32; as flag women, 98–99, 128–29, 135–36, 211n188; *pisse-en-lit* masquerade, 96–97, 113, 116, 124, 209n112; political purposes of behavior, 97–99, 118–19, 135, 140–41; and propriety, 97–98, 113–16, 131–32, 140–41, 209n130; and sexuality, 107, 117, 119, 124–26; in slavery, 104–17; surveillance of, 116–17, 119, 124
jangala, 77
Janniot, Alfred, 11
Jardin des Plantes (Paris), 10
Jaycees Carnival Queen (Trinidad), 133, *134*, 140
jazz, 31–32, 145, 151, 154–58, 160, 172. *See also* Baker, Josephine; Douglas, Aaron
Jazz Age, 30, 144, 160, 163
Jean and Dinah (Hall), 130, 132–33, 136, *136*, *pl. 5*
"Jean and Dinah" (Mighty Sparrow), 131
"Jean in Town" (calypso character), 131–32
Jeffers, Audrey, 130
Johnson, James Weldon, 26, 31, 58
Johnson, Marguerite. *See* Angelou, Maya

Jonkonnu (Jamaican festival), 106
Jordan, Louis, 151
Jugendstil, 31
Ju Ju Warrior masquerade, 138
jungle, 7–10; in Lam's tropical landscapes, 10, 62–63, 72–77, 85, 88, 92, 94, *pl. 3*; simulated decor in Parisian music halls, 144–49, *149*, 154; as Western construct, 77, 156–57. *See also* Baker, Josephine; tropics
Jungle, The (Lam), 62–63, 72–77, 79, 88, 92–94, *pl. 3*
"jungle rhythm," 157

kalinda songs, 98, 118, 122, 152, 208n87
Kansas, 39
knowledge production, 89–90
Kongo (precolonial African kingdom), 75
Ku Klux Klan (KKK), 37, 39

Lam, Wifredo, 4, 6, 15, 16, 59, 60–95, 99, 154, 185; and Africa, 62, 65, 69, 81–82; and anthropomorphic forms, 73–75, 84–85, 86, *pl. 3*, *pl. 4*; *Autel pour Elegua*, 63, 82–85, *83*, 94, 203n109; Aimé Césaire's assessment of, 86; color palette, 75, 79, 91–92; in Cuba, 61–63, 65, 69–70; and Cuban landscape, 19, 60–64, 72, 77–78, 81, 94; and decolonization, 19, 60, 84, 91; and Douglas, 60–61; garden photographs, 70, 72; *Harpe Astrale*, 63, 85–87, *86*; hybrid plant-human figures, 61, 71, *pl. 3*; and jungle, 10, 62–63, 72–77, 85, 88, 92, 94, *pl. 3*; *The Jungle*, 62–63, 72–77, 79, 88, 92–94, *pl. 3*; and masks, 65, 80, 82, 203n105; and negritude, 61–63, 65–68, 85–95; photograph of, 70, 72; and pointillism, 79–80, 83–84; and political, 19, 65, 202n59; and *Sans titre*, 82; *La Sombre Malembo, Dieu du Carrefour*, 63, 79–81, 84, *pl. 4*; spirituality, 79–85; *El Tercer Mundo*, 63, 91, 91–93; and surrealism, 85–95; visual language of, 60, 71–74, 87, 93–95. *See also* Cuba

land: in Afro-Cuban religion, 74–75, 81; capitalist exploitation of, 37–38; and empowerment, 85; privileging of, 4; public territories claimed by *jamettes*, 103; reclamation of, 5–6, 40, 62, 79, 93, 145, 153, 189, 194
landscape: and American identity, 25; antispace, 11; as character, 53–54, 58, 78, 86; and community, 58, 78, 85; Eurocentric views, 14, 198n52; imagistic features of, 9, 42, 74; tropicalization of, 6–11, 63. *See also* geography; place; tropicality
landscape painting, 15; Douglas and legacy of, 26–40; Duval-Carrié's, 186–91; European American values of, 10, 36, 38; foliage/landscape as character, 53–54; Hudson River School, 9–10, 28, 32; industrialization in, 34–35; nineteenth-century portrayals, 186; Ohio River valley tradition of, 33–36, *34*; political dimensions of, 61, 72–74, 77; women in, 56, *56*–57
language, visual, 60, 71–74, 87, 93–95, 183
Revue Nègre, La, 154–65, *156*; "Danse des Sauvages," 154, 158–60, *159*, 169; "Mississippi Steam Boat Race," 154, *155*, 156; poster art for, 161–65, *162*, *164*
Latin America, 71, 185. *See also* Brazil; Cuba; Tropicalism movement (Brazil)
latinité, Black, 145, 174–75
Lawrence, Jacob, 58
Leighten, Patricia, 48
Leiris, Michel, 157
Lent, 96, 100
Roman d'un Spahi, Le (Loti), 158–59
Folies Bergère, Les, 15, 154, *166*, 166–67
Tumulte Noir, Le, 163
Lévi-Strauss, Claude, 65
liberation: cultural, 66, 85; sociospatial, 16, 86, 87, 95, 117–18, 128–29, 177
Linsley, Robert, 93